The Ernst & Young Tax-Saving Strategies Guide 1995

By Ernst & Young LLP

Peter W. Bernstein, Editor

John Wiley & Sons, Inc.

New York   Chichester   Brisbane   Toronto   Singapore

In the preparation of this book, every effort has been made to offer current, correct, and clearly expressed information. Nonetheless, inadvertent errors can occur and tax rules and regulations often change.

Further, the information in the text is intended to afford general guidelines on matters of interest to taxpayers. The application and impact of tax laws can vary widely from case to case, however, based upon the specific or unique facts involved. Accordingly, the information in this book is not intended to serve as legal, accounting, or tax advice. Readers are encouraged to consult with professional advisors for advice concerning specific matters before making any decision, and the author and publishers disclaim any responsibility for positions taken by taxpayers in their individual cases or for any misunderstanding on the part of readers. The information included in this book is based on the Internal Revenue Code as of August 15, 1994.

Copyright © 1995 by Ernst & Young LLP

Published by John Wiley & Sons, Inc.

ISBN: 0-471-05776-2 regular edition
ISBN: 0-471-11536-3 special edition

Printed in the United States of America

10 9 8 7 6 5 4 3 2 1

The Ernst & Young Tax-Saving Strategies Guide 1995

Editorial Board

Chairman: Harvey B. Wishman

Lorraine Bell
Noreen A. Bracken
Marisa J. Bryce
Pamela B. Burke
Brian R. Burns
Diane C. Carruthers
Stephen A. Cohen
James B. Conley
Robert B. Coplan
Mark C.J. Fisher
D. Susan Gard
Karen E. Gilbreath
Frederick Gordon

Michael J. Grace
Gregory A. Harman
David H. Helmer
Richard G. Larsen
Herbert J. Lerner
Patrick J. Meyer
Robert A. Midler
S. Theodore Reiner
Robert K. Samson
Byron K. Strother
Seth H. Tievsky
Scott W. Vance

Special thanks to Philip A. Laskawy, Chairman of Ernst & Young LLP; William J. Lipton, Vice Chairman–Tax Services; Herbert J. Lerner, National Director—Tax Policy and Standards; Richard S. Bobrow, National Director—Technical and Industry Tax Services; Robert J. Garner, National Director—Personal Financial Counseling; Patrice Ingrassia, Howard Freedman, and Jody A. Bieze.

With approximately 3,500 tax practitioners, Ernst & Young LLP has one of the largest professional tax practices in the United States. This book draws upon the experience of many of those professionals for its content.

About the Author

Ernst & Young LLP is a member of Ernst & Young International, the leading worldwide organization of professional service firms. Ernst & Young LLP has 20,000 people in 100 U.S. locations. The firm's principal areas of practice are accounting, auditing, tax, and management consulting. Ernst & Young's tax professionals provide personal financial and tax services to thousands of individuals, and furnish tax services to hundreds of businesses, ranging in size from small companies to the largest of the Fortune 500.

About the Editor

Peter W. Bernstein is executive editor of *U.S. News and World Report* and the editor of *The Ernst & Young Tax Guide.*

Contents

Ask Ernst & Young

Questions and Answers About Your Taxes

Q. My brother and I contribute to the support of our parents. Can I claim them as dependents?

A. Yes, if you and your brother meet certain tests. For example, if together you provide more than 50% of their total support and individually you contribute over 10% of the support, you may be able to claim your parents as dependents on your return. Only one of you, however, can make the claim. Also, if your income is too high you may not get any tax benefit. See Chapter 2, What You Can Deduct, for more about multiple support agreements and the phaseout of dependents exemptions.

Q. My employer is setting up a 401(k) plan this year. If I contribute to the plan, will I still be able to make deductible contributions to my IRA?

A. Whether contributions to your IRA are deductible after your employer establishes a 401(k) plan depends upon whether: (1) you are an active participant in the plan and (2) your salary. Even if you do not qualify for a tax deduction, you can still contribute to your IRA and the earnings on these contributions will accumulate tax-deferred until you withdraw it. See Chapter 4 for more on 401(k) plans and IRAs.

Q. I will be moving to take a new job in a different city. I understand there are new rules for 1994.

A. You're right, a number of the rules have changed starting in 1994. You will still be able to deduct traveling expenses for you and your family as well as expenses for moving household goods and personal effects. You will not be able to deduct such things as the cost of house hunting trips and the costs incidental to the sale of your old home. Other new rules also apply for the first time in 1994. See Chapter 2 for more about deducting moving expenses.

Q. My company can defer paying me a part of my compensation until next year. Is that a good idea?

A. Compensation generally is income to you when you receive it, not when it is earned. Unless you anticipate a tax rate increase next year, you will generally find it to your advantage to defer recognizing the income until next year.

You should arrange with your employer before the amount is earned that you will not be paid until next year. For more, see Chapter 1, What You Have to Include as Income, and Chapter 8, Year-End Planning for Individuals.

Q. Under the current tax law, how will my Social Security benefits be taxed?
A. For 1994, up to 85% of benefits received can be subject to tax. This represents a significant tax increase for middle income retirees. Last year, up to one-half of a taxpayer's Social Security benefits were subject to tax. For more, see Chapter 1.

Q. Home mortgage rates are now lower than my existing rate. Should I refinance my mortgage?
A. It depends. You need to consider the following factors: 1) what it will cost to refinance; 2) how much longer you plan to own your house; and 3) whether an Adjustable Rate Mortgage (ARM) is a good idea. See Chapter 3, Tax Planning and Your Home, for more about refinancing a home mortgage.

How to Use this Book

The Ernst & Young Tax-Saving Strategies Guide 1995 is a user-friendly year-end and year-round tax planner with easy-to-follow, money-saving tax strategies from one of the nation's foremost tax authorities, Ernst & Young LLP. This book, with its concise explanations of key provisions of federal tax law—including the 1993 changes which are first effective in 1994—can also be used for quick reference to provide guidance on important personal and business transactions. It is not intended to give you line-by-line instructions on how to prepare your federal tax returns. A separate Ernst & Young LLP publication—*The Ernst & Young Tax Guide*—is available for that purpose.

The book is organized into three sections:

Part I, Tax Strategies for Individuals, contains chapters that tell you what to include as income, what you can deduct, and how you calculate your tax. This year we've added four additional chapters that cover in greater detail charitable contributions; your home; retirement plans, such as IRAs and 401(k)s; and capital gains and losses. In addition, sprinkled throughout all the chapters are money-saving tips about options and strategies you might consider to cut your tax bill. There is also a chapter on year-end planning for individuals.

Part II, How to Improve Your Financial Future, should help you with some of the tax considerations guiding your current investments. In addition, options you might consider to ensure yourself a comfortable and secure retirement are also presented here. The chapter on estate planning offers advice on gifts, estate, and generation-skipping taxes.

Part III, Tax Strategies for Businesses, discusses many of the fundamental tax questions that confront the owner of any business. There is a special chapter on S corporations. The last chapter contains year-end planning suggestions that can save businesses money.

Among its many benefits, this book offers the following special features:

- *E&Y Focus.* This new feature considers topics of current interest, such as leasing a car or deferred compensation plans. Special Focus will suggest smart money moves that you may want to consider.
- *TaxSavers.* Highlighted throughout every chapter in the book are numerous TaxSavers, specific strategies and recommendations that can help you cut your tax bill.

- *TaxOrganizers.* Do you need to save that receipt for tax purposes? TaxOrganizers point out things you need to do now to make it easier to file your taxes later.
- *TaxAlerts.* This feature highlights recent changes in the tax law that you should know about. Tax law changes that have been enacted recently, are included. If you are aware of a new development in the law before the end of the year, you can often take timely and appropriate action and save yourself some money.
- *Special chapters on year-end tax planning for individuals and businesses.* The prudent taxpayer must make decisions before December 31 about a number of important tax questions—for example, whether to report income now or defer it to next year and whether to pay a deductible expense this year or in the future.
- *Important information on the tax aspects of "life-cycle events."* These are the occasions, transactions, and eventualities that most of us will almost certainly have to deal with at some time during our adult lives. A special index to the "life-cycle events" discussed in this book follows this introduction.
- *Concisely presented rules of the tax law pertaining to individuals, estates, gifts, and business entities.* Included in each section are examples that show you how the rules work and "TaxSavers"—strategies to help you plan better.

The Ernst & Young Tax-Saving Strategies Guide contains two more features that will be of year-round use to individuals and businesspeople alike:

- *Up-to-date tax tables*—the ones that you will use most often can be found at the end of this book; and
- *Tax calendar*—a month-by-month reminder of important tax action dates for individuals and businesses.

Index to Life-Cycle Events

This special index can be used to locate the sections of the text that contain important information on the tax aspects of "life-cycle events"—those milestones that most adults will be facing at one time or another during the course of their lives. By reading this information, you'll get off to a good start in understanding and planning for the tax consequences associated with various life-cycle events.

10 Smart Tax Planning Tips

1. Start your planning early. This allows you time to take advantage of strategies that may not be available later in the year because of law changes, because it takes several months to realize the maximum benefits, or because there isn't enough time to implement the strategy.

2. Make your contributions to an IRA or Keogh plan early in the year. The combination of making contributions early in the year and compounding will make your money grow faster than if you wait until the last minute. See page 44.

3. Contribute the maximum to your 401(k) plan early in the year. If you wait too long, you may not be able to contribute the full amount because of limitations. See page 153.

4. Consider tax-smart investments for your portfolio. You should focus on the after-tax yield when comparing the returns on different investments. See page 32.

5. You should replace personal debt with mortgage debt to the extent possible. Interest expense on mortgage loans is—subject to some limitations—deductible; personal or consumer interest is not. See page 51.

6. Think about the effect of refinancing your home mortgage to take advantage of low interest rates. If you refinance, your deduction for interest expense will probably be lower. Therefore, you may have to increase your estimated tax payments to avoid underpayment penalties. See page 145.

7. If you roll over a pension distribution to an IRA account, be sure you do it in a timely fashion. Caution: there is a 20% withholding tax on lump-sum distributions. See page 25.

8. If you plan to work after your normal retirement date, consider how it will affect your Social Security benefits. Also, consider whether you would be better off applying for your benefits by age 62 or waiting until you are 65. See page 184.

9. Consider giving gifts to your children. You may be able to shift income to them since children are usually in lower tax brackets and so they often pay less in taxes. However, if your children are under age 14, their income above certain levels will be subject to the special "kiddie tax" rates. See page 136.

10. Remember that charitable deductions are subject to certain limitations. Some of your contributions to charities may not be tax deductible if you exceed the prescribed limits or do not meet the substantiation requirements. See page 54.

Changes in the Tax Law You Should Know About

Introduction

Congress regularly considers adding new wrinkles to the tax law. In addition, changes passed into law in earlier years sometimes become effective in later years. This was so for a number of tax law changes included in the Omnibus Budget Reconciliation Act of 1993 (the 1993 Tax Act), which was signed into law on August 10, 1993. A brief summary of these tax provisions is included below. A more detailed discussion of changes can be found in the relevant sections of this book.

Other tax law changes you should be aware of are those provisions that expired in 1993 or will expire during 1994. These changes are also discussed here. In addition, it may be helpful to be aware of the more significant proposals being considered by Congress that could be enacted in 1994. It is always wise to check with your tax advisor near the end of the year about last-minute legislative or regulatory changes that might affect your tax planning. For help in preparing your 1994 tax return, you should consult the 1995 edition of *The Ernst & Young Tax Guide,* which is available in bookstores beginning in January 1995.

1994 Tax Changes Affecting You and Your Family

The 1993 Tax Act included numerous changes that did not become effective until 1994.

Estimated Taxes for Individuals. Starting in 1994, the general safe-haven rule for avoiding an underpayment penalty by paying 100% of the prior year's tax liability is repealed. A taxpayer can be certain that there will be no limitation on the 100% of last year's tax only if his or her previous year's adjusted gross income is $150,000 or less ($75,000 or less if married filing separately). If your previous year's adjusted gross income exceeds $150,000, you must pay 110% of last year's tax liability to be certain of avoiding any underpayment penalties. (For more details, see page 244.)

Medicare Tax Increase. The dollar limit on wages and self-employment income subject to Medicare taxes for wages and other earned income received after 1993 has been eliminated. Thus, the 1.45% rate for employees (2.9% for self-employed individuals) will apply to all earned income in 1994. (For more details, see page 270.)

Taxation of Social Security Benefits. A new tier of Social Security benefit inclusion in gross income is in effect as of 1994. The new tier applies to taxpayers with *provisional income* in excess of between $25,000 and $34,000 for unmarried filers, and for joint filers with provisional income between $32,000 and $44,000. (For more details, see page 22.)

Reduced Compensation for Qualified Retirement Plan. In 1994, additional limitations are imposed on the benefits which can be provided to highly compensated employees. The new limitations reduce the amount of compensation which can be taken into account for qualified retirement plan purposes. The new limit is $150,000, indexed annually for inflation. (For more details, see page 88.)

Withholding Rate on Supplemental Wages. Withholding on supplemental wage payments, such as bonuses, commissions, and overtime pay, will be computed at a rate of 28%, if the employer elects to withhold in this manner.

Travel Expenses for Spouses, Dependents, and Other Individuals. Limitations on a taxpayer's ability to take a business deduction for travel expenses for his/her spouse or other family member have been tightened. In 1994, a deduction is allowed *only* if the spouse, dependent, or other individual is a bona fide employee of the person paying or reimbursing the expenses and the expense incurred would otherwise be deductible. (For more details, see page 59.)

Substantiation Requirements for Charitable Contributions. You must now obtain a contemporaneous written acknowledgment from any charitable organization to which a contribution of $250 or more is made in order to deduct that contribution. *Contemporaneous* for this purpose means that the written acknowledgment must be obtained by the taxpayer on or before the earlier of (1) the date on which the return is actually filed for the year in which the contribution was made or (2) the due date for the return, including extensions. (For more details, see page 114.)

TaxAlert

Retroactive Relief for Home Buyers. One of the more prominent 1994 tax changes that could affect you is the IRS decision to relax the tax treatment of seller-paid mortgage points. In April 1994, the IRS decided that buyers may deduct seller-paid mortgage points. In general, a taxpayer who purchases a new home and incurs mortgage indebtedness may treat amounts paid by a seller in connection with the acquisition of such principal residence as deductible mortgage points in the taxable year paid. The new rules apply to points paid during taxable years beginning after December 31, 1990. You may change your method of accounting for points paid during years beginning after December 31, 1990, and before January 1, 1994, for filing amended returns.

Earned Income Tax Credit (EITC). The EITC is a refundable credit available to lower-income workers, including domestic help. As of 1994, the EITC is comprised of two different credits: (1) the basic credit; and (2) a supplemental credit for health insurance premiums paid for qualifying children. The most significant difference in the EITC from 1993 to 1994 is that in 1994 a taxpayer is not required to have a child living with him or her to qualify for the basic credit, so long as the taxpayer is not claimed as a dependent by another taxpayer. The maximum amount of the credit for a taxpayer with no children is $306, with one child is $2,038, and with two or more children is $2,527. (For more details, see page 142.)

1994 Tax Changes Affecting Your Business

Business Meals and Entertainment. In 1994, taxpayers can deduct only 50% (down from 80%) of the cost of business meals and entertainment expenses. (For more details, see page 62.)

Club Dues. In 1994, taxpayers cannot deduct club dues. This applies to all clubs organized for pleasure, recreation, or other social purposes. Taxpayers can still deduct specific business expenses (such as meals) that they incur at a club, subject to the other rules for meals and/or entertainment expenses. (For more details, see page 63.)

Corporate Estimated Tax Rules. For tax years beginning after 1993, a corporation's estimated tax payments must be based on the lesser of (1) 100% of the tax shown on the corporation's return for the preceding tax year, or (2) 100% of the tax for the current year.

Lobbying Expenses. The business deduction for lobbying expenses will not be allowed for amounts paid or incurred after December 31, 1993, for:

- Influencing legislation;
- Participating or intervening in any political campaign for, or against, any candidate for public office;
- Attempting to influence the general public, or segments of the public, about elections, legislative matters, or referendums; or
- Communicating directly with covered executive branch officials in any attempt to influence the official actions or positions of such officials.

Taxpayers also cannot deduct amounts paid or incurred for research, preparation, planning, or coordination of any activity described in the previous list.

Executive Compensation Restrictions. Subject to numerous exceptions (including allowable compensation tied to performance and payments made to a qualified plan), a publicly held corporation may not take a deduction for compensation in excess of $1 million paid to its chief officer or to any of its four most highly compensated officers.

TAXALERT

The 25% deduction for health insurance premiums for self-employed persons, their spouses, and dependents expired as of December 31, 1993. Congress is expected, however, to increase the percentage (in some proposals to 100%) and to retroactively revive the deduction back to the expiration date. All of the health reform plans currently being debated by Congress include such a provision.

Supplemental Wage Withholding Rate. The withholding rate for supplemental wages has been increased to 28 percent for payments made after December 31, 1993.

Moving Expense Reimbursement. Beginning January 1, 1994, reimbursed and employer-paid moving expenses that are deductible by the employee are not included in employee income. Many of the deductions for moving expenses have been eliminated. Reimbursed and employer-paid moving expenses that are not deductible by the employee are included in income and subject to employment taxes and income tax withholding. (For more details, see page 36.)

Educational Assistance. The exclusion of employer-provided educational assistance programs from employee income has been extended through December 31, 1994.

Interest on Tax Refunds. Effective January 1, 1994, no interest shall be allowed on refunds of employment tax if refunded within 45 days of the date the tax return was filed. Effective January 1, 1995, if a refund on a claim is paid within 45 days of the date the claim is filed, no interest will be paid for the period after the claim was filed.

Jobs Credit Extended. Employers can still claim the targeted jobs credit for wages (up to $6,000) paid or incurred for qualified employees who begin work by December 31, 1994.

Tax Changes Currently Under Consideration

Although it is impossible to predict what changes to the tax law may occur, it is still important to stay informed of possible changes that could be enacted later this year.

Health Reform. Almost any health reform plan Congress may enact in 1994 would impose substantial changes in the tax law. In general, however, most of the changes are put off to later years (i.e., 1996 and beyond). The one exception to this is an increase in the excise tax on tobacco products. If health care reform is enacted in 1994, it will likely include some early increase in tobacco excise taxes.

Nanny Tax. Congress is likely to enact legislation simplifying the rules for individuals employing domestic workers, the so-called "nanny-tax" legislation. The high-profile problems of some prominent political nominees have raised the importance of and likely approval of this legislation. In general, the legislation would increase the threshold above which individuals who hire domestic employees are required to withhold and pay employment taxes for Social Security.

Tax Simplification/Technical Corrections. This legislation contains provisions to simplify the tax treatment of individuals, pensions, partnerships, international operations of U.S. corporations, tax-exempt bonds, and estate and gifts. It also includes a number of technical corrections that fix or clarify tax provisions enacted after 1989. In order to offset revenue loss associated with the simplification proposals, the bill includes revenue-raising proposals that would, among other things:

- Require tax withholding of 28% on gambling winnings from bingo and keno when the winnings exceed $10,000.
- Require owners who rent homes for less than 15 days per year to include the proceeds as taxable income.

I

Tax Strategies for Individuals

"How can I pay less in taxes?" Following the retroactive 1993 tax increase, the question is particularly timely for many American taxpayers. Fortunately, there are numerous tax-saving strategies you can use to lower your tax bill. This book has been organized in a way that will assist you in developing and implementing tax saving strategies. Step 1, as anyone who has collected information for an annual tax return knows, is to determine what portion of your income is subject to tax and what may not be. Income, of course, is not just the money you get in your paycheck. It includes interest and dividends, rent and royalties, pensions and annuities, alimony and separate maintenance payments, among many other things—all of which are explained in Chapter 1. We've also pointed out numerous ways you can reduce the amount of income you have to report.

The second step (described in Chapter 2) is to figure out which of the expenses you incurred during the year can be deducted from your taxable income. We've included suggestions about how you can maximize your deductions and therefore lower the amount of tax you owe. This year, we've added four new chapters—Charitable Contributions, Tax Planning and Your Home, IRAs and 401(k) Plans, and Capital Gains and Losses—that explain in greater detail strategies that can help you deal with these important topics.

Many people consider the third step, the calculation of your tax explained in Chapter 7, to be the trickiest part of the process. It involves several calculations—you need to figure out, for example, whether or not you may be subject to the alternative minimum tax, and whether to claim the standard deduction or to itemize. We've tried to describe the process in as simple and straightforward a way as possible. The results—some of which can help to lower your bottom line—can be richly rewarding.

The last step represents both an end and a new beginning. The sophisticated taxpayer can take steps at the end of the tax year that can defer taxes until next year. This is the primary focus of Chapter 8. If you can shift the tax from April 1995 to April 1996, you have saved the use of those deferred funds for a year. More importantly, Chapter 8 illustrates how a taxpayer can start planning so that less tax will have to be paid in future years.

1

What You Have to Include as Income

Introduction

The first step in determining how much in taxes you'll have to pay is to figure out your *taxable income*. That is an amount figured by subtracting from your gross income certain adjustments and allowable deductions. Gross income includes income from whatever sources derived, including:

- Alimony and separate maintenance payments
- Compensation for services, including fees, commissions, and certain employee benefits
- Gains from dealings in property
- Gross income from a business
- Income from an interest in an estate or trust
- Income from paying off a debt
- Certain income from life insurance and endowment contracts
- Interest and dividends
- Pensions and annuities
- Rents and royalties
- Your share of income from a partnership or S corporation, whether it is distributed or not.

This chapter discusses what you have to include in calculating your taxable income. Along the way, you'll find many tax-saving suggestions that should help you lower your taxable income—and your tax bill.

Wages, Salaries, and Other Earned Income

As a general rule, you must include in your gross income everything you receive as payment for personal services including wages, salaries, commissions, and tips. If you receive property or services as compensation, you generally should include the fair market value of the property or services as wages in the year you receive it.

Unless you anticipate a tax rate increase next year, you will generally find it to your advantage to defer recognizing income and paying the tax for an additional year. Usually the date of receipt determines the year income is taxable. Failure to cash a check or refusal to accept a payment will not defer income.

E&Y FOCUS: Deferred Compensation Plans

Deferred compensation plans are designed by employers for executives who can afford to defer a portion of their earnings. Under such plans you make an election to defer some portion of your income until a stated time; you are taxed on the deferred income only when it is received.

Deferrals can be made from your regular salary or from bonuses. You must make an election to defer income before that income is earned. Furthermore, you and your employer must enter into a written deferral agreement.

Deferred compensation plans serve one or two functions, depending on whether they are short-term or long-term plans:

- Short-term arrangements are generally most effective when used to take advantage of tax-rate changes. For example, in 1987 the top rate on taxable income was 38½%. In 1988, the top rate dropped to 28%. You might have used a deferred compensation plan to shift income to 1988 so that is was taxed at a lower rate.

- Long-term arrangements are aimed primarily at providing key employees with bonuses and retirement income in excess of the amounts allowed by law under the employer's qualified pension and profit-sharing plans. Some experts are dubious about the benefits of long-term deferrals, chiefly because they believe tax rates will be higher in the future than they are currently. If they're right, the deferred income would be taxed at a higher rate—defeating one of the primary purposes of deferring the income. But, deferred plans do enable you to earn tax-deferred income on pre-tax dollars. And more and more restrictions are being placed on qualified retirement plans. In addition, deferred plans force you to save money. Not a bad thing to do if you want a safe and secure retirement.

TaxSaver

How to Make Sure You Collect Your Deferred Compensation. Many traditional "nonqualified" (i.e., un-funded) deferred compensation plans are based on an unsecured promise from your employer to pay compensation in the future. But how can you be sure your company will pay up?

Various arrangements have been developed to provide the employee with an additional sense of security that the promise will be honored without causing the income to be immediately taxable. One such device is known as a "rabbi trust," so named because the first arrangement approved by the IRS was developed by a synagogue for its rabbi.

Under a rabbi trust arrangement, amounts sufficient to pay the deferred compensation are placed into an irrevocable trust by your employer. Once in the trust, these amounts can be accessed by the employer's creditors only upon the employer's bankruptcy or insolvency; the amounts are not otherwise available for use by the original employer or a successor employer. This means that, unless the employer becomes bankrupt or insolvent, amounts in the rabbi trust will be available to pay the deferred compensation in future years.

"Noncash" Compensation. The following are some of the more common forms of noncash compensation that are subject to tax:

1. *Employer-provided automobile for personal use.* If your employer provided you with a car, your personal use of the car is considered taxable noncash compensation.
2. *Educational assistance.* You generally must include in income any educational expenses your employer paid for you, unless the courses are required by your employer, are job-related, or the expenses are paid for under a special plan meeting IRS requirements.

TaxAlert

Note: A special exclusion for educational expenses expires on December 31, 1994.

3. *Bargain purchase of employer's assets.* If you are allowed to purchase property from your employer at a price below its fair market value as compensation for your services, you must report as income the difference between the property's fair market value and the amount you paid for it.
4. *Stock options.* The difference between the stock's fair market value and the option price should generally be

reported as additional income when you exercise an option to buy stock from your employer. A special rule, however, applies to certain stock options. This rule usually delays the tax until you sell or exchange your stock. (See page 34 in this chapter.)

5. *Group life insurance premiums for over $50,000 of coverage.* Employer's payments for group term life insurance premiums for coverage over $50,000 are considered to be additional income to you unless the beneficiary of the "over $50,000 life insurance" is an organization to which a contribution would be a charitable contribution.

6. *Club memberships.* If your employer provides you with a membership in a country club or similar social organization, you are subject to tax on the value of the membership.

Tax-Free Fringe Benefits.   Certain fringe benefits you receive from your employer are specifically excluded from taxation. These include:

1. *No-additional-cost service.* If you receive services from your employer that are regularly offered for sale to customers and your employer incurs no substantial additional cost in providing them to you, you do not have to include the value of these services as income. *Example:* Stand-by flights for airline employees.

2. *Qualified employee discount.* You do not have to report additional income if the discount your employer extended to you is less than the discount he would regularly offer his customers. For the purchase of services, the discount must be less than 20% of the price regularly charged to customers. *Example:* Appliance manufacturers discounted sales of their products to their employees.

3. *Working condition fringe benefits.* You do not have to include in income the value of property or services provided to you by your employer if you would be entitled to a business deduction for such items on your personal return had you paid for these items. *Example:* Business periodical subscriptions.

4. *De minimis fringe benefits. De minimis* fringe benefits are items so small in value that it would be unreasonable or administratively impractical for your employer to account for them. *Examples:* Personal use of copying machine, occasional parties for employees.

We've mentioned just a few examples. You should consult with your employer and your tax advisor to find out how to treat a particular item.

401(k) Plans.   If your employer has a 401(k) plan or another plan that allows you to postpone income, you can elect to defer a certain amount of your salary on a pre-tax basis. Such amounts are withheld from your salary and are not reported as income until withdrawn from the plan. For further information about 401(k)s and other retirement plans see Chapter 4.

TAXSAVER

A key element of tax planning is reducing your adjusted gross income (AGI). One way to do that is to take advantage of your employer's 401(k) plan, particularly if the deductible amount you are permitted to contribute to an IRA is limited (see page 27). With a 401(k), you can elect to defer up to a maximum of $9,240 in 1994.

TAXSAVER

Although the funds in your 401(k) plan are meant to be set aside for your retirement, you may still have access to them if you need money. Your plan may permit you to borrow from the plan, subject to strict rules. Despite the restrictions, you may be better off borrowing from your retirement fund than getting a loan from your bank. If the loan from the bank is for personal purposes, it will result in nondeductible interest. While a loan from your 401(k) plan does not generate deductible interest, it allocates the interest payments you make to your account.

Interest and Dividends

Interest that you receive from bank accounts, from loans that you have made to others, or from other sources is taxable. However, interest received from obligations of a state or one of its political subdivisions, the District of Columbia, or a possession of the United States or one of its political divisions, is tax-exempt for federal purposes.

TAXSAVER

Generally, the interest rates paid on tax-exempt state and local obligations are lower than those paid on taxable bonds. However, you may find these lower rates attractive when you compare them with the after-tax yield from other taxable instruments (see page 33).

Interest is paid by the IRS on a tax refund arising from any type of original tax return if the refund is not issued by the 45th day after the later of the due date for the return (determined without regard to any extensions) or the date the return was filed. Interest you receive from the IRS is taxable. (The rates on such payments are set periodically by the IRS.)

U.S. Saving Bonds

U.S. saving bonds are direct obligations of the United States government. Two series of bonds are available: Series EE bonds and Series HH bonds. Both are subject to federal income tax, though in some circumstances (explained below) interest on Series EE bonds may be deferred for many years, and if used for certain educational purposes may even be exempt from tax. Both series of bonds, however, are not subject to state or local income taxes.

Series EE Bonds. These are bonds that are issued at a discount—that is, they're purchased at a fixed amount, and are redeemed at a higher amount depending upon how long the bonds were held. Cash method taxpayers have the option of reporting income on the bonds when the bonds are redeemed or reporting it annually as it accrues. Accrual method taxpayers must report the income as it accrues.

TAXSAVER

Series EE bonds can be an interesting tax-sheltered investment in two ways. First, because most individuals are cash-method taxpayers paying taxes on income as it is received, interest income from Series EE bonds is not recognized until it is received when the bonds are redeemed. But, there is a second way you can shelter your interest income from Series EE bonds for an even longer time. If, instead of redeeming the bonds when they come due, you exchange them for Series HH bonds (that pay interest semiannually), you can avoid recognition of the accumulated Series EE bond interest until the Series HH bonds are redeemed.

__Example:__ Sam purchases $7,500 worth of Series EE bonds, which pay interest at the guaranteed minimum 4 percent per year. In slightly more than seven years, the bonds will have grown in value to $10,000. Instead of redeeming them at that point, Sam exchanges them for $10,000 worth of Series HH bonds, which pay interest at the rate of 4 percent per year. The $2,500 of interest income earned over the years on the Series EE bonds would not be taxable at the date of exchange but would be deferred. Sam will receive $400 of taxable interest income per year on the Series HH bonds—or a 5.3% return on his original $7,500 investment. The $2,500 of deferred interest income on the Series EE bonds would not be taxable until the Series HH bonds reach final maturity or are redeemed.

There is, however, a limitation on the purchase of EE bonds. An individual may purchase only up to $15,000 per year.

When held five years or longer, EE bonds become eligible to receive a market-based interest rate, retroactive to the first day of the month of issue. They receive interest at either 85% of the average return during that time on marketable Treasury securities with five years remaining to their maturity, or the minimum guaranteed rate in effect at the time the bond is purchased, whichever is greater. The guaranteed minimum rate on newly purchased Series EE bonds is 4%.

TAX*SAVER*

EE bonds purchased beginning January 1, 1990, may be exempt from federal tax on the interest income, if their redemption proceeds are used for certain educational purposes. To be eligible for the tax exemption, the purchaser of the bonds must be at least 24 years of age, and the proceeds from the sale of the bonds must be used to pay for the qualified higher educational expenses of either the purchaser, his/her spouse, or dependents. The tax break phases out for married taxpayers filing jointly who have adjusted gross income beginning at $61,850 in 1994. For single taxpayers and heads of household filers, the phaseout begins at $41,200. The break is not available if you are married filing separately. A little good news, a little bad news: a young couple whose income increases significantly may find that by the time their child is ready for college, they are no longer eligible to claim the tax exemption.

Series HH Bonds. These are current income securities: interest is paid at a fixed rate semiannually. Interest must be reported in the year in which it is paid. Since March 1, 1993, new issues have paid a 4% rate of interest.

TAX*SAVER*

Both Series EE and HH bonds are subject to estate, inheritance, gift, or other excise taxes—whether federal or state—but they are exempt from all other taxes imposed on the principal or interest by any state, U.S. possession, or local taxing authority.

TAX*SAVER*

Millions of Series (single) E and (single) H saving bonds continue to be held by the public. Most are earning interest. Some, however, have reached final maturity and no longer earn interest; others are nearing their final maturity dates. The chart below shows the extended maturities that have been announced by the U.S. Treasury. Series E bonds that have reached final maturity should be redeemed or exchanged for Series HH bonds.

Extended maturities

Series	Date of Issues	Interest-bearing Life
E	May 1941–Nov. 1965	40 years
	Dec. 1965 and later	30 years
H	June 1952–Jan. 1957	29 years, 8 months
	Feb. 1957 and later	30 years
EE	All issues	30 years
HH	All issues	20 years

Dividends. Dividends are distributions of money, stock, or other property paid to you by a corporation. You may also indirectly receive dividends through a partnership, an estate, or a trust. In most cases, dividends are taxable as ordinary income. Some dividends, however, are treated as capital gain distributions. The distributions are nontaxable if the distribution is considered to be a return of capital or if the distribution is in the form of stock or stock rights. You should be informed by the corporation making the distribution about the nature of the dividends at the time of distribution. For further information, see Chapter 9, Investment Planning.

Stock Dividends and Stock Rights. Generally, the receipt of stock dividends or stock rights in a company is not taxable, unless the shareholder is permitted to choose between stock (or stock rights) and cash or other property (e.g., a dividend reinvestment plan).

If you receive a nontaxable distribution from a company, the adjusted basis of your old stock must be apportioned between the old and the new stock (or stock rights) based on their relative market values.

Example: If you owned 100 shares of XYZ Company which you purchased at $10 a share and you then received another 100 shares as a stock dividend, your adjusted basis for your 200 shares would be $5 a share. For further discussion, see Chapter 9, Investment Planning. You are not required to allocate basis to nontaxable stock rights received if the value of the rights is less than 15% of the fair market value of the stock on the date of distribution.

Mutual fund dividends declared in October, November, and December to shareholders of record in those months are considered paid on December 31 of that year even if the distribution isn't actually paid until January of the next year.

Rental Income and Expenses

Rental income includes any payment you receive for the use or occupation of property. If you receive property or services as rent, the fair market value of the property or services you receive is rental income. (See Chapter 3 for a discussion of rentals of vacation homes and depreciation.)

Capital Gains and Losses

For the most part, everything you own and hold for personal and investment purposes is a capital asset. See Chapter 6, Capital Gains and Losses, for a discussion of how sales of capital assets are taxed.

Selling Your Home

A gain on the sale or exchange (including condemnation) or your principal residence is taxable. If you have a loss on the sale, you cannot deduct it. (See Chapter 3 for more information about the tax consequences of home ownership as well as for tax-saving strategies that involve your home.)

Income from Business and Other Investments

Sole Proprietorship, Partnership, and S Corporation Income

In a sole proprietorship, you and your business are one and the same taxpayer. You report gross profit or loss for the year from the sole proprietorship on Form 1040, and it becomes part of your adjusted gross income. In contrast with a sole proprietorship, a partnership is an entity that is separate from the individual taxpayers that are its owners. A partnership is not a taxable entity that is subject to federal income tax. However, if you are a member of a partnership, you are liable individually for tax on your share of partnership income, even if such income is not distributed to you. S corporations generally do not pay federal income tax. Instead, S corporation income typically is taxed directly to the shareholders based on their respective ownership percentage, regardless of whether such income is distributed to them. Like partnerships, S corporations separately report items of income, gain, deduction, and loss that may be subject to special treatment by their shareholders. For a more complete discussion about the taxation of business income, see Part III, Tax Strategies for Businesses, especially Chapter 13, Determining Income, Deductions, and Taxes for Your Business.

"At Risk" Limitation Provisions

The deduction for business and other investment losses held directly or through partnerships or S corporations is generally limited to the amount by which you are considered to be "at risk" in the activity. You are considered at risk for the amount of cash you have invested in the venture and the basis of property invested plus certain amounts borrowed for use in the activity.

Borrowed amounts that are considered at risk are (1) loans for which you are personally liable for repayment or (2) loans secured by property, other than that used in the activity. Generally, liabilities that are secured by property within the activity for which you are not otherwise personally liable are not considered to be at risk. An exception: if nonrecourse financing is secured against real property used in the activity, you may be considered at risk for the amount of the financing.

If you are a partner in a partnership or a shareholder in an S corporation, you are also considered to be at risk for your undistributed share of partnership or S corporation income. The at-risk provisions apply to individuals and closely held corporations (corporations in which five or fewer individuals own more than 50% of the stock). For S corporations or partnerships, the at-risk rules apply to the shareholder or the partner. An exception: closely held corporations engaged in certain equipment leasing and active qualifying businesses are not subject to the at-risk rules.

The law provides a broad list of activities (including the holding of real estate acquired after 1986) that are subject to the at-risk provisions. Each investment activity is considered separately. However, S corporations and partnerships can aggregate investments in similar activity categories. If the "at-risk" provisions apply to you, you should consult with your tax advisor.

Passive Activity Losses and Credits

Prior to 1987, individuals generally were allowed to use losses and tax credits generated by a particular business or investment activity to shelter income tax liability attributable to their other endeavors. Consequently, individuals with substantial salaries, business income, interest income, and dividends could significantly reduce their tax liabilities by investing in "tax shelters" (typically some form of limited partnership) that offered losses or tax credits. This opportunity did not depend on the taxpayer's level of participation in the shelter's day-to-day operations.

Individuals, estates, trusts, closely held corporations, and personal service corporations are prohibited from deducting net losses generated by passive activities. (Passive activities are discussed below.) In addition, tax credits from passive activities are generally limited to the tax liability attributable to such activities. Disallowed passive activity losses are suspended and carried forward to offset passive activity income generated in future years. Similar carryforward treatment applies to excess credits.

Defining an Activity.   The proper grouping of business operations into one or more activities is important in determining the allocation of suspended losses, measuring your material participation, separating rental and nonrental activities, and determining when a disposition of an activity has occurred. IRS proposed regulations define an activity as any "appropriate economic unit for measuring gain or loss." What constitutes an "appropriate economic unit" is determined by looking at all facts and circumstances. The regulations list five factors that are to be given the greatest weight. They are:

1. Similarities and differences in types of business;
2. The extent of common control;
3. The extent of common ownership;
4. Geographical location; and
5. Interdependence between the activities.

Generally, taxpayers must be consistent from year to year in determining the business operations that constitute an activity. Consult your tax advisor for more information.

Defining Passive Activities.   A passive activity involves the conduct of any trade or business in which you do not materially participate. You are treated as a material participant only if you are involved in the operations of the activity on a regular, continuous, and substantial basis. If you are not a material participant in an activity, but your spouse is, you are treated as being a material participant and the activity is not considered passive.

Seven Tests.   The IRS has seven different tests you can meet to be considered a material participant. If you satisfy one of these tests, you will be considered a material participant in an activity. These tests are:

1. You participate in the activity for more than 500 hours during the taxable year;
2. Your participation during the taxable year constitutes substantially all of the participation of all individuals;
3. You participate for more than 100 hours during the taxable year and no one else participates more;
4. The activity is a significant participation activity (SPA) for the taxable year, and your participation in all SPAs during the taxable year exceeds 500 hours. An SPA is

an activity in which an individual participates for more than 100 hours, but does not otherwise meet a material participation test;

5. You materially participated in any 5 of the 10 preceding taxable years;

6. The activity is a personal service activity, and you materially participated for any three preceding taxable years. A personal service activity involves performance of personal services in the fields of health, law, engineering, architecture, accounting, actuarial sciences, performing arts, consulting, or any other business in which capital is not a material income-producing factor; and

7. Based on all the facts and circumstances, your participation is regular, continuous, and substantial during the taxable year.

Rental Activities. Rental activities are generally considered passive activities. However, the personal use of a dwelling unit for the greater of 14 days or 10% of the time that it is rented out to others is considered use of a personal residence and is not considered a passive activity (see the discussion of rental income and expenses earlier in this chapter).

IRS rules provide other exceptions for which activities involving the use of tangible property are not deemed a rental activity.

> ### TAXALERT
>
> *Beginning after December 31, 1993, the passive activity limitations for certain real estate professionals were liberalized. Taxpayers who satisfy certain eligibility thresholds and materially participate in rental real estate activities may offset rental real estate losses against all sources of taxable income.*
>
> *Only individuals and closely held C corporations can qualify for this special rule. An individual taxpayer will satisfy the eligibility requirements for any tax year if more than one-half of the personal services (with more than 750 hours) performed in trades or businesses by the taxpayer during such a tax year are performed in real property trades or businesses in which the taxpayer materially participates. Personal services performed as an employee are not considered in determining material participation unless the employee has more than a 5% ownership in the employer. However, independent contractor realtor services would qualify for this purpose. For closely held C corporations, the eligibility requirements are met if more than 50% of the corporation's gross receipts for the tax year are derived*

from real property trades or businesses in which the corporation materially participates.

   Example: *During 1994, a self-employed real estate developer earned $100,000 in development fees from projects the developer spent 1,200 hours developing. In addition, the developer incurred rental real estate losses of $200,000 from properties which the developer spent over 800 hours managing during 1994. The developer performs no other personal services during the year, and has no other items of income or deduction. Because the developer (1) materially participated in the rental real estate activity, (2) performed more than 750 hours in real property trades or businesses, and (3) performed more than 50% of the developer's total personal service hours in real estate trades or businesses in which the developer materially participated, the developer will have a net operating loss of $100,000 to carry back (and the excess to carry forward) to offset any source of income.*

Limited Partnerships.   Limited partnership interests are considered passive because a limited partner is generally not a material participant. If you have an interest in a limited partnership, you should check with your tax advisor to see if exceptions apply.

   In general, working interests in any oil and gas property that you hold directly or through an entity that does not limit your liability is not considered passive, whether or not you are a material participant.

TAXSAVER

One way to increase the deductibility of your passive activity losses is to convert the interest expense from nondeductible passive activity interest to deductible residential interest. You can accomplish this shift by borrowing against your personal residence and using the proceeds to repay passive activity loans. Interest on borrowings of up to $100,000 secured by your personal residence is usually fully deductible regardless of how the proceeds are used.

Exception for Active Real Estate Participation.
An exception to the passive loss rules applies to real estate rental activities in which you are an active participant. For this purpose, "active" participation requires a significant but lesser amount of involvement than does "material" participation. Active involvement would include making management decisions such as approving new tenants or making capital expenditures. You are considered to have not actively participated in the rental activity if, at any time during

the tax year, you own less than a 10% interest in the activity. Each tax year, you can deduct up to $25,000 of passive losses (or claim the equivalent amount of credits) arising from real estate rental activities against income from nonpassive sources, such as salary, interest, and dividends. The $25,000 maximum deduction is reduced (but not below zero) by 50% of the amount by which your adjusted gross income exceeds $100,000. Thus, this deduction is completely phased out if your adjusted gross income is $150,000 or more. Adjusted gross income, for this purpose, is figured without taxable Social Security benefits, IRA contribution deductions, and any passive activity loss.

Example: Ron's adjusted gross income, figured without taxable Social Security benefits, IRA contribution deductions, and any passive activity loss, is $120,000. He has rental losses of $25,000. If Ron's income had been less than $100,000, he would have been able to deduct the full $25,000 rental real estate loss. Because his income is over $100,000, Ron's $25,000 loss is reduced by $10,000 [50% × ($120,000 − $100,000)]. The disallowed loss of $10,000 can be carried over to future years and deducted (based on these same limitations).

Dispositions of Passive Activities. If you completely dispose of a passive activity in a fully taxable transaction, you can then claim previously disallowed (i.e., suspended) losses. In addition, if you get rid of a "substantial part" of a passive activity in a fully taxable transaction, you can deduct the portion of your suspended losses attributable to that part of your investment—assuming that you can determine with reasonable certainty the amount of the losses attributable to that part of your investment. However, if you dispose of a passive activity by selling your interest to a related party, you will not be able to deduct any suspended losses until the related purchaser disposes of the interest in a taxable transaction to an unrelated person. You can also deduct suspended losses in a passive activity if your interest is disposed of in various other ways, including abandonment, death of the taxpayer, gifts, and installment sales of entire interests. Special rules may apply. You should consult your tax advisor for further clarification and requirements.

Social Security and Other Benefits

Social Security and Equivalent Railroad Retirement Benefits

For unmarried filers with base income between $25,000 and $34,000 and for joint filers with base income between $32,000 and $44,000, a portion of Social Security and equivalent railroad retirement benefits should be included in your taxable income. The amount to be included is the lesser of:

1. One half of the benefits received, or
2. One half of the "excess combined income" over a specified base. Excess combined income is adjusted gross income with certain modifications plus one half of the benefits received. The base is $32,000 if you are married filing jointly, $0 for married filing separately if you lived with your spouse at any time during the year, and $25,000 for other individuals.

For tax years beginning after December 31, 1993, existing rules for calculating the amount of Social Security benefits subject to income tax remain the same for unmarried filers with base income between $25,000 and $34,000 and for joint filers with base income between $32,000 and $44,000.

However, for taxpayers with income in excess of the new higher thresholds, the portion of Social Security benefits received that is subject to tax is calculated as the lesser of:

- 85% of Social Security benefits received; or
- The sum of the following amounts:
  a. The smaller of (1) the amount that would have been included in income under prior law; or (2) $4,500 (for unmarried taxpayers) or $6,000 (for married taxpayers filing joint returns), plus
  b. 85% of the excess of the taxpayer's base income over the new threshold amount.

For married individuals filing separately, taxable Social Security benefits are calculated as the lesser of 85% of benefits received or 85% of the taxpayer's base income.

The table below illustrates the portion of $10,000 in Social Security benefits received that would be includible in the taxable income of single and joint filers at various income levels.

Amount of $10,000 in Social Security Benefits Included in Taxable Income

Base Income	Single	Joint
$25,000	None	None
34,000	$4,500	$1,000
38,000	7,900	3,000
44,000	8,500	5,000
50,000	8,500	8,500

TaxSaver

The amount of combined income is what triggers the tax on your Social Security benefits. You may want to consider deferring the recognition of income by in-

vesting in U.S. Savings Bonds, Series EE, or growth stocks that pay little or no dividends.

TAXSAVER

Tax-exempt income is added to your adjusted gross income for purposes of calculating how much, if any, of your Social Security benefits will be subject to tax. Keep this in mind when evaluating the after-tax rate of return of tax-exempt investments versus taxable investments.

Disability

Generally, you must report as income amounts you receive for your disability through an accident or health insurance plan paid for by your employer.

TAXSAVER

If you pay part of the cost of a disability plan, then any amounts you receive that are attributable to your payments will not be taxed to you.

Employee Death Benefits

Certain amounts received by a beneficiary from or on behalf of an employer by reason of the death of an employee may be excluded from income. The total amount that can be excluded with respect to an employee who has died may not exceed $5,000, regardless of the number of employers or beneficiaries. This exclusion may not apply if the employee had a nonforfeitable right to receive the amounts while living. Benefits paid in a lump-sum distribution for a self-employed person who was treated as an employee for qualified retirement plan coverage can also be excluded, subject to the same limitation.

Pensions or Annuities

As a general rule, if you did not pay any part of the cost of your pension or annuity, and your employer did not withhold part of the cost of the contract from your pay while you worked, the amounts you receive each year are fully taxable. For more information about IRAs, Keoghs, and Simplified Employee Pensions (SEPs), see Chapter 4.

What to Exclude From Income. If you paid part of the cost of your annuity, the portion of an annuity payment representing the return of your "investment in the contract" can be excluded from your gross income. The excludable portion is the payment received times the "exclusion ratio," that is, the investment in the contract divided by the expected return under the contract. The "expected return under the contract" is the total amount that you or someone you designate can expect to receive under the contract based on actuarial considerations. The exclusion ratio is determined as of the first day of the first period for which an annuity payment is received. Once computed, the ratio ordinarily will not change.

For annuities that began payments before 1987, tax-free recoveries will continue even if the annuity owner outlives his or her life expectancy. However, if your first annuity payment was after 1986, the portion of a payment excluded from your gross income cannot exceed the unrecovered investment in the contract immediately before the receipt of such payment.

If annuity payments (from annuities with starting dates after 1986) cease because the annuity owner dies before his or her total contributions have been recovered, the amount of the unrecovered investment is allowed as an itemized deduction to the annuity owner for his or her last taxable year. The deduction is not subject to the 2% floor on miscellaneous itemized deductions. Similar rules apply where the contract provides for payments to be made to a beneficiary.

TaxSaver

Annuities are popular investments to earn income and defer taxes. Earnings accumulate and are not taxed until you receive payments. For more on annuities, please see Chapter 9, Investment Planning.

Lump-Sum Distributions. Lump-sum distributions you receive from a qualified retirement plan—an employer's pension, stock bonus, or profit-sharing plan—may qualify for special tax treatment. A lump-sum distribution is the distribution within a single tax year of an employee's entire balance, excluding certain amounts forfeited or subject to forfeiture, from all of the employer's qualified pension plans, all of the employer's qualified stock bonus plans, or all of the employer's qualified profit-sharing plans. The distribution must have been made:

1. Because of the employee's death,
2. After the employee reaches age 59½,
3. Because of the employee's separation from service (does not apply to self-employed persons), or
4. After a self-employed individual becomes totally and permanently disabled.

As with an annuity, you may recover tax-free your cost basis in the lump-sum distribution. In general, your cost basis is:

1. Your total nondeductible contributions to the plan;

2. The total of your taxable one-year term costs of life insurance;
3. Any employer contributions that were taxable to you; and
4. Repayments of loans that were taxable to you.

You must reduce your basis by amounts previously distributed to you tax-free.

You also may be able to receive special tax treatment on the remainder of the distribution:

Long-Term Capital Gain Treatment. If you were at least age 50 on January 1, 1986, you may choose to treat a portion of the taxable part of a lump-sum distribution as a long-term capital gain taxable at a 20% rate. This treatment applies to the portion you receive relating to your participation in the plan before 1974.

Capital gains treatment is not available for lump-sum distributions received after 1991 by individuals who were less than 50 years old on January 1, 1986.

Special Averaging Method. You may elect to use a 5-year special averaging method to calculate the tax on the ordinary income portion of a lump-sum distribution, including the capital gain portion for which you did not elect capital gain treatment. To use special averaging, you must be at least age 59½ (unless you were at least age 50 on January 1, 1986), elect to use special averaging for all lump-sum distributions received during the year, and have been a participant in the plan for five or more years. You can make this election only once in a lifetime.

If you were at least age 50 on January 1, 1986, the 59½ requirement does not apply and you may elect to use 10-year averaging rather than 5-year averaging. However, the tax rates used in the 10-year averaging calculation are the rates in effect for 1986.

To get an idea of how special averaging works, assume that your income was received equally by 5 different persons (10 for 10-year averaging) in the current year and that each of these people had no other income. As a result, most of the income is taxed at the lowest rates on the single taxpayer tax rate schedule. The tax for these fictional individuals is then added up and becomes your tax on the distribution.

TAXALERT

Legislation currently pending in Congress (H.R. 3419) would repeal 5-year income averaging for lump-sum distributions.

TaxSaver

The 5-year or 10-year averaging method may be so beneficial to you that you elect to have the long-term capital gain portion of the lump-sum distribution included in the 5-year or 10-year averaging computation rather than have it taxed as long-term capital gain. The tax should be figured both ways to see which is the lowest. If you are eligible to elect either 5-year or 10-year averaging, you should also figure your tax both ways to determine which is most beneficial.

Individual Retirement Arrangements (IRAs).

In general, distributions from an IRA are taxed in much the same way as an annuity. The portion of each distribution that is attributable to nondeductible contributions, if any, is excluded from your taxable income. The portion of each distribution to be excluded is determined by dividing undistributed nondeductible contributions by your total IRA account balance. If no nondeductible contributions have been made, then the entire distribution is considered ordinary income. (See Chapter 4 for more details about IRAs.)

Other Income

Interest-Free and Below-Market-Rate Loans

Certain interest-free and below-market-rate loans are required to be treated as loans bearing interest at a statutory rate.

An interest-free or below-market loan is a loan on which no interest is charged or on which interest is charged at a rate below the applicable federal rate (AFR), set monthly by the IRS. Such a loan is generally treated as an arm's length transaction in which you, as the borrower, are deemed (1) to have received a loan that requires the payment of interest at the applicable federal rate and (2) to have received an additional payment equal to the difference between the AFR and the no-interest or low-interest rate. The additional payment is treated as a gift, dividend, contribution to capital, payment of compensation, or other payment, depending on the nature of the transaction. In effect, two transactions are deemed to have occurred. One results in interest income to the lender and interest expense to the borrower to the extent that the interest at the statutory rate exceeds the actual interest paid. This is known as "foregone interest." In the second transaction, the lender is considered to have paid to the borrower the amount of "foregone interest" in the form of a gift, dividend, compensation, or other payment, depending on the nature of the relationship between the two parties.

Below-Market Demand Loans. If one party receives a below-market gift demand loan or other demand loan (one payable in full at any time upon the lender's demand), the lender will be treated as having made a transfer on the last day of the calendar year to the borrower of an amount equal to the "foregone interest." This amount will be treated as a gift, compensation, dividend, or other payment as appropriate. An identical amount will be treated as a payment of interest by the borrower at the same time. Therefore, the borrower may be entitled to deduct a part of that amount as interest expense. Loans with indefinite maturities are treated as demand loans.

Below-Market Term Loans. If one party receives a below-market "gift" term loan (one that is not a demand loan), the lender is treated as having made a gift on the loan date equal to the excess of the amount borrowed over the present value of all principal and interest payments required by the terms of the loan. The present value is determined using the applicable federal rate established monthly by the IRS. The borrower is then treated as though he or she has paid interest to the lender on the last day of the calendar year.

If one party receives a term loan (other than a gift term loan), the lender is deemed to have transferred an amount equal to the excess of the loan over the present value of all principal and interest payments to the borrower. The transfer is treated as having occurred on the date the loan was made. The amount will be considered a dividend, compensation, or other payment as appropriate. An amount equal to this excess will be treated as original issue discount. Accordingly, the original discount rules apply. The borrower and the lender will be treated as paying or receiving interest on an economic accrual basis over the term of the loan. (Original issue discount is discussed on page 230.)

The AFR used in the calculations discussed above is based on the average yield on U.S. Treasury obligations. Different rates will be used for short-, intermediate-, and long-term loans. Semiannual compounding is required for both term and demand loans.

Exceptions: The rules for below-market loans do not apply to:
1. Gift loans between individuals that in the aggregate do not exceed $10,000, provided the loan proceeds are not directly used to purchase or carry income-producing assets;
2. Gift loans between individuals not exceeding $100,000, where the borrower's net investment income does not exceed $1,000 and there is no motive to avoid paying tax;

3. Gift loans between individuals not exceeding $100,000, where the borrower's net investment income exceeds $1,000 and there is no motive to avoid paying tax (the amount of interest income and expense imputed is limited to the net investment income); and
4. Compensation or corporate/shareholder loans that in the aggregate do not exceed $10,000, provided the principal purpose of the loan is not avoiding taxes.

TaxSaver

Imputed interest sometimes results in one or both parties of the transaction recognizing taxable income without an offsetting deduction, even though no money changed hands. To avoid this, be sure that the loans carry an appropriate market interest rate and that interest payments are made when due. For term loans, the interest rate is the applicable federal rate in effect on the date the loan is made; for demand loans the interest rate is the applicable federal short-term rate in effect on each day the loan is outstanding.

Restricted Property Received for Services

The excess of the fair market value of restricted property received for services performed over the amount (if any) paid for such property should be included in income as compensation in the year your interest in the property becomes transferable or is not subject to a substantial risk of forfeiture. Restricted property includes both real and personal property that is subject to some form of restriction, such as a limitation on transferring the property or a risk of forfeiture upon leaving employment before a specified date. However, restricted property does not include either money or an unsecured promise to pay money or property in the future. Generally, the fair market value is determined at the time the property becomes transferable or nonforfeitable.

Instead of deferring the recognition of income until your interest in the property becomes transferable or is no longer subject to a substantial risk of forfeiture, you may elect in the year of transfer to include in your income the fair market value of the property at the time of receipt (disregarding restrictions other than ones that by their terms will never lapse) minus the amount (if any) paid for such property. Generally, this election must be made within 30 days after the transfer of the property. However, if this election is made and the property is subsequently forfeited, you may only deduct the excess of the amount originally paid for the property (if any) over the amount realized (if any) from the forfeiture.

TaxSaver

The election to include in your income the fair market value of the property at the time of receipt can produce tax savings if the property appreciates in value by the time the restrictions lapse. This election defers recognizing the gain on the appreciation until the property is sold. However, you need to consider the value of money over time for the taxes you will currently pay as well as the possibility of forfeiting the property.

The holding period for the restricted property begins on the first date on which your rights are either transferable or not subject to a substantial risk of forfeiture. If, however, you elect to include in your income the fair market value of the property, the holding period begins on the date of actual transfer.

If you perform services in return for restricted property, the person for whom you perform such services is allowed a deduction for the same amount and in the same year in which you report income. For transfers to employees, regulations generally require withholding by the employer.

Unemployment Compensation
Unemployment compensation benefits are fully taxable.

Health and Accident Benefits
Benefits received under a qualified employer-sponsored health or accident plan for the reimbursement of medical expenses and payments for permanent injury or loss of a bodily function can be excluded from your gross income. Reimbursements for medical expenses that you claimed as an itemized deduction in a previous year must be included in gross income.

Benefits received under an employer-funded self-insured medical reimbursement plan by employees who are officers, shareholders, or highly compensated individuals can be excluded from your income only if the plan does not discriminate in favor of these employees.

Life Insurance Contracts
Generally, amounts received under a life insurance contract paid by reason of the death of the insured, whether in a single sum or otherwise, is not included in your gross income.

Any interest paid along with life insurance death proceeds is taxable.

Any proceeds received upon the surrender of a life insurance contract by the insured are taxable to the extent that the amount received (including amounts recovered tax-free prior to the exchange) is in excess of the amounts paid in. A loss is not deductible.

TAXALERT

Some insurance companies are providing pre-death payments to terminally ill policyholders. The IRS generally is treating payments to terminally ill on account of imminent death as insurance proceeds at death. Therefore, they are not includible in the policyholder's income.

Modified Endowment Contracts

In general, a modified endowment contract is one in which the accumulated amount paid by the taxpayer under the contract at any time during the first seven contract years exceeds the sum of the average annual premiums for paid-up insurance that would have been paid within the first seven years.

Modified endowment contracts entered after June 21, 1988, are taxable as follows:

1. Amounts received under the contract are treated first as income and then as a recovery of investment in the contract.
2. Loans under the contract, as well as loans secured by the contract, are treated as amounts received under the contract except for certain loans relating to funeral expenses.
3. An additional 10% tax is imposed on amounts received that can be included in income. This additional tax does not apply to any distribution: (a) made on or after you turn 59½; (b) due to your becoming disabled; or (c) that is part of a series of substantially equal periodic payments made over your life or life expectancy or for the joint lives or life expectancies of you and your beneficiary.

Certain Living Expense Contracts

You can exclude from your gross income amounts received under an insurance contract that pays you for living expenses in excess of your normal living expenses resulting from the loss of the use of your principal residence due to a casualty.

Dividends on Life Insurance and Endowment Policies

Dividends on most unmatured life insurance or endowment policies are a partial return of the premiums paid and are not included in your gross income until they exceed the accumulated net premiums paid for the contract.

Alimony and Similar Payments

If you receive cash payments of alimony or separate maintenance, you must include them in figuring your gross income. Conversely, if you pay alimony or separate maintenance to a former spouse, you may deduct such payments from your gross income. Payments received from a property settlement or for child support are not considered alimony and therefore are not considered income to the recipient (or deductible to the payor).

TAXSAVER

The tax consequences of alimony versus other payments need to be carefully considered in working out divorce or separation agreements. For example, if you receive property with a tax basis that is substantially less than its current value, you will be subject to tax when you sell the property on the difference between the tax basis of the property and what you receive. You should consult your tax advisor on such matters. (See page 45 for a further discussion of alimony.)

Tax-Exempt Interest

Interest on certain obligations of a state, territory, U.S. possession, or any political subdivision of the foregoing can be excluded from your gross income. In addition, if you earn interest on tax-exempt bonds issued in your home state, the interest will generally not be subject to state or local tax. Special rules apply to interest on arbitrage and industrial development bonds. Tax-exempt interest on certain municipal bonds issued after August 7, 1986, are tax preference items for alternative minimum tax purposes. (See discussion on page 138.)

TAXSAVER

Higher income tax rates increase the appeal of tax-exempt bonds and mutual funds that invest in these bonds, especially for taxpayers in the 39.6% top marginal tax bracket. As tax rates rise, taxable securities must provide a higher yield in order to match the tax-effected yield offered by tax-exempt bonds of similar quality and time to maturity. For example, to a taxpayer in the 31% bracket, a taxable bond yielding 8.69% is comparable to a municipal bond with a 6.0% tax-exempt yield. However, a taxpayer in the new 39.6% bracket would need almost a 10% yield on a taxable bond to match the municipal bond's 6.0% return. And considering the fact that some states have income tax rates over 10%, the combined federal and state mar-

ginal tax rate, taking phaseouts and other back door tax increases into account, can exceed 50%. Thus, an investor living in such a high tax state would need a 12% taxable bond to achieve the same after-tax return as a 6% municipal bond.

The following table demonstrates the yield you would have to earn on a taxable bond in order to generate the same after-tax earnings as a tax-exempt bond would provide at a correspondingly lower yield.

Equivalent Yield Needed from a Taxable Bond

Tax-Exempt Yield	Your Combined Federal, State & Local Marginal Tax Bracket						
	28%	31%	33%	36%	39.6%	42%	46%
4.00	5.56	5.80	5.97	6.25	6.62	6.90	7.41
4.50	6.25	6.52	6.72	7.03	7.45	7.76	8.33
5.00	6.94	7.25	7.46	7.81	8.28	8.62	9.26
5.50	7.64	7.97	8.21	8.59	9.11	9.48	10.19
6.00	8.33	8.70	8.96	9.38	9.93	10.34	11.11
6.50	9.03	9.42	9.70	10.16	10.76	11.21	12.04
7.00	9.72	10.15	10.45	10.94	11.59	12.07	12.96

Group Term Life Insurance Paid by Employers

Generally, the cost for group term life insurance paid by an employer for the benefit of employees can be excluded from your gross income, as long as the premiums do not exceed the cost for $50,000 of life insurance.

If the group term life insurance plan discriminates in favor of highly compensated employees, then the cost of this insurance is fully taxable to such employees. For purposes of this rule, highly compensated employees include certain officers of the corporation and certain shareholder-employees.

E&Y FOCUS: Employee Stock Options

Many employers grant stock options to employees as a reward for services rendered or to be rendered. Stock options allow an employee to buy a specified amount of stock of his or her employer at some set price, and for a stated period of time. For example, your employer might grant you an option to purchase stock in the company at $10 per share—its market price at the time of the grant. If the market price of the stock rises to, say, $15 per share, you would be able to buy the stock at a discount of $5 per share— that is, at the $10-per-share option price rather than the $15 market value. But if the value of the stock never goes above the $10 exercise price, you would let your option lapse.

Merely being able to hold unexercised options may be viewed as providing the option holder with significant economic benefits. Options can be seen as an opportunity to "ride the market" without committing personal capital to a risk that the value of the stock may fall. If the market price of the employer's stock increases, the holder of unexercised options benefits from this appreciation just as a shareholder would. That's because the option holder can acquire the appreciated stock for a known bargain price simply by exercising the option.

Incentive Stock Options

An incentive stock option (ISO) can be received and exercised without recognition of income if certain requirements are met. An incentive stock option (ISO) has the following tax consequences:

1. No taxable income will be recognized by the employee when the ISO is granted or exercised.
2. The income will be taxed as a capital gain when the employee sells stock acquired under an incentive stock option plan, provided the holding period requirements are met.
3. The employer will not be able to deduct the bargain element of the option as an expense, as long as the gain on the option is treated as a capital gain.
4. The difference between the option price and the fair market value at the time the option is exercised is an adjustment for the alternative minimum tax.

This favorable treatment for incentive stock options is available provided that:

1. You do not dispose of the stock within two years after the option is granted and you hold the stock for at least one year from the date the option is exercised. If these requirements are not met, you will recognize ordinary income on the difference between the option price and the fair market value at the date the option is exercised or the sales price on the date the shares are sold, if lower. Any amount realized in excess of the fair market value on the date the option is exercised will be considered a capital gain. In such a case, your employer would be entitled to deduct as a compensation expense the ordinary income portion of your gain.
2. For the entire time from the date the option is granted until three months before it is exercised, you must be an employee either of the company granting the option, a parent or subsidiary of that corporation, or a corporation that has assumed the option of another corpora-

tion as a result of a corporate reorganization, liquidation, or similar transaction.

Nonstatutory Stock Options

Nonstatutory stock options (NSOs) are options that do not meet certain requirements and are not afforded the special tax treatment given to ISOs (see the preceding paragraphs). Generally, these options are taxed at ordinary income rates. Depending on the particular characteristics of the option, it may be taxed (1) when the option is granted, (2) when it is exercised, (3) when it is sold, or (4) when restrictions on the disposition of the stock lapse. Typically, most nonstatutory stock options are taxed when exercised.

E&Y FOCUS: When to Exercise Stock Options

Incentive Stock Options. If you expect your company stock to appreciate over the long term, it generally makes sense to postpone exercising incentive stock options (ISOs) until their expiration date is imminent. By waiting you can watch the stock appreciate as long as possible before having to pay the option price.

In the following situations, however, it may make sense to exercise ISOs before they expire:

- If you believe the company's stock price has peaked and you intend to sell the stock as soon as you can after exercising the options (i.e., before the required long-term capital gain holding period);
- If the annual dividends paid on your company's stock exceed the carrying cost of the funds needed to exercise the options, that is, the option price plus any taxes due (this strategy would, of course, subject you to the risk that the stock price may fall); or
- If you have a need for cash now or in the near future that can be satisfied by exercising the options and subsequently selling the stock. You may not want to take the risk of a lower market price in the future.

Nonqualified Stock Options. Generally, if you expect the company stock to appreciate over the long term, it makes sense to postpone exercising NQSOs until their expiration date is imminent. By waiting, you can continue to benefit from the appreciation on all of the options without having to liquidate other assets or some of the stock. Remember, however, that when the options are exercised, you have to surrender cash (or, in some cases, stock) to pay the option price and the tax on the option spread. By deferring the exercise at the option, you can earn more appreciation before you have to cough up the option price and pay the tax bill.

In the following situations, however, it may make sense to exercise options before they expire:

- If you believe the company's stock price has peaked, and you intend to sell the stock as soon as you can after the exercise;
- If the annual dividends paid on your company's stock exceed the carrying cost of the funds needed to exercise the options, that is, the option price plus any taxes due (this strategy would, of course, subject you to the risk that the stock price may fall);
- If you have a need for cash now or in the near future that can be satisfied by exercising the options and subsequently selling the stock. You may not want to take the risk of a lower market price in the future;
- If you expect that ordinary income tax rates will increase in the future; or
- If you are subject to the alternative minimum tax but will not be entitled to a minimum tax credit carryover for the full amount of the AMT. The ordinary income from exercising the option will be subject to the AMT tax rate of 26 or 28%, which is substantially below the regular tax rate.

Prizes and Awards

Generally, contest prizes and awards are included in gross income.

The value of an employee achievement award for length of service or safety performance can be excluded from your gross income to the extent your employer can deduct the expense. Special rules apply to limit the total awards you can exclude from your income in any one tax year. The maximum yearly exclusion is generally $400. However, if the awards received are under a plan that satisfies certain conditions specified by the tax law, you may be able to exclude up to $1,600 in total annual awards from income.

Reimbursements for Moving Expenses

The 1993 law substantially rewrote and restricted the benefits of the rules for moving expenses. In addition to other changes, after 1993 qualified moving expenses paid or reimbursed by your employer are excludable from gross income and are not included on your Form W-2. (For a discussion of the qualified deductions allowed for employment-related moving expenses, see pages 56–58.)

Gifts and Inheritances

Your gross income does not include the value of property acquired by gift or inheritance. (See Chapter 11 for a discussion of the gift and estate tax.)

Scholarships and Fellowship Grants

You can exclude from gross income the amount received as a qualified scholarship or fellowship grant provided you are a degree candidate and the monies are used strictly for qualified tuition, fees, books, supplies, and required equipment.

Cafeteria Plans

A cafeteria plan is an employee benefit plan under which a participant may choose between two or more benefits consisting of cash and qualified benefits. You may generally exclude from gross income employer contributions for nontaxable benefits selected under the plan (unless you are a "highly compensated participant" in a discriminatory plan). The exclusion from gross income does not apply to "key employees" where the statutory benefits provided to them exceed 25% of the total nontaxable benefits provided for all employees under the plan.

TaxSaver

Cafeteria plans can be used effectively to increase the tax benefits of certain deductions and credits. For instance, ordinarily only medical expenses in excess of 7.5% of your adjusted gross income can be deducted. However, if you contribute to your employer's cafeteria plan (in pre-tax dollars), you can then be reimbursed by the plan for certain medical benefits if the employer's plan provides this as an option. You will not be taxed on the reimbursement you receive. There are some risks for employees because money left over at the end of the year is forfeited. So consult your tax advisor.

Similarly, dependent care payments you make qualify you for the dependent care credit. Depending on your income level, you may get a tax credit for at least 20% of the payments you made. However, if your contribution to your employer's cafeteria plan is made in pre-tax dollars, the benefit of reimbursement of child care expenses from the plan can be as high as 39.6%, depending on your tax bracket.

Example: *Assume you have medical expenses of $1,000. If your expenses are paid through a cafeteria plan, the cost to you will be $1,000 in reduced wages. If you are in the 31% bracket and pay the medical expenses after tax you will have to earn $1,450 to have enough left over to pay the $1,000 of medical expenses.*

TaxALERT

Note that the rules relating to cafeteria plans could be affected by pending health care reform legislation.

2

What You Can Deduct: Exemptions, Adjustments, and Deductions

Introduction

This chapter discusses most of the deductions and exemptions that you can claim to lower your taxable income. Deductions include medical and dental expenses, charitable contributions, non-business casualty and theft losses, and home mortgage interest payments, as well as amounts you pay for state and local income and property taxes, certain other interest payments, and a variety of miscellaneous items. In addition, you are entitled to exemptions for yourself, for children, and for other dependents.

The amount of income tax you owe is figured by taking your gross income minus allowable adjustments, deductions, and exemptions. The adjustment amounts reduce your gross income to arrive at a figure known as *adjusted gross income* (AGI). Then, deductions and exemptions are subtracted from your AGI to arrive at your taxable income, the amount on which income tax is imposed. After you have figured your adjusted gross income, you are ready to subtract the deductions used to figure taxable income. You may subtract the greater of either the standard deduction (which is explained in this chapter) or you may itemize your deductions. For the most part, itemized deductions are for various kinds of personal and investment expenses.

If your income level is above a specified amount, the tax benefits of some personal and dependent exemptions are phased out. In addition, certain deductions are only available to you if your expenses exceed a certain percentage of your income. This chapter will help you sort out those expenses you can deduct and those you can't. In the process, it will help you focus on possible ways to lower your tax bill.

Standard Deduction

Individuals who do not itemize their deductions are entitled to a standard deduction amount. This amount varies according to your filing status. The standard deduction that you are entitled to is subtracted from your adjusted gross income in arriving at your taxable income. You can choose between itemizing your deductions or claiming the applicable standard deduction amount in figuring your taxable income depending on which produces the greatest tax benefit.

The standard deduction amounts available to individuals are listed in Table 2.1, below.

For married individuals (filing jointly or separately where neither spouse itemizes) and surviving spouses, an "additional standard deduction" of $750 is allowed for each spouse over the age of 65 and for each spouse who is blind. The additional standard deduction is $950 for elderly or blind individuals who are unmarried and are not surviving spouses ($1,900 in the case of an elderly and blind taxpayer). These additional standard deductions are adjusted annually by a cost-of-living adjustment.

If you are eligible to be claimed as a dependent on another taxpayer's return, you may not claim the full standard deduction. Rather, your standard deduction would be limited to the greater of either $600 or your earned income (not to exceed the appropriate standard deduction amount). For taxpayers who are age 65 or over or blind and who are eligible to be claimed as a dependent on another taxpayer's return, the standard deduction is limited to the greater of either $600 or earned income, plus any additional standard deduction available because of age or blindness. In calculating the limitation, earned income includes taxable scholarship and fellowship monies you receive.

The following are specifically excluded from using the standard deduction:

TABLE 2.1   Standard Deductions

Filing Status	1994*
Single	$3,800
Head of household	5,600
Married filing jointly and surviving spouses	6,350
Married filing separately	3,175

*These amounts are adjusted annually by a cost-of-living adjustment.

1. A married individual filing a separate return where the other spouse itemizes deductions;
2. A nonresident alien; or
3. An individual whose return covers less than 12 months due to a change in the annual accounting period.

Personal and Dependent Exemptions

Personal and dependent exemptions reduce your taxable income. Each exemption for the taxable year 1994 equals $2,450. (The amount is adjusted annually to reflect increases in the cost-of-living.) You are entitled to:

1. One exemption for yourself. (This exemption is not available to individuals who can be claimed as a dependent on another taxpayer's return.)
2. One exemption for your spouse if (a) a joint return is filed or (b) a joint return is not filed and your spouse has no gross income and is not the dependent of another.
3. One exemption for each dependent whose gross income is less than $2,450 or who is your child, if he or she is: (a) a full-time student under the age of 24 at the end of the year or (b) not yet 19 years old at the end of the year.

TaxSaver

You may consider the option of taking a dependent exemption for your married child (if he or she so qualifies) and have the child file "Married filing separately." In some cases, the benefit of a dependent exemption may outweigh the benefit of the child filing a joint return with his or her spouse.

Personal and Dependent Exemption Phaseout

The tax benefit of the personal and dependent exemptions are phased out for taxpayers whose adjusted gross income exceeds specific amounts. The phaseout is accomplished by reducing the exemption amount allowed by 2% for each $2,500 (or fraction thereof) of AGI in excess of certain levels. In 1994, the phaseout of personal exemptions begins at an *adjusted gross income* of $167,700 for married taxpayers filing a joint return; $83,850 for married filing separately; $139,750 for head of household; and $111,800 for single taxpayers.

Example: Bill and Martha Brown file a joint return. They have three dependent children. For 1994 they have adjusted gross income of $204,800. The dependency exemption amount for 1994, before any reductions, is $2,450. Because their AGI exceeds $167,700 by $37,100, each of their exemptions will be reduced by $735 [($37,100 ÷ $2,500 rounding up to the nearest whole number) × 2% × $2,450]. Thus, each exemption is only $1,715, or a total of $8,575 for their two personal exemptions and three dependency exemptions.

The impact of this provision for affected taxpayers is the same as if their marginal tax rate were increased. Consequently, it raises the 36% rate by about .68%, and the 39.6% rate by .74%, for each exemption claimed. Thus, a taxpayer in the 39.6% bracket with four exemptions will pay tax at an effective marginal rate of 42.56% on a portion of their income after the phaseout is taken into account.

Children cannot claim a personal exemption for themselves if they are eligible to be claimed as an exemption on their parents' return. As discussed earlier, parents with adjusted gross income in excess of $167,700 on joint returns, $139,750 for heads of households and $111,800 for single individuals begin to phase out the exemptions. So there may be a point where your dependent child could recognize a greater tax benefit if he or she could claim a personal exemption rather than your taking the exemption on your own return. But to shift the exemption to your child, you will have to take steps to disqualify your child as your dependent. Generally, this can only be accomplished if your child receives less than half of his or her support from you.

Social Security Numbers. Taxpayers must report on their income tax return the Social Security number of any dependent claimed who is age one or older before the close of the tax year.

Definition of Dependents

A dependent is any person listed below who receives more than half of his or her support from the taxpayer and who does not file a joint return with his or her spouse:

1. A son or daughter of the taxpayer, or a descendant of either;
2. A stepson or stepdaughter of the taxpayer;
3. A brother, sister, stepbrother, or stepsister of the taxpayer;
4. A father or mother of the taxpayer, or ancestor of either;

5. A stepfather or stepmother of the taxpayer;
6. A son or daughter of the taxpayer's brother or sister;
7. A brother or sister of the taxpayer's father or mother;
8. A son-in-law, daughter-in-law, father-in-law, mother-in-law, brother-in-law, or sister-in-law of the taxpayer;
9. Any individual (other than the taxpayer's spouse) who for the entire taxable year has as his or her principal place of abode the home of the taxpayer, as a member of the taxpayer's household, unless the relationship is in violation of local law.

Dependents of Divorced or Separated Parents. The dependent exemption for qualifying children of divorced or separated parents is generally allowed to the custodial parent (the parent who has custody of the child for the greater portion of the year) unless: (1) a multiple support agreement exists; (2) a pre-1985 divorce or separation agreement shifted the exemption to the noncustodial parent; or (3) the custodial parent releases the claim to the exemption to the noncustodial parent. To transfer the exemption, the custodial parent must sign a written declaration releasing the exemption to the noncustodial parent. The custodial parent may make the declaration annually, for one or more calendar years, or permanently.

TaxSaver

In giving up the exemption for a dependent child, the custodial parent does not forfeit the right to claim head-of-household status, the earned income credit, or the child and dependent care credit if the individual otherwise qualifies. These are discussed on pages 133, 142, and 143.

The word "dependent" does not include any individual who is not a citizen or national of the United States, unless the individual is a resident of the United States, Canada, or Mexico. A legally adopted child need not be a U.S. citizen to qualify as a dependent if the child is a member of a household of a taxpaying U.S. citizen.

Multiple Support Agreements

An individual supported by several persons, none of whom alone furnishes more than one half of his or her support, may qualify as a dependent. In this case, the dependency deduction may be claimed by any one individual (otherwise entitled to do so) contributing over 10% of the support, provided that:

1. over one-half of the support was contributed by persons who, except for the support test, would be entitled to claim the supported individual as a dependent, and

2. each other person described in (1) contributing over 10% of the dependent's support files a written declaration (Form 2120) with the return of the person who claims the exemption, stating that he or she will not claim a deduction for the same dependent for that year.

TAX*SAVER*

If you provide less than 50% but more than 10% of the support to a dependent (e.g., your parent), it may be more beneficial to give the right to claim the exemption to the supporter to whom it will yield the highest tax benefit.

TAX*SAVER*

If your dependent maintains his or her own home and you paid the mortgage and real estate taxes, neither of you will be entitled to the mortgage interest or real estate taxes deduction. You may consider taking a partial interest in the property in order to secure the deductions subject to the mortgage interest limitation (page 51) on your return. Another option would be to give cash to your dependent so that he or she can pay the mortgage and real estate taxes directly. In turn, the dependent can deduct such payments on his or her own return.

Individual Retirement Arrangements (IRAs)

An individual retirement arrangement (IRA) is a personal savings plan that lets you set aside funds for your retirement, using pre-tax dollars. (See Chapter 4 for details.)

Simplified Employee Pensions

A simplified employee pension (SEP) is a written plan that allows an employer to make contributions toward an employee's retirement without becoming involved in more complex retirement plans. If you are self-employed, you can contribute to your own SEP. For more information see Chapter 10, Retirement Planning.

Keogh (HR 10) Plans

If you are self-employed and own your own business, you may set up a retirement plan, commonly known as a Keogh or HR 10 plan. You must have earned income from the trade or business for which the plan was established to take a deduction for a contribution to the plan. A Keogh plan may be either a "defined contribution plan" or a "defined benefit plan." (For more information on this type of plan, see Chapter 4.)

Divorce or Separation

Alimony

Alimony is an amount paid to a spouse or former spouse under a divorce or separation agreement. You are allowed a deduction for alimony payments you make. (See page 32 for an explanation of how alimony you receive is taxed.)

What Qualifies as Alimony. To qualify for a deduction as alimony, payments stipulated in the divorce or separation agreement should not be designated as something other than alimony. In addition, the parties to the divorce or legal separation must not be members of the same household at the time of payment, and there must be no liability for payments to continue after the death of the spouse receiving the money. Payments made under a divorce or separation decree executed after 1984 must be in cash or its equivalent. For example, transferring securities to satisfy payments due under a divorce or separation agreement does not qualify as alimony. Cash payments made to a third party, however—such as medical expenses paid to doctors or hospitals, on behalf of the spouse or former spouse at his or her request—will qualify as alimony, assuming all other requirements are met.

> ### *TaxSaver*
>
> *If you pay medical expenses for your spouse or former spouse, you should deduct the payment as alimony, not as medical expenses. Alimony is fully deductible from your adjusted gross income (whether or not you itemize your deductions), whereas only the portion of your medical expenses that exceed 7.5% of your adjusted gross income will be deductible.*

Deductible alimony payments made under divorce or separation agreements executed after 1984 are subject to recapture rules when payments are "front loaded." In other words, if the payments decrease by more than a designated amount during the first three post-separation years, you may be required to recapture and include in your gross income some portion of alimony that you deducted in a prior tax year. On the other hand, if you received the payment, you deduct any recaptured amount from your income in the computation year.

Exceptions to the recapture rules apply when alimony payments end because either party dies, the spouse receiving the payments remarries before the end of the third post-separation year, or the payments are subject to fluctuation because they are tied to the payer's compensation or income from a business or property.

Child Support

Child support payments are neither deductible by the payor nor included as income by the spouse who receives them. If any portion of payments that were agreed to be alimony could be reduced because of circumstances relating to a child (e.g., the child's leaving school or the family household, becoming employed, getting married, or dying), that portion may be reclassified as nondeductible and nontaxable child support. This can occur even when the divorce or separation agreement specifically provides for separate child support payments.

Payments are presumed to be child support if a reduction is scheduled to occur within six months before or after a child reaches age 18, 21, or the local age of majority, or when two or more reductions are scheduled within one year of a child reaching an age between 18 and 24 that is designated in the agreement. Payments that represent property settlements or child support are not treated as alimony.

TAXSAVER

Deciding whether payments should be classified as alimony, a nontaxable property settlement, or child support is relevant if the spouse who will be making the payments will be in a higher tax bracket than the spouse receiving them. The spouse making the payment typically wants it to be tax-deductible alimony to minimize his or her out-of-pocket costs. At the same time, the spouse receiving the payment doesn't want to see it eaten up by taxes.

A way to solve the problem is to share the overall tax saving realized by treating the payment as alimony. For example, if the spouse making the payment offered to "gross up" the payment to cover the taxes the recipient would owe, both on the amount of the payment originally expected and the "extra" alimony offered, the payor could wind up paying less out-of-pocket (after deductions) than if the initially-agreed-to level of the payment was treated as a nondeductible property settlement.

Transferring Property

Generally, a transfer of property from one spouse to the other "incident to the divorce" is tax-free—no gain or loss is recognized by the transferor spouse. Such transfers can include sales or exchanges of property between ex-spouses within one year after the marriage ends and transfers pursuant to a divorce or separation agreement generally occurring within six years after the marriage ends.

These transfers are treated as gifts for tax purposes even if there were actually a bona fide sale. That is, the transferor spouse's basis in the property carries over to the transferee spouse, who will be required to recognize gain or loss when the property is ultimately sold or otherwise disposed of. (See Chapter 3, Tax Planning and Your Home, for more details.)

TaxSaver

Remember, when dividing up appreciated property in a divorce settlement, that the value of a particular property may be overstated if it does not take into account potential taxes that would be due on the built-in gain if the property is subsequently sold. The spouse receiving the property should consider having the divorce or separation agreement provide for reimbursement when the property is actually sold or otherwise disposed of.

Medical and Dental Expenses

Deductible Expenses

You may claim as itemized deductions certain medical and dental expenses for yourself, your spouse, and your dependents. You may also deduct medical expenses that you pay for any person whom you could have claimed as a dependent on your return if that person had not received $2,450 or more of gross income or had not filed a joint return. A child of divorced parents is treated as a dependent of both spouses for the purpose of computing medical expenses. However, you may deduct only the part of your medical and dental expenses that is more than 7.5% of your adjusted gross income. Medical expenses are not subject to the reduction in itemized deductions for taxpayers with adjusted gross incomes in excess of $111,800 discussed on page 68.

What to Include as Medical and Dental Expenses. Medical expenses include the costs of related transportation, hospitalization insurance, Medicare supplemental insurance, certain capital expenditures if they exceed any increase in property value, and certain expenses incurred by a physically handicapped individual for removing structural barriers to accommodate the disability. You may also include the cost of hearing aids, dentures, eyeglasses, and so on, and wages you paid for nursing services. The cost of elective cosmetic surgery is not deductible. However, cosmetic or plastic surgery to correct a deformity or personal injury or to treat an illness or disease will qualify as a deductible medical expense. Prescription drugs and insulin are the only medications that are considered medical expenses.

TaxSaver

If you make a medically related capital improvement to your home, such as an elevator, you should request a written recommendation for the improvement from your doctor. In addition, obtain a reliable written appraisal from a real estate appraiser or a valuation expert. Be prepared to prove to what extent the value of your property was not increased by the expenditure of the improvement, because only that amount is deductible.

TaxSaver

Certain medical expenses may qualify for the dependent care credit. (See page 142.) However, the same expense may not be used for both benefits. You should analyze each benefit based on your marginal tax rate and your medical expense deduction limitation (7.5% of adjusted gross income) to determine how best to classify the expense.

When seeking medical care away from home, you can deduct lodging expenses of up to $50 per night per individual, as a medical expense. Lodging expenses can include the person seeking treatment and other qualified individuals, such as a parent traveling with a sick child.

TaxAlert

Until January 1, 1994, self-employed individuals could deduct 25% of their health insurance premiums directly from self-employment income rather than as a medical deduction. There is a good chance that Congress will reinstate this deduction—and possibly make it more generous—as it considers health care reform legislation.

Separate Returns. If you and your spouse do not live in a community property state and you file separate returns, each of you may claim only the medical expenses you actually paid. Any medical expenses paid out of a joint checking account in which you and your spouse have the same interest are considered to have been paid equally by each of you unless you can show otherwise.

TAXSAVER

Because you may deduct only the part of your medical and dental expenses that is more than 7.5% of your adjusted gross income, you should consider filing separate returns whenever the medical expenses of either spouse substantially exceed those of the other spouse. Figure your tax filing jointly and separately before deciding which alternative to choose.

When to Deduct. You may deduct medical expenses only in the year you paid them. If you charge medical expenses to your credit card, deduct the expenses in the year the charge is made even if you pay the charge in a later year.

Reimbursements. You must reduce your total medical expenses for the year by the total reimbursements you receive from insurance or other sources for medical expenses during the year before you apply the 7.5% adjusted gross income limit. Reimbursements include payments received from Medicare.

TAXSAVER

If you are reimbursed in a later year for medical expenses you deducted in an earlier year, you must report the reimbursement as income in the later year. However, do not report more than the amount you previously deducted as medical expenses. In making the calculation, you may also exclude the amount of expenses in the previous year that did not reduce the amount of income taxes you paid. For example, if you had a taxable loss in the year of the deduction, you would not have had a tax benefit from your medical deductions and any subsequent reimbursement is not considered income. This same rule would apply if the expenses did not produce any benefit in the earlier year because they did not exceed 7.5% of your adjusted gross income in that year.

Taxes

Deductible Taxes

If you itemize deductions, you can deduct state, local, and foreign income taxes and real property taxes and state and local personal property taxes. You can generally deduct property taxes only if you are the property owner.

You may deduct only those taxes paid during the calendar year for which you file a return. Deductible taxes are subject to the overall limit on itemized deductions for taxpayers with adjusted gross income in excess of $111,800. See discussion on page 68.

See page 68.

TAXSAVER

See page 140 for the discussion about how state, local, and foreign taxes affect your alternative minimum tax calculations.

Nondeductible Taxes

Taxes that cannot be deducted include the federal income tax; state and local sales taxes; social security taxes; estate, gift, and inheritance taxes; gasoline, cigarette, and liquor taxes; automobile registration fees (unless based on the automobile's value); and driver's license fees. Certain taxes paid in connection with the acquisition or disposition of property, such as transfer taxes associated with a purchase, must be capitalized.

Half the self-employment taxes you pay may be deducted and treated as attributable to a trade or business that you conduct. Most otherwise nondeductible state, local, foreign, and excise taxes are deductible if incurred in a trade or business or in the production of income.

Deduction vs. Credit

You may elect to have foreign income taxes (including withholding) on dividends or other income credited directly against your U.S. tax liability (subject to a limitation based on the effective U.S. rate of tax). However, you cannot take a deduction or credit for foreign income taxes paid on income that is exempt from tax under the foreign earned income exclusion.

TAXSAVER

It is usually better to take a credit for foreign taxes than to deduct them as itemized deductions, because credits reduce your U.S. tax on a dollar-for-dollar basis, while a deduction just reduces the amount of income subject to tax.

Refunds of Taxes

If you receive a refund of state or local (or foreign) income taxes in a year after the year in which you paid them, you may have to include all or part of the refund in income in the year you receive it. This includes refunds resulting from taxes that were overwithheld, not figured correctly, or decreased as a result of an audit. If you did not itemize your deductions in the previous year or if the portion of the claimed deduction that is refunded did not provide a tax benefit, you do not have to include the refund in income.

Interest Expenses

If interest paid during the taxable year is deductible it will be as an itemized deduction, a passive activity deduction, or a business expense. However, several limitations apply. Deductions for personal interest are not allowed. There are also limitations on the deduction of passive activity interest (page 18) and investment interest (page 52). Your deduction for interest paid during the year is limited to the amount that represents the cost of using the borrowed funds for that year or a preceding year. An exception to this rule applies for points paid to obtain a loan to purchase or to improve a principal residence as long as the payment of points is an established business practice in your area.

Interest expense, except for investment interest, is subject to the overall limit on itemized deductions for taxpayers with adjusted gross income in excess of $111,800. See discussion on page 68.

Personal Interest

Interest on personal loans is not deductible on your individual tax return. Personal interest generally includes all interest other than:

- Interest incurred in connection with a trade or business (other than the trade or business of performing services as an employee);
- Investment interest;
- Interest taken into account in computing your income or loss from a passive activity;
- Qualified residence interest; and
- Interest on certain estate taxes that have been deferred.

> ### TAXSAVER
>
> *You should ordinarily pay off personal debts because the related interest expense, unless qualified residence interest, is not deductible. One way to accomplish this objective is to use a home equity loan (discussed below) to pay off your personal debt. This interest is fully deductible up to certain limits.*

Home Mortgage Interest

Generally mortgage interest is any interest you pay on a loan secured by your home. This includes a mortgage, second mortgage, a line of credit, and a home equity loan. Most home mortgage interest is deductible, subject to limitations discussed in Chapter 3, Tax Planning and Your Home.

Investment Interest

There are specified limits on the deduction of investment interest by individuals. Investment interest is interest paid on indebtedness properly allocable to property held for investment. Property held for investment includes any property that produces interest, dividend, annuity, or royalty income not derived in the ordinary course of a trade or business, and any property held by a taxpayer in an activity involving the conduct of a trade or business that is not a passive activity (pages 18–20) and in which the taxpayer does not materially participate. Investment interest does not include qualified residence interest (see above) or interest taken into account in computing your income or loss from a passive activity.

The deduction for interest on investment indebtedness is limited to your net investment income—the excess of investment income over certain directly connected expenses.

Investment interest deductions that are disallowed solely by these provisions may, in most cases, be carried forward and deducted in subsequent years, subject to the annual limits.

TaxAlert

A net capital gain attributable to the disposition of property held for investment is no longer includable in the definition of investment income for purposes of computing the investment interest deduction limitation. However, you may elect to include net capital gain amounts in investment income for this purpose if you also agree to reduce your net capital gain eligible for the 28% maximum capital gains rate by the same amount.

TaxSaver

Deciding whether to make the election depends on how long you would otherwise have to wait to take your deduction. Here are some general guidelines:
- *Take the deduction now if your marginal rate on ordinary income is 28% and is expected to stay at that rate. In this case, waiting won't produce a greater benefit.*
- *You may be better off waiting and carrying forward the investment interest deduction if your rate may soon increase, and you expect to have more non-capital gain investment income in the short term.*

There is no substitute for running the numbers for your situation.

TaxSaver

You should regularly review the mix of your investment portfolio to be sure that your assets generate enough investment income so you can deduct all the interest you incur on your margin account. A margin account is money you borrow from a broker to purchase additional securities.

Tax-Exempt Securities

Interest paid on money borrowed to purchase or carry tax-exempt securities or certain life insurance contracts is not deductible. In addition, the deduction of interest paid for money borrowed to purchase or carry investments in stock of certain regulated investment companies will be limited if the company makes a distribution of tax-exempt interest during the taxable year.

Other Interest

Below-Market Interest Rate Loans. If you are the recipient of an interest-free loan, you can deduct interest imputed on the loan, subject to the applicable interest expense limitations. The interest is calculated using specified rates based on the average market yields of U.S. Treasury obligations. With certain exceptions, interest is imputed on loans payable upon demand of over $10,000 outstanding after June 6, 1984, and on term loans made after June 6, 1984. (For further discussion, see pages 27 and 229.)

Interest to Carry Discount Bonds and Investments. Special rules limit your deduction for interest expense incurred to purchase or carry bonds that were acquired at a market discount. For debt obligations issued after July 18, 1984, the interest expense deduction is limited to the sum of:

1. the interest income received from the bonds during the tax year, and
2. the interest expense in excess of the interest income received in item (1) plus accrued market discount.

The disallowed interest is deferred until the bond is sold or matures, and is then deducted. If you elect to include the accrued market discount in your current income, you can fully deduct the interest instead of deferring it.

Example: Tom buys a $100,000, 9% interest-bearing bond for $90,000 on January 2, 1994. The bond was originally issued at face value in 1989. It matures in 2004, 10 years after Tom purchased it. Tom borrowed to acquire the bond. In 1994, Tom paid $10,200 in interest on the loan. The allowable interest deduction for 1994 is figured as follows:

(a) Interest expense	$10,200
(b) Interest income ($100,000 × 9%)	(9,000)
(c) Net interest expense	1,200
(d) Accrued market discount ($10,000 ÷ 10 yrs.)	(1,000)
(e) Net interest expense allowable as a deduction	$ 200

Total allowable interest expense deduction is $9,200 [(b) + (e)]. The remaining $1,000 will be allowed as a deduction in the year the bond matures or is sold.

The same limitation applies to interest expense arising from the purchase of short-term obligations. The interest deduction for an amount equal to the daily accrual of the obligation's discount income will be deferred until the short-term obligation is redeemed or sold. If you elect to include the accrued discount in income, you can fully deduct the interest instead of deferring the interest deduction.

TaxOrganizer

How you characterize interest expense depends on how you used the debt proceeds. You must keep detailed records so that the IRS can trace the ultimate use of borrowed dollars that give rise to each dollar of interest expense.

__Example:__ You purchase through your broker $40,000 worth of stock. Several months later you need $20,000 to purchase a car. You borrow the $20,000 by collateralizing your stock. The interest on that loan is considered to be consumer interest (generally nondeductible). On the other hand, if you had purchased the stock on margin for $20,000—that is, you borrowed the money for the purchase from your broker— and spent your remaining personal funds of $20,000 on the car, the interest attributable to the margin debt is investment interest and potentially deductible.

Qualified mortgage interest is deductible in full, regardless of how the loan proceeds are actually used.

Charitable Contributions

You are allowed to take a tax deduction for charitable contributions you make to qualified organizations. (See Chapter 5, page 100.)

Casualty and Theft Losses

A casualty is the damage, destruction, or loss of property resulting from an identifiable event that is sudden, unexpected, or unusual. A sudden event is one that is swift, not gradual or progressive. An unexpected event is one that is ordinarily unanticipated and one that you do not intend. An unusual event is one that is not a day-to-day occurrence and one that is not typical of the activity in which you were engaged.

Defining a Loss. A deduction is allowed for losses of business property, investment property, or nonbusiness property caused by fire, storm, or other casualty, including theft. Generally, the deduction is the lesser of either the adjusted basis of the property before the casualty or the actual loss measured by its fair market value before and after the casualty. If you recover any amount of the loss by insurance, you must reduce the deduction you take accordingly. A special rule applies to business or income-producing property that is completely destroyed because of a casualty loss. Your loss is your basis in the property (without regard to fair market value), less any amount you receive from insurance payments.

Deductions for casualty losses of nonbusiness property are limited to the amount of each loss in excess of $100. A husband and wife filing a joint return are treated as one individual for purposes of the $100 limitation. If each spouse sustains a loss from the same casualty, only one $100 limitation will apply. After considering the $100 floor applicable to each separate loss, your total personal casualty losses are deductible in full to the extent they are offset against any casualty gains. A casualty gain occurs when your insurance reimbursement is more than your basis in the property, even if the decrease in the fair market value of the property is more than its basis.

Example:

Value of the property before the casualty	$100
Value after the casualty	75
Loss	25
Insurance reimbursement	20
Basis in property	15
Gain	$ 5

Any excess loss is deductible as an itemized deduction only for the amount that exceeds 10% of your adjusted gross income. If casualty gains exceed casualty losses, the 10% floor is not imposed, and the gains and losses are treated as arising from the sale of capital assets. You are not permitted to deduct nonbusiness casualty losses unless an insurance claim for the damage to the insured property is filed on a timely basis.

Casualty losses occurring in federally declared disaster areas at any time during the taxable year may be deducted on the tax return for the year preceding the year of the loss. This may enable you to get an immediate refund of taxes you already paid.

If you have a casualty or theft on nonbusiness property, you must use Section A of Form 4684, *Casualties and Thefts*, to figure and report your gain or loss. Be sure to attach Form 4684 to your return.

TAXSAVER

If you are going to claim a casualty or theft loss, it is important that you gather as much supporting evidence as possible. Newspaper clippings about a storm, police reports, and insurance reports may all be helpful in proving the nature of the casualty or theft loss and when it occurred. You have the burden of proof to establish that a casualty occurred and that your loss was a direct result of a casualty.

Establishing the amount of your loss may be difficult, but the time you spend documenting the loss may help reduce your tax. You should make a list of all lost, damaged, or destroyed items as soon after the disaster or casualty as possible. IRS Publication 584, Nonbusiness Disaster and Casualty Loss and Theft Workbook, may be useful. It has schedules to help you figure a loss on your home and its contents and on your car, van, truck, or motorcycle.

Casualty and theft losses are not subject to the overall limit on itemized deductions for taxpayers with adjusted gross income in excess of $111,800. See discussion on page 68.

Moving Expenses

Under certain circumstances, expenses you incur in connection with changing the location of your employment are deductible. The expenses can be deductible if the distance between your new job and your residence is at least 50 miles more than the distance between your old job and your residence. In addition, if you are an employee, you must work full-time during at least 39 weeks of the 12-month period after relocating. If you are self-employed, the standard is stiffer. You must work full time at least 78 weeks during the 24-month period after relocating. In addition, you must work full-time for at least 39 weeks during the immediate 12-month period after relocating.

If you are fired or laid off, involuntarily lose your job (for other than willful misconduct), or are required to move again by your employer before the 39 weeks are up (or 78 weeks, if applicable), you can still deduct your moving expenses. You may also be exempted from the 39-week or 78-week requirement because of death and disability.

TaxSaver

If you file a joint return, the time test may be met by either spouse. However, weeks worked by both husband and wife cannot be added together to meet the time test.

If you and your spouse live together and both of you have been working full-time but one of you loses your job, you will obtain the maximum tax benefits by filing a joint return, even if you reside in a community property state. Moving expenses paid by both husband and wife may be aggregated and are deductible in full, subject only to the overall dollar limitations discussed below.

The deduction for moving expenses is allowed for the following:
1. Travel expenses (including lodging) for an employee or self-employed person and his or her family to the new residence
2. Expenses for moving household goods and other personal effects

The deduction for expenses that fall into categories (1) and (2) is unlimited. Expenses that qualify as moving expenses that are not paid or reimbursed by the taxpayer's employer are allowable as a deduction in calculating adjusted gross income (AGI). Thus, moving expenses are no longer an itemized deduction. Reimbursement or payment of moving expenses by an employer are excludable from gross income of the employee, and are not included in the employee's Form W-2.

Use Form 3903, *Moving Expenses,* to report your moving expenses if your move was within or to the United States or its possessions.

Starting in 1994, deductible moving expenses no longer will include the following:
- the cost of meals;
- the cost of pre-move house-hunting trips;
- the cost of temporary living expenses;
- the costs incident to the sale or lease of the old residence, including settling of an unexpired lease; and

- the costs incident to the purchase or lease of a new residence.

Employee Business Expenses and Other Expenses

This section covers a variety of expenses that you are allowed to deduct on your individual return. These personal business expenses can be broken down into three broad categories: deductible employee expenses, deductible expenses of producing income, and other deductible expenses.

The general rule is that you may deduct any business expense incurred by you personally that is related to your trade or business, connected with producing income, or paid to determine your tax. Expenses other than these are generally considered personal and typically may not be deducted. But, with careful and proper planning, you may be able to deduct more than you think.

Deductions Subject to the 2%-of-Adjusted-Gross-Income Limit

Most miscellaneous itemized deductions are deductible only to the extent the total of all these deductions is more than 2% of your adjusted gross income. Miscellaneous deductions that are not subject to this limitation are discussed later in this chapter.

Your deduction is the excess of the total of the allowable deductions over 2% of your adjusted gross income. The 2% limit is applied after any other deduction limit (such as the 50% limit on meals and entertainment) is applied.

Unreimbursed employee business expenses are also subject to the overall limit on itemized deductions for taxpayers with adjusted gross income in excess of $111,800. See discussion on page 68.

Employee Business Expenses

If you are an employee, including an outside salesperson, you may deduct as an adjustment to income only the amount reimbursed by your employer for work-related business expenses. To the extent that the reimbursements are included in your income, any expenses that are not reimbursed by your employer are deductible only as a miscellaneous deduction (subject to the 2% limit) on Schedule A, Form 1040.

If you claim a deduction for any employee business expenses, you must complete Form 2106 and attach it to your Form 1040. You do not have to complete the form if your business expenses were equal to the reimbursements you received from your employer, the reimbursements were not included in your W-2 form, and you adequately accounted to your employer for those expenses. If none of your employee business expenses are reimbursed by your employer, however, and you are not claiming any meal, entertainment, travel, or transportation expenses, you do not have to complete Form 2106. Instead, list your employee business expenses on Schedule A.

TaxSaver

If you can get your employer to reimburse you for what would otherwise be unreimbursed business expenses in lieu of an equal amount of salary, you should do so. You gain at no additional cost to your employer. Reimbursed employee business expenses are not subject to the 2% floor that might otherwise limit their deductibility.

Travel and Transportation

Travel expenses that are directly related to business or income-producing activities, including those incurred by outside salespersons and other employees, are usually deductible. Travel expenses include transportation fares, automobile expenses, costs of meals and lodging, baggage charges, and miscellaneous business expenses (e.g., telephone charges) incurred while away from home. The cost of transportation (including automobile expenses) between your home and your regular place of business is not deductible, but the cost of local transportation between business locations during the day is generally deductible.

You cannot deduct travel expenses when the sole purpose of the travel is educational.

TaxAlert

A deduction is allowed for travel expenses paid or incurred with respect to a spouse, dependent, or other individual accompanying a person on business travel only if the spouse, dependent, or other individual is a bona fide employee of the person paying or reimbursing the expenses and the following apply:

- *The travel of the spouse, dependent, or other individual is for a bona fide business purpose.*
- *The expenses incurred would otherwise be deductible.*

***Example:** Mrs. Smith, an employee of an investment advisory firm, is accompanied on a business trip by her husband Mr. Smith, who is not an employee of the firm. Because Mr. Smith assisted his wife on the trip by en-*

tertaining clients, helping her conduct a seminar, and performing other substantial business services, Mr. Smith's presence on the trip had a bona fide business purpose. The firm paid all of Mrs. and Mr. Smith's travel expenses. Under the prior law, the firm may have been able to deduct the costs of Mrs. and Mr. Smith's travel as an ordinary and necessary business expense. Under the new law, the company may not deduct the costs of Mr. Smith's travel because he is not an employee of the company.

Automobile Expenses

The deduction for automobile expenses can be calculated in one of the following two ways:

■ *Actual expenses:* Automobile depreciation is added to the actual expenses related to use of the automobile. Depreciation deductions for certain luxury automobiles may be limited. For automobiles first placed in service in 1994 and for which business use exceeds 50%, the depreciation deduction is limited to $2,960 in the first year, $4,700 in the second year, $2,850 in the third year, and $1,675 for each succeeding year. These amounts will be indexed annually for inflation.

Maximum Depreciation Deduction Allowed (business use > 50%)

Year placed into service	Tax Year			
	1st	2nd	3nd	4th++
1987	$2,560	$4,100	$2,450	$1,475
1988	2,560	4,100	2,450	1,475
1989	2,660	4,200	2,550	1,475
1990	2,660	4,200	2,550	1,475
1991	2,660	4,300	2,550	1,575
1992	2,760	4,400	2,650	1,575
1993	2,860	4,600	2,750	1,675
1994	2,960	4,700	2,850	1,675

These amounts are further limited if the auto is used for both business and personal use. If a vehicle is used for business 50% or less of the time, the alternative depreciation system (ADS) must be used.

■ *Standard rate:* The deduction is computed using the standard mileage rate of 29 cents per mile for all miles of business use. The basis of the vehicle must be reduced (but not below zero) by 12 cents per mile for all miles for which the standard mileage rate is used.

TAXSAVER

If you own an expensive business car, the standard mileage rate is probably inadequate to cover your op-

erating costs. You should keep detailed records of your total expenses so that you may claim a larger deduction than you would be able to by using the standard mileage rate.

TAX*SAVER*

Interest paid on loans to purchase a car—even if used by an employee for business—is considered personal interest and is not deductible. However, if you finance the car by taking out a home equity loan, the interest will be fully deductible as home mortgage interest. The after-tax cost of home equity payments will often be lower than the best car loan available. If you don't own a home or have enough equity available, consider leasing because to the extent the car is used for business, the deductible portion of your lease payments includes the implicit financing costs as well as depreciation.

E&Y FOCUS: Leasing a Car

If you lease a car, you can deduct the part of each lease payment that is for the use of the car in your business or work. Normal operating costs and maintenance may also be deducted. Special rules apply to reduce the annual lease deduction for leased cars similar to the limitations of depreciation that apply to luxury automobiles.

Should you buy or lease a car?

Here are some of the things you need to know before deciding:

1. The financing cost and monthly payments on a loan. (Can you finance with a home equity loan and deduct the interest? See TaxSaver above.)
2. The monthly payments on the lease.
3. How many miles you expect to drive the car and the additional charges at the end of the lease term if the mileage exceeds the amount set out in the contract. If you drive many fewer miles than provided for in the lease contract, you probably will be paying for something you will not use. On the other hand, if you drive much more, although you have to pay for the extra miles, remember that you pay for them at the end of the lease term, so 5,000 extra miles over 4 years at 15 cents per mile equals $750. In today's dollars, assuming 6% rate of return, that comes to $594.
4. An estimate of the car's value when you would normally sell or trade it in.

5. What you think you could earn on your payments if it were available for investment.

You would then compare the costs of buying versus leasing a car in today's dollars. To do that you need to calculate the present value of the payments on the lease or on a loan if you decide to borrow some or all of the purchase price. Present value is the financial term for what a dollar paid or received in the future is worth to you today ($1,000 paid five years from today effectively really costs you less than $1,000 paid out today. That's because you could earn money with that $1,000 during the five years before you pay it.)

A few other points should be noted:

■ Know your obligations under a lease contract for early termination and wear and tear to the car. Leasing car companies will generally make you pay dearly if you want out of your lease early, or if you don't return the car in good shape.

■ Know whether insurance will cover your remaining contract obligation if the car were totally destroyed during the lease term.

Most often the purchase price of a car is negotiable, and so are the lease terms. Shop around.

Purchasing a car outright should be the least expensive way to go if you can't earn more on your money than you would have to pay in finance charges. Purchasing the car with financing is usually next and leasing is generally the most expensive. However, these generalizations will vary depending on dealer incentives, interest rates, and other factors applicable to your situation.

Meals and Entertainment

Individual expenses for meals or entertainment directly related to or associated with the active conduct of a trade or business, including those incurred by an employee, are deductible. To be associated with the conduct of a trade or business, such entertainment must take place directly before or after substantial and bona fide business discussions.

The deduction for business meal and entertainment expenses is limited to 50% of the amount incurred (a change from the former limitation of 80%), except for the following items:

■ Expenses treated as compensation or otherwise included in your gross income

■ Reimbursed meal and entertainment expenses

■ Traditional recreational expenses that benefit employees (e.g., company picnic or Christmas party)

- Services or facilities made available to the general public (e.g., food samples distributed at a supermarket)
- *De minimis* fringe benefits (e.g., holiday turkey/ham)
- The cost of a ticket package to certain sporting events organized to benefit tax-exempt organizations

Deductions for expenses related to entertainment facilities (such as yachts, apartments, skybox rentals, and resort cottages) are generally not allowed. In addition, no deduction is usually allowed for the expenses of attending foreign conventions. However, if you can show that it is just as reasonable that the convention could be held abroad rather than at a domestic location, all business expenses are deductible. A foreign convention is one held outside North America, which comprises the United States and its possessions, the Trust Territory of the Pacific Islands, Jamaica, Barbados, Bermuda, Grenada, Canada, and Mexico.

Cruise ship expenses directly related to the active conduct of a trade or business are deductible up to $2,000 per year per individual as long as the cruise ship is registered in the United States and all ports of call are located in the United States or in U.S. possessions. Cruise expenses must be substantiated by written documentation, including proof of business activities and time devoted to them. Such documentation must include proof and explanation of business activities signed by you and an officer of the organization sponsoring the meeting.

Business Gifts

Deductions for business gifts are limited to $25 per individual recipient per year.

TaxSaver

It is usually to your advantage to define a particular item as an entertainment expense rather than as a gift. Although entertainment expenses are subject to a 50% limitation in 1994 and must be considered ordinary and necessary, there is no fixed dollar limitation on the deduction.

Club Dues

Starting in 1994, no deduction is allowed for club dues. This rule applies to all types of clubs, including business, social, athletic, luncheon, sporting, hotel, and airport clubs. Specific business expenses, such as meals and entertainment that may occur at a club, would be deductible to the extent that they otherwise satisfy the standard for deductibility.

Documenting Expenses

Business expense deductions for away-from-home traveling expenses, gifts, and entertainment expenses must be supported by adequate records or by sufficient evidence, oral or written, which corroborates the deductions.

In general, records in support of travel and entertainment expenses must indicate the following:

- The amount of each separate expenditure (certain items, e.g., the cost of daily meals, gasoline and oil, and daily telephone calls, may be aggregated)
- The time and place of the travel or entertainment including dates of departure and return, number of days away, location and type of entertainment
- The business purpose or benefit derived (or expected to be derived) from the activity
- The business relationship of the person(s) entertained or receiving the gift

Receipts are required to support all expenditures for lodging while traveling away from home and for any other expenditure of $25 or more, except where such receipts are not readily available for transportation expenses (such as cab fares).

Other Expenses

Dues, business publications, subscriptions, the cost of uniforms, and other expenses you incur as an employee or in the production of income are allowed as deductions. These are treated as miscellaneous deductions and can only be deducted to the extent that your total miscellaneous deductions exceed 2% of your adjusted gross income.

Educational Expenses

In general, educational expenditures, such as tuition, books, supplies, lab fees, and certain travel and transportation costs, are deductible (whether or not the education leads to a degree) if the education (1) maintains or improves skills required in your employment or business or (2) meets the express requirements of your employer, or applicable law, imposed as a condition of employment. However, educational expenditures that are made to meet minimum educational requirements or that qualify you for a new trade or business are not deductible. Therefore, only expenses for education relating to your present work are deductible.

Office-in-Home Expenses

The IRS rule is that no deduction is allowed for office-in-home expenses unless the portion of the residence used in connection with your trade or business is used exclusively on a regular basis (1) as your principal place of business, (2) as a place of business for meeting or dealing with patients, clients, or customers in the normal course of business, or (3) is a separate structure that is not attached to your residence and is used in connection with your trade or business. (For more details, see Chapter 3.)

Computers. You may be able to claim an accelerated depreciation deduction and a Section 179 deduction (page 226) for your home computer provided you use the computer over 50% of the time for business (in your work as an employee) and the computer was placed in your home for the convenience of your employer, as a condition of your employment, so that you can properly perform your duties as an employee. Thus, your employer does not have to explicitly require you to buy the computer as long as its purchase spares the employer the cost of providing suitable equipment with which to perform your job responsibilities.

Reporting Reimbursements and Expenses

Normally, amounts you receive from your employer as reimbursement for travel, entertainment, and other employee business expenses under "a reimbursement or other expense allowance arrangement" (also known as an "accountable plan") are not included in your gross income. In order to qualify as an accountable plan, your employer's plan must meet the following requirements:

1. *Business connection.* The plan must provide for reimbursements, advances, or allowances for business expenses paid or incurred by you in connection with your performance of services as an employee. Advances to cover expenses must be made within a "reasonable period" before you incur the expense.
2. *Substantiation.* The plan must require you to provide substantiation for the expenses to your employer within a "reasonable period" after the expenses are incurred. Alternatively, your employer may have a plan wherein you are deemed to have substantiated an amount of expenses equal to the lesser of either (1) the amount of reimbursement or (2) a standard mileage rate or per diem amount specified by the IRS.
3. *Mandatory return of excess expenses.* The plan must require you to return to your employer, within a "reasonable period" of time, any amount advanced or reimbursed in excess of the substantiated expenses covered under the arrangement. However, under so-called "substantiation plans," some excess per diem amounts are treated as having been returned to your employer, even though you are entitled to keep such excess amounts.

In general, if your employer's plan meets the requirements described above, all amounts paid under the plan are excluded from your gross income, are not supposed to be reported on your W-2, and are exempt from withholding and payment of employment taxes (income tax, FICA, FUTA, and RRTA).

Amounts in excess of substantiated expenses that you fail to return to your employer, notwithstanding the requirement to do so under an accountable plan or, alternatively, because you are entitled to keep such amounts under the deemed "substantiation" rules, are included in your gross income and must be reported to you on Form W-2. These amounts will be subject to withholding and payment of employment taxes (for amounts received on or after July 1, 1990, relating to expenses paid or incurred after such date). You may deduct such expenses, and any actual expenses in excess of employer reimbursements made under an accountable plan, only as miscellaneous itemized deductions. Such deductions are subject to all applicable limitations, including the 50% meal and entertainment expenses limitation and the 2% of adjusted gross income floor.

Expenses to Produce Income and Other Expenses

You may deduct certain other expenses as miscellaneous itemized deductions to the extent that the total amount of these deductions exceeds 2% of your adjusted gross income. These include expenses you pay:
1. To produce or collect income,
2. To manage, conserve, or maintain property held for producing income, or
3. To determine, contest, pay, or claim a refund of any tax.

These expenses must be ordinary and necessary and bear a reasonable and proximate relation to the income or income-producing property and the income must be taxable to you.

Indirect Deductions of Pass-Through Entities (Partnerships and S Corporations).
Deductions of pass-through entities, such as a partnership or S corporation, are passed through to the partners or shareholders. If the deductions are miscellaneous itemized deductions, they are usually deductible only to the extent that they exceed 2% of your adjusted gross income.

Investment Counsel Fees.
Amounts paid for managing your investments are deductible subject to the 2% limit if they relate to investments that produce taxable income.

Trustee's Administrative Fees.
Fees that are billed separately and that you paid in connection with your Individual Retirement Account or Arrangement (IRA) are deductible, subject to the 2% limit, provided that they are ordinary and necessary.

TAXSAVER

If the trustee of your IRA takes his or her fee out of your $2,000 contribution, there will be less money in your IRA account that can be invested. You should consider paying the fee separately from your IRA contribution. For more about IRAs see Chapter 4.

Legal Expenses. Legal fees that you pay to produce taxable income are usually deductible subject to the 2% limit. You may deduct legal expenses for tax advice related to a divorce if your lawyer's bill specifies how much is for tax advice and if the amount is determined in a reasonable way. Generally, legal expenses of a personal nature are not deductible.

Safe Deposit Box Rent. If you use a safe deposit box to store taxable income-producing stock, bonds, or investment-related papers or documents, the rent is deductible subject to the 2% limit.

Tax Preparation Fees. Amounts paid for tax preparation are usually deductible in the year you pay them. Thus, you may deduct, subject to the 2% limit, your fees paid in 1994 for preparing your 1993 return.

Deductions Not Subject to the 2% Limit
Some expenses can be deducted as miscellaneous itemized deductions whether or not the total of your miscellaneous expenses exceeds 2% of your adjusted gross income. Some of the expenses not subject to the 2% limit include the following:

Federal Estate Tax on Income in Respect of a Decedent. You may deduct the federal estate tax attributable to "income in respect of a decedent" that is ordinary income and that you, as a beneficiary, include in your gross income. Income in respect of a decedent is gross income that the decedent had a right to receive, could have received had death not occurred, and that could not have been properly included in the decedent's final income tax return.

Federal estate tax on income in respect of a decedent is subject to the overall limit on itemized deductions for taxpayers with adjusted gross income in excess of $111,800. The other items discussed below are not. See discussion on page 68.

Gambling Losses to the Extent of Gambling Winnings. You may not deduct more gambling losses than the gambling winnings you report.

Other Adjustments to Income

Early Withdrawal from Savings Accounts. Penalties paid because of the premature withdrawal of funds from time savings accounts or certificates of deposits are allowed as a deduction against your total income in figuring your adjusted gross income.

Forestation/Reforestation Amortization Expenses. If you can claim an amortization deduction for the costs of forestation or reforestation but you do not have to file the *Business Income Form* (Schedule C) or *Farm Income Form* (Schedule F), you can claim such deductions as an adjustment to income in figuring your adjusted gross income.

Supplemental Unemployment Benefits. If, during the tax year, you repaid supplemental unemployment benefits that you have previously reported as income because you became eligible for payments under the Trade Act of 1974, you can deduct the repayment as an adjustment to your gross income. Alternatively, if the amount you repay is more than $3,000, a tax credit is available.

Net Operating Loss Deduction

The net operating loss (NOL) deduction permits a taxpayer to use a loss from one year against income from another year. A net operating loss is determined by making specific adjustments to eliminate certain nonbusiness items in the loss year.

NOLs incurred in taxable years ending after 1975 may be carried back 3 years and then forward 15 years. You may also elect to forgo the carry-back period for NOLs incurred in taxable years ending after 1975 and only carry the loss forward for 15 years. Special rules apply to the determination of the NOL deduction under the alternative minimum tax. (See page 138.) Net operating loss for businesses is discussed in Chapter 12.

Overall Limit on Itemized Deductions

Itemized deductions—i.e., deductions claimed on your return—are phased out by 3% of the excess of your adjusted gross income over $111,800 (married filing separately, $55,900), adjusted annually for inflation. This means that a taxpayer with AGI of $180,000 would lose $2,046 [($180,000 − $111,800) × 3%] of itemized deductions.

This overall limitation is imposed *after* any other limitations affecting specific categories of itemized deductions are applied. For example, miscellaneous itemized deductions will be subject to both the 2% floor discussed on page 67 and the additional 3% phaseout.

Medical expenses, casualty, theft, and gambling losses, and investment interest expense are not subject to this limitation. And in no case can the reduction be more than 80% of your otherwise allowable deductions. Also, the limitation does not apply if you are subject to the alternative minimum tax.

TAX*SAVER*

If you can reduce your 1994 AGI to below $111,800 you will avoid having your itemized deductions reduced at all. For every $1,000 of AGI in excess of $111,800 your itemized deductions are reduced by $30. So if you have AGI in excess of $111,800, you save $30 in deductions if you can reduce your AGI by $1,000.

3

Tax Planning and
Your Home

Introduction

Your home is often your most significant asset. For this
reason, if no other, you will want to do everything you can
to maximize your after-tax return on this investment. Fortunately, your home can also be your biggest tax shelter.
The tax code allows you to deduct interest paid on a home
mortgage, within certain limits, from your adjusted gross
income. This chapter discusses numerous tax-saving strategies that involve your home. It discusses ways you can
maximize your deduction for home mortgage interest; ways
to minimize the gain and recognize loss when you sell your
residence; and what tax deductions you may be able to take
if you own a second home. It suggests different methods
by which you may divide jointly owned property because of
a divorce, what you can deduct if you have an office at home,
and ways you may generate charitable contributions using
your home.

Selling Your Home

A gain on the sale or exchange (including condemnation) of
your principal residence is taxable. If you have a loss on
the sale, you cannot deduct it.

TAXSAVER

*If you believe your home will decline in value before
you sell it, you may want to convert it to rental property
before the value declines so that the loss, if any, may
be deducted.*

TAXSAVER

*Selling expenses and any home improvements you've
made over the years will reduce the amount of gain
that is taxable. You need to keep good records of such*

expenses in order to figure the lowest taxable gain you must report.

If certain conditions are met, however, the tax on the gain from the sale or exchange of your principal residence is postponed. For you to be eligible to postpone the tax, the cost of your new residence must exceed the adjusted sales price of your old residence, and the new residence must be purchased and occupied within a period beginning two years prior to the date of the sale of the original residence and ending two years after such date. For certain members of the armed forces and individuals whose tax home is outside of the United States, the time period is longer.

TaxSaver

If you want to defer tax on the gain from the sale of your old home, make absolutely sure you occupy the new home as your principal residence in time. You are not allowed any additional time even if conditions beyond your control keep you from moving in.

When Your New Home Costs Less than the Sales Price of Your Old One. If the two-year rule is met, but the cost of the new residence is less than the adjusted sales price of your old residence, you may have to recognize gain to the extent that the adjusted sales price of the old residence exceeds the cost of the new residence. Any gain not recognized on the sale of the old residence reduces the tax basis of the new residence.

The term "adjusted sales price" means the selling price minus the sales expenses of the sale and fixing-up expenses incurred in putting the residence into condition for sale. For example, expenses of sale could include broker's fees, fees for drafting a contract of sale, fees for drafting the deed, escrow fees, and mortgage title insurance. Fixing-up expenses include decorating and repair expenses you have incurred to sell the old home and must be for work done during the 90 days prior to signing the sale contract and paid within 30 days after the sale.

Example: Your old home had a basis of $75,000. On January 5, 1994, you signed a contract to sell the old home for $160,000 and on January 6, 1994, you purchased a new home for $138,000. You incurred selling expenses of $8,000 and fixing-up expenses of $3,000 on the sale of your old home. Your calculations would be:

1. Selling price of old home	$160,000
2. Minus: Selling expenses	(8,000)
3. Amount realized	$152,000
4. Basis of old home	(75,000)
5. Gain on old home [(3) minus (4)]	$ 77,000
6. Amount realized on old home	$152,000
7. Fixing-up expenses	(3,000)
8. Adjusted sales price	$149,000
9. Cost of new home	138,000
10. Gain not postponed [(8) minus (9)]	$ 11,000
11. Gain postponed [(5) minus (10)]	$ 66,000
12. Cost of new home	$138,000
13. Minus: Gain postponed (11)	(66,000)
14. Basis of new home	$ 72,000

One-Time Exclusion for Taxpayers 55 and Older. If you are 55 or older, you are allowed a one-time exclusion of a gain up to $125,000 ($62,500 in the case of a married individual filing a separate return). To qualify, you must be 55 before the date of the sale and must have owned and occupied the residence for three out of the previous five years.

There is an exception to the three-out-of-five-year rule for certain incapacitated taxpayers. If you are physically or mentally incapable of self-care during the five-year period, time that you spend in a licensed facility (including a nursing home) can qualify as use of the residence for up to two of the three required use years as long as you own the property during the period of incapacitation. Because this exception only applies for two years of the three-year period, you must still use the property as a residence for a period of at least one year.

Special rules also apply when the property sold was acquired as a result of an "involuntary conversion"—the forced disposition of property as a result of condemnation. In such cases, the holding period of the residence is added to the holding period of the property sold to determine whether the three-out-of-five-year test is satisfied.

Married individuals are entitled to only one lifetime exclusion per couple. For example, if a taxpayer used the election in a prior marriage, this same taxpayer could not use the election in a new marriage, even though his or her new spouse had not previously used the election. However, if each spouse had made an independent election prior to marriage, neither has to repay the tax on the gain previously excluded by either one. Any gain in excess of $125,000 may be deferred if you reinvest the money in a new residence within a certain period, as explained.

Example: A 55-year-old taxpayer sells his residence for $250,000 on July 21, 1994, and purchases a smaller home. The original residence was purchased more than three years ago for $120,000. The new home is purchased by July 10, 1996, and costs $160,000. There is no tax on the $130,000 gain, and the basis of the new residence is $155,000, computed as follows:

Gain Realized and Not Excluded:

Sales price	$250,000
Basis of original residence	(120,000)
Realized gain	$130,000
One-time exclusion (55 years old)	(125,000)
Gain not subject to exclusion	$5,000

Gain Recognized:

Sales price	$250,000
One-time exclusion	(125,000)
Adjusted sales price	$125,000
Cost of new residence	(160,000)
Gain recognized (not less than zero)	$0

Basis of New Residence:

Cost of new residence	$160,000
Gain not excluded and not recognized	(5,000)
Basis of new residence	$155,000

E&Y FOCUS: The Split-Gain Technique

A married couple that plans to sell their jointly owned principal residence and plans to buy a replacement residence that costs less than the adjusted sales price of their former home—e.g., they are retiring and moving to a lower-cost area or downsizing after the children have moved out—can reduce the amount of capital gain recognized on the sale of the former home by a planning approach known as a "split-gain technique." In essence what is done is that the ownership of the residence is changed from joint ownership where the two own all of the property to an ownership structure in which each owns one half. When the property is sold each one takes their half of the proceeds. Then one spouse purchases a new replacement residence with his or her half of the proceeds. The other spouse does not purchase a replacement residence but reports all the gain from the sale of their old home. This is best understood through this simplified example:

A husband and wife jointly own their principal residence, which is worth about $800,000 and cost them $400,000 when they bought it. The plan to sell their house and purchase a retirement home that will cost them $400,000. They have a $400,000 gain on the sale of the first house. Because the cost of new house is much less that the proceeds of the old house, they will recognize a $400,000 gain and pay a capital gains tax of about $112,000. If instead of their owning the property jointly, they each own one-half, each will get $400,000 from the sale, and each will have a $200,000 gain. If the wife purchases the replacement residence, her $200,000 gain will not be recognized. The husband's $200,000 gain will be recognized. His capital gains tax will be $56,000 (28% of $200,000).

The wife's basis in the new house will be only $200,000. If she sells the house in the future, she may have to pay taxes on that deferred gain. But, deferring the payment of tax to the future is better than paying taxes currently.

This technique to reduce the amount of gain that a married couple would have to recognize currently is effective only if the excess of the adjusted sales price of the former home over the cost of the replacement residence is greater than one-half of the realizable gain.

Example: Assume in the example above that the cost of the replacement residence is $900,000. If Bob and Mary purchase the new home jointly, only $100,000 of the gain would have to be currently recognized. However, if Bob purchased the home alone, then Mary's entire $250,000 share of the gain would have to be recognized.

If you are thinking of taking advantage of the "split-gain" technique, you should consider the following preparatory steps:

- Converting title in your residence from joint tenancy to tenants in common before selling the old home;
- Having the settlement attorney issue separate Forms 1099 reporting one-half of the gain to each spouse;
- Filing as married filing separate for the year of sale with each spouse completing a Form 2119 (*Sale of Your Home*); and,
- Having the spouse that takes title individually to the new home (or, in a community property sale, as separate property) use only his or her sale proceeds and

other separate funds, if necessary, to purchase the new home.

Real Estate Taxes. The deduction for real estate taxes on any real estate sale is apportioned between the seller and the buyer based on the number of days in the real-property tax year that the property is owned by each.

Below Market Interest. In certain instances the seller of a personal residence may be required to acknowledge additional interest income for debt obligations issued with a below-market interest rate. (See page 53.)

Home Mortgage Interest

Generally, mortgage interest is any interest you pay on a loan secured by your home. This includes a mortgage, second mortgage, a line of credit, and a home equity loan. Most home mortgage interest is deductible, subject to the following limitations:

The loans secured by your principal residence and a second residence cannot exceed $1 million. In addition, in order to be deductible, the debt has to qualify as "acquisition indebtedness." Acquisition indebtedness is debt incurred in acquiring, constructing, or substantially improving a qualified residence. Acquisition indebtedness is reduced by principal payments made on such debt. If you have repaid some of your "acquisition debt" (most commonly by making mortgage payments), it cannot be restored through refinancing. You can refinance your mortgage up to the balance remaining on the old mortgage and still deduct the interest. If you refinance in an amount in excess of the old mortgage, the interest allocable to the excess is not deductible unless the excess was used to substantially improve your home or it qualifies as home-equity indebtedness (discussed below).

Acquisition indebtedness that was incurred prior to October 14, 1987, is not subject to the $1 million limitation. However, the amount of such debt reduces (but not below zero) the $1 million limitation on subsequent acquisition debt. Such debt includes that which was incurred on or before October 13, 1987, and was secured by a qualified residence as of that date and at all times thereafter.

Home mortgage interest is deductible on a home-equity loan if the loan does not exceed $100,000. The home-equity debt must not exceed the fair market value of a qualified residence that is reduced by the amount of acquisition indebtedness for that residence. Home-equity loans may provide you with deductible interest on debt incurred for personal purposes, such as the purchase of a family car. (See Chapter 2, page 39.)

> **TAXSAVER**
>
> *If you own more than two homes, you may not deduct as home mortgage interest, interest on more than two of these homes during any one year. You must include your main residence as one of the homes. You may choose any one of your other homes as a qualified residence and may change this choice in a different tax year.*
>
> *However, you cannot choose to treat one home as a second residence for part of a year and another home as a second residence for the remainder of the year if both of these homes were owned by you during the entire year and neither was your main residence during that year.*

Before You Refinance

Here are some questions you should consider when you are thinking about refinancing your mortgage:

1. What will it cost to refinance the mortgage?
2. How much longer do I plan to own my home?
3. Will my financial condition in the future allow me enough cash flow to continue paying the mortgage?
4. Should I consider an Adjustable Rate Mortgage (ARM), or a fixed rate mortgage? Because of current low interest rates, ARMs may require smaller monthly payments than a fixed rate mortgage. However, monthly payments on an ARM will increase if interest rates go up and could, at some time, exceed the amount of a fixed rate mortgage.

If the rates stay low you can be ahead with an ARM. However, if you are on a fixed income there is always a risk that rates will go up beyond what you can afford.

Points

"Points" are certain charges sometimes paid by a borrower. They are also referred to as loan origination fees, maximum loan charges, or premium charges. If the payment of any of these charges is only for the use of money, it is interest.

Because points are, in effect, interest paid in advance, generally you may not deduct the full amount for points in the year paid. Points that represent prepaid interest generally must be deducted over the life of the loan.

Exception: You may deduct the entire amount you pay as points in the year of payment if the loan is used to buy or improve your principal residence and is secured by that home. This exception will apply only if:

1. The payment of points is an established business practice in the area where the loan was made, and

2. The points paid do not exceed the number of points generally charged in this area.

Furthermore the points charged on a mortgage obtained to purchase your principal home are immediately deductible whether paid out of separate funds or, if the following additional conditions are satisfied, incorporated into the mortgage note. These additional requirements are:

1. Your lender prepares a Form HUD-1, *Uniform Settlement Statement,* that explicitly states the points incurred on the loan. Points may be identified as "loan origination fees," "loan discount," "discount points," or simply, "points,"
2. The points must be computed as a percentage of the principal amount of the loan,
3. The total of your downpayment plus other cash paid by the time you close is at least as much as the amount of points charged.

To be immediately deductible, points paid on home improvement loans must be paid from separate funds at closing—that is, they cannot be included in the borrowed amount.

Points paid on a loan to purchase or improve your second home do not qualify for full, immediate deduction. Generally, points paid on the refinancing of a principal residence must be spread over the life of the loan.

TaxAlert

If a buyer does not have enough cash to close the purchase of a house and pay points, the mortgage lender will very likely require a higher interest rate. But, the purchaser might not be able to afford payments with the higher interest, so the seller pays the points. The question then is "if there is a deduction who gets it?"

The IRS decided in 1994 that a borrower (the purchaser) may treat amounts paid by the seller in connection with the acquisition of a principal residence as mortgage points that are deductible in the taxable year paid. The new rule applies back to points paid after December 31, 1990. If you are affected by this new rule, you may file amended returns deducting the points paid during years beginning after December 31, 1990 and before January 1, 1994.

TaxSaver

A borrower may deduct points paid by the seller if the following conditions are satisfied:
- *The rule only applies to points—that is, to financing costs described on the HUD-1 or similar settlement*

statement as "loan origination fees," "loan discount," "discount points," or "points."

■ Points must be described as a percentage of the loan amount.
■ The amount of the points must be reasonable for the local market.
■ Points are only deductible to the extent of the amount of funds brought to the table by the buyer. Furthermore, the buyer must reduce his or her basis in the home by the amount of seller-paid points deducted.

As noted above, this rule is retroactive and applies to all primary residences purchased since January 1, 1991 that involved seller paid points.

TaxSaver

Generally, each point adds about 1/8% to the interest rate on a 30-year mortgage. However, the effect is much greater if the loan is for a shorter period of time. Therefore, if you expect to sell your property well before the mortgage is paid off, it could be better to pay a higher interest rate and fewer points.

TaxSaver

Generally, costs for your children's dormitory space at college are not deductible. However, if you purchase a condominium in which your college-age dependent child lives while at school, you may be able to generate a deduction. This is possible because the interest expense for a qualified second residence is deductible. The interest portion of the mortgage and any related property taxes would be deductible. Obviously, appreciation or depreciation potential and other factors must be considered when looking at this idea, but in the right circumstance it could make sense.

Alternative Minimum Tax Consequences. Home mortgage interest is allowed as a deduction for AMT purposes. However, the definition of such interest is narrower than that of "qualified residence interest" for regular tax purposes. Refinanced home mortgage interest that is applicable to any mortgage in excess of the outstanding mortgage before refinancing is not deductible for AMT purposes. (See page 75 for further discuss.)

Second Homes
Vacation Homes and Other Dwellings. Benefits may be derived from the ownership of a second home. You may significantly reduce your taxable income by increasing

your home mortgage interest deduction, subject to certain limitations (see page 75). If you rent your property, you may reduce your taxable income further through the deduction for rental expenses (see page 17).

Domicile vs. Residence. Where you actually establish your domicile can have a tremendous impact on your tax bill. While you may have numerous residences, theoretically, you may have only one domicile. Traditionally, the critical element of domicile is physical presence in a state with the intent to establish that state as a home.

TaxSaver

You should try to establish a domicile in a state where the income and estate taxes will be the lowest.

Example: A New Yorker who has a residence in New York City retired to Florida for five years before his death. The man kept an office in New York but spent most of his time (more than six months) in Florida. New York claimed that the man was a resident of New York because he died there and was buried there. The New York estate taxes would have equaled $4 million. However, the man had arranged his will through a Florida attorney and took numerous steps to declare Florida as his new domicile. It was determined that he was, indeed, a resident of Florida and a nonresident of New York. His nonresident estate taxes in New York were less than $20,000.

E&Y FOCUS: Establishing Your Domicile

Where you actually establish domicile can have a tremendous impact on your tax bill. For instance, New York and Massachusetts have significant state income taxes while Florida and Texas have none. States also have differing rules governing certain estate matters, such as the division of property when someone dies without a will.

To Establish Your New Domicile
- Register and vote in your new state whenever possible. Advise the Board of Elections where you formerly voted that you have moved, and cancel your old registration.
- File a declaration of domicile. Some states, such as Florida, have a special form you can file to establish permanent residency.

- File, as a resident, all state and local tax returns required by your new state—and use your new address on all future tax returns.
- Change your car's title and registration.
- Obtain a driver's license in your new state.
- Take advantage of homestead exemptions if your state offers them—they're an excellent way to help establish a change of domicile and reduce real estate taxes.
- Open bank accounts in your new state.
- Become a member of organizations in the new state, rather than continue memberships in the old state.
- Execute a new will in which you refer to your domicile.
- Spend more time in your state of domicile than in any other state.
- Declare your new state as your domicile on all forms that require a statement of residence. Examples are passports, contracts, credit applications, and hotel registrations.
- Use your new address in all formal agreements.
- Register securities at your new address.
- Change insurance policies that do not relate specifically to property located outside your new state.
- Change your address with the Social Security Administration.
- Change credit cards, particularly those which are national in scope.

Rental Income and Expenses

Rental income includes any payment you receive for the use or occupation of property. For example, if you rent the loft above your garage or a room in your house, you will have rental income. If you receive property or services as rent, the fair market value of the property or services you receive is rental income.

Deductible Rental Expenses. Repairs, advertising, janitorial and maid service, rental of equipment, utilities, fire and liability insurance, taxes, interest, commissions for the collection of rent, and travel and transportation expenses—all of these expenditures, if they are incurred in renting property, may be deductible. Repairs are expenses incurred to keep your property in good operating condition. Repair expenses include repainting property inside or out, fixing gutters or floors, and fixing leaks. Repairs are different from improvements. Improvements must be "capitalized" and depreciated—that is, the cost of the item is written off as a business expense over a period of years. (See the discussion of depreciation later in this chapter.) Improvements are expenditures that either add to the value of your property or prolong the property's useful life. Improvements include such items as building an addition, putting in new plumbing or wiring, and installing a new roof.

TaxSaver

You may deduct expenses on your rental property during a period in which it is not being rented as long as it is actively being held out for rent. This rule applies to a period between rentals as well as to the period during which a property is being marketed as a rental property for the first time. The IRS can disallow these deductions if you are unable to show that you were actively seeking a profit and had a reasonable expectation of achieving one. However, the deduction cannot be disallowed merely because your property was difficult to rent.

Rental of Vacation Homes and Other Dwellings. If you rent out part or all of a vacation home or other dwelling unit, and you also use any part of the unit for personal purposes during the year, you must divide your expenses between the rental use and the personal use.

TaxSaver

When Rental Income Isn't Taxed. *If a residence is rented out for fewer than 15 days during the taxable year, the rental income is not taxable. This is one of the few instances in which the IRS considers rental income to be nontaxable. Consequently, if you live near the site of a major annual sporting event—say, The Masters Golf Tournament in Augusta, Georgia—and you rent out your residence during the event (for 14 days or less), any income you receive will be tax-free. However, expenses attributable to the rental of your residence, such as depreciation, insurance, and so on, are not deductible except for interest, taxes, and casualty losses that are deductible on Schedule A, Form 1040, if you itemize. (There are pending legislative proposals to eliminate this TaxSaver for less-than-15-day rental income.)*

Figuring Rental Expenses. If you rent out a dwelling unit for 15 days or more, the income you receive is taxable. Expenses related to the property rental are deductible, subject to certain limitations based on the number of days you personally use the dwelling unit. Generally, your deductions can be found by applying this formula: Expenses × rental days ÷ total days used for all purposes.

Example: You own a ski chalet that is used only during the winter ski season. During the year, the dwelling unit is rented out for 80 days and used personally by you for another 10 days. Total utility expenses are $1,800. You can deduct $1,600 of the utility expenses against rental income ($1,800 × 80 ÷ 90). The remaining $200 is considered a nondeductible personal expense.

If You Use a Rental Property for More Than 14 Days.

When you use a dwelling unit for personal purposes for more than the greater of 14 days or 10% of the number of days that the dwelling unit was rented at a fair market rate during the year. A further restriction applies to the deduction for rental expenses. In this case, the dwelling unit is treated as a residence. The rental expense deductions are limited to the amount of gross rental income, reduced first by any allocated expenditures that would otherwise be deductible, such as interest and taxes, and then by other deductible expenses, such as allocated utilities and depreciation.

Generally, a dwelling unit is used for personal purposes only on days that it is:

- used by you or by any other person who has an interest in it;
- used by a member of your family or by a family member of any other person who has an interest in it, unless that family member uses the dwelling unit as his or her main home, pays a fair rental price, and arranges the rental pursuant to a shared equity financing agreement. For purposes of this rule, your family includes only brothers and sisters, spouses, ancestors (parents, grandparents, etc.) and lineal descendants (children, grandchildren, etc.);
- used by another under an arrangement that lets you use some other dwelling unit; or
- used by anyone at less than a fair rental price.

TaxSaver

Note that this rule relating to personal use does not apply to use by an in-law of the taxpayer who owns the property. Thus, a son-in-law could lease property at a fair value to his mother-in-law, and it would not be treated as personal use.

Some days that you spend at the dwelling unit are not counted as days of personal use. For example, any day that you spend repairing and maintaining your property on a full-time basis is not counted as a day of personal use. In addition, the fact that family members used the dwelling for personal purposes on the same day that you are repairing or maintaining it does not make the day a personal day. You also do not have to count days on which you used the property as your main home as days of personal use, if you used the property as your main home before or after renting it or offering it for rent, and either (1) you rented or tried to rent the property for 12 or more consecutive months, or (2) you rented or tried to rent the property for a period of less than 12 consecutive months and the period ended because you sold or exchanged the property.

TaxSaver

The IRS method for allocating expenses between personal and rental use requires a strict allocation between the total number of days the unit was used during the year and the number of rental days. Taxpayers, however, have successfully challenged this method in a number of Tax Court cases. Using the Tax Court method, you can allocate interest and taxes based on the number of days in the year rather than the number of days rented as prescribed by the IRS. Depending upon the method you chose for allocating expenses between personal and rental use, you may be able to increase your total expense deductions.

Vacation Home and the Passive Activity Rules

Vacation homes and other rental properties considered rental activities are subject to the passive activity rules discussed on page 19. Consequently, when making decisions regarding renting, financing, and selling properties, you must consider the impact of rental losses being disallowed and the $25,000 rental loss limitation deduction that is applicable to certain taxpayers. (See discussion of exception for active real estate participation in Chapter 1.) Losses that are not deductible as a result of the passive activity rules can be carried forward to later years and, subject to the same income limitations, deducted in those years.

TaxSaver

When the cash flow from your rental property is not enough to meet your operating costs, you should determine if the expected growth in the value of the property will make up for the losses you are incurring each year. If it doesn't, you may want to reconsider your investment. Remember, what has to be made up includes what you could earn on the proceeds from the sale if the property were sold today.

Depreciation

Depreciation is the annual deduction you are entitled to take to cover the cost of certain capital expenditures for property held for business or investment purposes. The depreciation deduction is claimed over "the recovery period" of the property, which varies depending upon the type of property. For example, the recovery period for the cost of a new roof on a rental home is longer than the recovery period for furniture bought for the home. Depreciation is calculated in the same way whether you report income on the cash or accrual method.

Several factors determine how much depreciation you can deduct. The main factors are: (1) your cost basis in the property and (2) the recovery period for the property.

The total of all your annual depreciation deductions cannot be more than your cost or other basis of the property. For this purpose, the total depreciation must include any depreciation that you were allowed to claim, even if you did not claim it.

For more information about depreciation see Chapter 12, Some Basic Planning Strategies for Businesses.

TAX**S**AVER

The Tax Act of 1993 generally extended the recovery period for nonresidential real estate from 31.5 years to 39 years for property placed in service on or after May 13, 1993. One effect of the change will be to modify the investment return one can expect on nonresidential real estate.

Charitable Contributions

Contribution of Property. A transfer of an undivided interest in property qualifies as a charitable contribution and may be deducted. You may deduct the fair market value of the property at the time of contribution if the property would qualify for long-term capital gain treatment if sold. Generally, the contribution of your residence will qualify for such treatment. However, if you have owned your residence for less than a year, your deduction is its fair market value minus the amount that would be ordinary income or short-term capital gain. See page 100 for a discussion of charitable contributions.

Contribution of Property Subject to a Mortgage. If you contribute your residence to a charity and it is subject to a mortgage, you will be allowed a partial deduction. In determining the amount of the contribution, the contribution will be treated as a bargain sale—the amount of the charitable deduction is the difference between the fair market value of the property and the amount of the mortgage. Further, you must include the full amount of the mortgage as income when you make the charitable gift.

Partial Interest in Property. Generally, no deduction is allowed for a charitable contribution of less than your entire interest in property. For example, the owner of property will not get a deduction for giving a "life estate interest" in a property to charity. (A life estate interest is an interest in property that terminates upon the death of the life estate's owner.) A contribution of the right to use property is a contribution of less than your entire interest in that property and is not deductible.

Exceptions: There are some situations in which you may claim a deduction for a charitable contribution that is less than your entire interest in the property:

1. *Undivided part of your entire interest.* A contribution of an undivided part of your entire interest in property must consist of a part of each and every substantial interest or right you own in the property. It must extend over the entire term of your interest in the property.
2. *Remainder interest in a personal residence or farm.* You may take a charitable deduction for a gift to a qualified organization of a remainder interest in a personal residence or in a farm, if the gift is irrevocable.

TaxSaver

If you give a remainder interest in a personal residence (or a farm) to a qualified charity, the present value of the remainder interest is deductible as a charitable contribution. One significant advantage of such a gift is that you suffer no loss of income or increase in expense from the gift, but you still gain a current income tax deduction. The gift may be made without the use of a trust. In addition, you continue to use and enjoy the home for life.

To qualify for the deduction, the gift must be a gift of your personal residence. The home does not have to be your principal residence. Thus, the gift may be your vacation home.

The charity receives no immediate benefit; however, the opportunity for future benefits can be substantial.

Example: *A 62-year-old woman owns a personal residence with a fair market value of $162,000. The land on which the residence is located is valued at $42,000. The residence has a remaining useful life of 35 years and an estimated salvage value of $30,000. According to IRS tables, the value of the remainder interest in the*

*home and the land is approximately $40,000, which is
currently deductible as a donation of the interest. Besides a substantial income tax deduction, the donor
will receive an estate tax deduction for the value of
the interest that passes to charity at her death.*

Divorce and Separation

The tax effects on the sale or transfer of one's residence
incident to a divorce can vary substantially depending on
whether the couple retains ownership, sells, or transfers
the property.

If title is given to your spouse or former spouse, incident
to divorce, no gain or loss is recognized on a transfer. A
transfer of property is incident to divorce if the transfer
occurs within one year after the date on which the marriage
ends, or if the transfer is related to the ending of the marriage. The transfer is treated like a gift, and the spouse
receiving the property takes the basis of the transferring
spouse. This results even if the spouse that retains the
residence pays cash and the transaction mirrors the form
of a sale.

Alternatively, couples may decide to sell the house to a
third party and split the proceeds. In this circumstance,
both parties will recognize gain upon the sale of the house
unless they qualify for the rollover exception or the
$125,000 exclusion (see page 33).

TaxSaver

*If both of you are over 55, and if you choose to sell
your property, you should wait until after the divorce
to do so. At this time, you and your former spouse
each may elect the $125,000 exclusion, if applicable
(see page 33). If you sell the property while you are
married, you may elect the exclusion as a couple; you
will not each receive the $125,000 exclusion.*

Yet another alternative is to retain your interest in the
residence even though you no longer live there. This option
may be attractive if there are not enough assets to com-
pensate you for your interest in the residence. Under this
alternative, you and your spouse could agree, pursuant to
the settlement, that the residence subsequently will be sold
(i.e., when the children no longer live there) and the proceeds from the sale divided between the two of you. However, when the residence is later sold, you will not qualify
for the $125,000 exclusion nor will you be able to roll over
any gain from the sale into the purchase of another residence because it is no longer your principal residence.

TaxSaver

If you decide to retain your interest in the residence, you should consider transferring it to your spouse and as part of the divorce settlement require him or her to divide the proceeds upon sale. Consequently, any applicable exclusions may be used toward the entire proceeds.

Office-in-Home Expenses

To qualify for a deduction for office-in-home expenses, you must use the home office exclusively as an office and it must be your primary place of business. In determining whether you meet this standard, you must look at: (1) the relative importance of the activities performed at each business location; and (2) the amount of time spent at each location. The IRS has indicated that it will first look to the "relative importance" test. If it does not produce a definitive answer, then the amount of time spent at each location is the determining factor. This test may result in a taxpayer having no specific office which can be deemed the principal place of business and, thus, being denied a deduction for home-office expenses.

The allowable deduction is limited to the gross income generated from the use of the residence, reduced first by any expenditures otherwise deductible, such as taxes and interest, and then reduced by other deductible trade or business expenses, such as prorated utilities and depreciation. Any disallowed expenses can be carried forward to future years, subject to the gross income limitation in those years.

You are not entitled to office-in-home deductions for expenses attributable to the rental of all or part of your home to your employer for performing services as an employee. An independent contractor is treated as an employee under these rules. (Also see pages 58.)

Moving Expenses

Certain moving expenses to one's new residence are deductible. For a discussion of moving expenses, see page 56.

Estate Tax Consequences

For a discussion of planning techniques to minimize estate tax consequences on your residence, see page 186.

4

IRAs, 401(k) Plans, and Other Retirement Plans

Introduction

Ask a financial planner what's the best way to save money for your retirement, and chances are he or she will recommend that you contribute as much as you can to a 401(k) plan, an individual retirement account or annuity (IRA), a Keogh plan, a Simplified Employee Pension (SEP)—or some combination of the four, if you're eligible. Within certain limitations, all these retirement plans give you the ability to contribute before-tax dollars to an account or trust and receive a tax-deferred accumulation of funds, which will not be taxed until the amounts are withdrawn—generally, when you are retired and quite possibly in a lower tax bracket. This chapter will explain in more detail what these retirement plans are and how they operate. In addition, it will suggest strategies you can use to make the most of your retirement funds.

IRAs

An IRA is a personal savings plan that lets you set aside funds for your retirement. Subject to the limitations discussed below, you may be able to make and deduct from your gross income on your tax return a cash contribution paid to an IRA.

Your annual IRA contribution is limited to the lesser of $2,000 or 100% of your compensation (or earned income from self-employment). Alimony is treated as compensation for this purpose. The amount you can contribute to your IRA is determined on an individual basis. Therefore, if you and your spouse each receive compensation over $2,000, then each of you can contribute $2,000 to your respective

IRAs. Earnings in your IRA are not taxable until they are distributed to you.

Although anyone with compensation or earned income may contribute to an IRA, a deduction is not permitted on your tax return if:

1. You or your spouse is an active participant in a qualified retirement plan provided by one of your employers, and
2. Your adjusted gross income exceeds $50,000 ($35,000 for single filers and $10,000 for married persons filing separately).

If you or your spouse is an active participant in an employer's qualified retirement plan, you can claim a reduced IRA deduction if your adjusted gross income is less than the dollar amount described above but more than $40,000 ($25,000 for single filers and $0 for married filing separately). For married couples filing separately, if one spouse is an active participant in a qualified retirement plan, then the other spouse will also be treated as a member of the plan, unless the couple has lived apart throughout the entire year.

TaxSaver

Contributing before-tax earnings to an IRA account can make a big difference in your retirement savings. For example, assume you are in the 36% tax bracket and that you are earning 6% interest on your savings. You can earn approximately 1.3 times more money after paying taxes on the distribution (payable at the time of withdrawal) on a $2,000 IRA contribution held for 20 years than if you did not make that before-tax contribution. If your tax rate drops after your retirement because you have less income, your savings could amount to an even bigger nest egg.

__Example:__ If you contributed $2,000 a year to an IRA for 20 years and the IRA earned 6% each year, at the end of 20 years you would have about $78,000. If you deposited $1,280 ($2,000 less $720 in tax) each year in an account earning 6% and paid tax on the interest you earned each year, you would have about $39,000 in the account at the end of 20 years. Even paying 36% tax on the $78,000, you would have about $50,000 left as opposed to $39,000 without the IRA. If after retirement your tax rate is 28%, you would have about $56,000 left from the IRA as opposed to $39,000 without an IRA.

Nondeductible IRA Contributions. Even if you do not qualify for a tax-deductible contribution to your IRA, you can still make an after-tax contribution. The earnings on these contributions accumulate tax-deferred until you withdraw the money from your IRA. The maximum non-deductible contribution you can make to your IRA is determined as though the contribution were deductible, minus the amount of any deductible contribution you may make. See Table 4.1.

Spousal IRAs. If you can make a deductible contribution to an IRA and are married, you can also establish an IRA for a non-working spouse. The spousal IRA must be kept separate from your IRA, i.e. one for you and one for your spouse or one IRA with separate sub accounts, one for you and one for your spouse. The most you can contribute to a spousal IRA is the *lesser* of $2,250 or 100% of your compensation. And, you can allocate the contribution in any way you want as long as not more than $2,000 is allocated to one person.

For example: Joe and Joan have a spousal IRA to which $2,250 is contributed. The contribution can be divided $2,000 for Joe and $250 for Joan, $250 for Joe and $2,000 for Joan or any combination in between such as $1,125 for Joe and $1,125 for Joan.

When to Make Your IRA Contributions. Contributions to an IRA can be made starting from the first day of the tax year through the due date (without extensions) of your tax return for that tax year. This means that IRA contributions can generally be made until April 15 of the year following your tax year.

TABLE 4.1   IRA Deductions

Adjusted Gross Income (In $)		Allowable Deduction	
Married Filing Jointly*	Single	Not an Active Participant	Active Participant
0–39,999	0–24,999	2,000	2,000
40,000– 48,999	25,000– 33,999	2,000	200– 2,000**
49,000– 49,999	34,000– 34,999	2,000	200***
50,000 and over	35,000 and over	2,000	0

*A married couple filing separately is subject to a special limitation (see above).

**The $2,000 amount is reduced by a percentage equal to your adjusted gross income in excess of the lower adjusted gross income limits divided by $10,000. For example, a single individual with an adjusted gross income of $32,000 is allowed an IRA deduction of $600.

***The IRA deduction will not be reduced below $200 until it is reduced to $0 at $50,000 (married filing jointly) and $35,000 (single) of adjusted gross income.

You can maximize your savings by funding your IRA as early as possible for any given tax year. By contributing to your IRA at the beginning of a tax year instead of waiting until April 15 of the following year, your contribution can earn as much as 15½ months worth of additional interest. The interest earnings will not be taxed until the money is withdrawn from the account.

IRA Custodial Fees. Annual custodial fees paid to maintain an IRA, as well as the initial fee to establish an IRA, are deductible if you pay for the fees separately rather than having the costs charged to the IRA account itself. Such IRA expenses are deductible as miscellaneous itemized deductions subject to 2% of the adjusted gross income floor.

401(k) Plans

If your employer has a 401(k) plan or another plan that allows you to set aside income (e.g., a tax-sheltered annuity or 403(b) plan, which is generally available to employees of tax-exempt and educational organizations), you can elect to defer a certain amount of your salary on a before-tax basis. Such amounts are withheld from your salary and are not reported as income until withdrawn from the plan. Income earned on your 401(k) investment is also tax-deferred. Unlike an IRA, you may be able to borrow from your 401(k) plan without penalty. Subject to nondiscrimination tests which apply to 401(k) plans, you can elect to defer your wages up to a maximum of $9,240 in 1994. Also, many employers provide a matching contribution in their 401(k) plans. For example, a 401(k) plan may provide that for each $1 you contribute, the employer will contribute 50¢. With this kind of plan, you would receive an immediate return on your investment of 50%.

Because funds in a 401(k) plan accumulate tax-free, it is usually a good idea to make as large a contribution to your 401(k) plan as possible. In addition, because contributions to your 401(k) plan are made on a before-tax basis, any contributions made to the plan reduce your adjusted gross income.

Although the funds in your 401(k) plan are meant to be set aside for your retirement, you may still have access to them if you need money at an earlier time. Your plan may permit you to borrow from your account, subject to strict rules. Despite the restrictions, you may be better off borrowing from your retirement

*fund than getting a loan from your bank. If the loan
from the bank is for personal purposes, it will result in
nondeductible interest. A loan from your 401(k) plan
does not generate deductible interest, but the interest
you pay is allocated directly back to your account.*

In addition to the general qualified plan distribution rules
discussed below, 401(k) plans are also subject to special
rules regarding certain distributions. Specifically, employee
deferrals cannot be distributed prior to one of the following
events:
- retirement
- death
- disability
- separation from service with the employer
- attainment of age 59½
- termination of the plan
- disposition of corporate assets or disposition of subsidiary
- hardship.

Distributions From IRAs and 401(k) Plans
The rules governing the taxation of distributions from IRAs
and 401(k) plans are very complex. Not only can the tax
rules for ordinary retirement withdrawals be confusing, but
the tax law also provides for complicated penalty taxes if
distributions are received too early (generally before age
59½), if distributions exceed an annual allowable amount,
and if distributions begin too late (generally after April 1
of the year following the year you turn age 70½).

Tax Rules for Ordinary Withdrawals. In general,
distributions from IRAs and 401(k) plans are taxed as ordinary income. If nondeductible contributions have been
made to an IRA, however, distributions are taxed in much
the same way as an annuity. The portion of each distribution
that is attributable to nondeductible contributions, if any,
is excluded from your taxable income. The ratio of each
distribution to be excluded is determined by dividing undistributed nondeductible contributions by your total IRA
account balance. If no nondeductible contributions have
been made, then the entire distribution is considered ordinary income. (Nondeductible contributions to IRAs have
only been allowed since 1987.)

With 401(k) plans, lump-sum distributions may qualify
for special tax treatment. A lump-sum distribution is the
distribution within a single tax year of an employee's entire
balance, excluding certain amounts forfeited or subject to
forfeiture, from all of the employer's qualified pension, stock
bonus, or profit-sharing plans. The distribution must have
been made:
1. Because of the employee's death;

2. After the employee reaches age 59½;
3. Because of the employee's separation from service (does not apply to self-employed persons); or
4. After a self-employed individual becomes totally and permanently disabled.

As with an annuity, you may recover tax-free your cost basis in the lump-sum distribution. In general, your cost basis is:

1. Your total nondeductible contributions to the plan;
2. The total of your taxable one-year term costs of life insurance;
3. Any employer contributions that were taxable to you; and
4. Repayments of loans that were taxable to you.

You must reduce your basis by amounts previously distributed to you tax-free.

If a lump-sum distribution is received from your 401(k) account, two types of special tax treatment may be available. These two types are discussed below.

Long-Term Capital Gain Treatment. If you were at least age 50 on January 1, 1986, you may choose to treat a portion of the taxable part of a lump-sum distribution as a long-term capital gain taxable at a 20% rate. This treatment applies to the portion you receive relating to your participation in the plan before 1974.

Special Averaging Method. You may elect to use a 5-year special averaging method to calculate the tax on the ordinary income portion of a lump-sum distribution, including the capital gain portion for which you did not elect capital gain treatment. To use special averaging, you must: be at least 59½ (unless you were at least age 50 on January 1, 1986), elect to use special averaging for all lump-sum distributions received during the year, and have been a participant in the plan for five or more years prior to the distribution. You can make this election only once in a lifetime.

If you were at least age 50 on January 1, 1986, the age 59½ requirement does not apply and you may elect to use 10-year averaging rather than 5-year averaging. However, the tax rates used in the 10-year averaging calculation are the rates in effect for 1986.

To get an idea of how special averaging works, assume that your income was received equally by 5 different persons (10 for 10-year averaging) in the current year and that each of these people had no other income. As a result, most of the income is taxed at the lowest rates on the single taxpayer tax rate schedule. The tax for these fictional individuals is then added up and becomes your tax on the distribution.

TAXSAVER

The 5-year or 10-year averaging method may be so beneficial to you that you elect to have the long-term capital gain portion of the lump-sum distribution included in the 5-year or 10-year averaging computation rather than have it taxed as long-term capital gain. The tax should be figured both ways to see which is the lowest. If you are eligible to elect either 5-year or 10-year averaging, you should also figure your tax both ways to determine which is most beneficial.

Lump-sum distributions from an IRA do not qualify for either long-term capital gain treatment or the special averaging method.

Penalty Tax for Early Distributions. Most distributions from qualified retirement plans made to employees before they reach age 59½ are subject to an additional tax of 10% on the taxable part of the distribution. For this purpose, a qualified retirement plan means: (1) a qualified employee retirement plan (including a 401(k) plan); (2) a qualified annuity plan; (3) a tax-sheltered annuity plan for employees of public schools or tax-exempt organizations; or (4) an IRA.

This additional tax does not apply, under the following circumstances, to distributions that are:

1. Made to a beneficiary or to the estate of the participant on or after his or her death;
2. Made because the participant is totally and permanently disabled;
3. Made as part of a series of substantially equal periodic (at least annual) payments over the participant's life expectancy or the joint life expectancies of the participant and his or her beneficiary. (This exception does not apply to non-IRA distributions unless the distribution begins after you've left your job);
4. Made to an employee who left his or her job in or after the year in which he or she reached age 55;
5. Paid to the employee, to the extent the employee has deductible expenses for medical care (whether or not the employee itemizes deductions for the tax year);
6. Paid to another person designated in a qualified domestic relations order; and
7. Made to an employee who, as of March 1, 1986, left his or her job and began receiving benefits from the qualified plan under a written election designating a specific schedule of benefit payments.

Exceptions 4, 5, and 6 above do not apply to IRAs.

Penalty Tax for Excess Distributions. There are currently two ways to determine the rate at which excess distributions are taxed.

1. *The general rule:* Under the Tax Reform Act of 1986, annual non-lump-sum distributions from qualified plans (including pension annuities and IRA withdrawals) are subject to a 15% excise tax to the extent that the distributions in total exceed $150,000 in any year. The taxable portion of a qualified lump-sum distribution that exceeds $750,000 will also be subject to this tax. The tax also is applied to excess amounts remaining in a qualified plan or an IRA at death, including the value of payments to any beneficiary after your death.

2. *The grandfather rule:* Anyone whose total accrued taxable benefits and balances in all qualified plans and IRAs were at least $562,500 as of August 1, 1986, could have elected to grandfather (that is shelter from the excise tax) the total amounts accrued in the plans as of that date. Individuals who did not elect the grandfather rule are governed by the general rule as described above. The grandfather election must have been made on Form 5329 no later than when you filed your 1988 federal income tax return.

Basically, the amount that is covered under the grandfather rule is not subject to the 15% excise tax. If you took advantage of the grandfather rule, the grandfathered amount recovered each year depends on which recovery method you elected: the discretionary method or the attained age method. The grandfathered amount is recovered at a different rate each year under each recovery method.

Under the discretionary method, 10% of the annual distributions you receive are considered to be a recovery of the grandfathered amounts. You may also irrevocably elect to accelerate this percentage to 100% in the future. With this acceleration there will be no 15% excise tax until the grandfathered amount is completely recovered.

Alternatively, under the attained age method, a percentage of your annual distributions is considered the recovery of grandfathered amounts. This method results in a decreasing percentage of annual distributions being treated as the recovery of the grandfathered amounts as you grow older. However, you may not use this method if your 35th birthday is after August 1, 1986.

Under the grandfather rule, annual non-lump-sum distributions are subject to the 15% excise tax to the extent that the distributions in total exceed the greater of the remaining, unrecovered grandfathered amount or $140,276 (as adjusted for annual inflation). For lump-sum distributions, the limit is the greater of the remaining, unrecovered grandfathered amount or $701,380 (as adjusted for annual inflation).

Penalty Tax for Late Distributions.
Distributions from qualified pension, profit-sharing (including 401(k)),

stock bonus, IRA, and tax-sheltered annuity plans generally must begin by April 1 of the year following the calendar year in which the employee reaches age 70½, without regard to the employee's retirement.

As a minimum distribution, the individual must either; (1) receive his or her entire interest in the plan by the required beginning date, or (2) begin to receive regular partial distributions by the beginning date in an amount large enough to use up the entire interest over the employee's life expectancy or over the joint life expectancies of the employee and a designated surviving beneficiary. The payout can also be over a period that is less than the employee's life expectancy.

If the required minimum distribution is not made, an excise tax, equal to 50% of the amount required to be (but not actually) distributed, is imposed. This excise tax may be waived if you establish that the shortfall in distributions was due to reasonable error and that reasonable steps are being taken to remedy the shortfall.

Nontaxable Distributions. Some distributions from an IRA or 401(k) plan are not taxed. These include: (1) rollovers (discussed below), (2) withdrawals of IRA contributions by the due date (including extensions) of the return for the year the contributions are made, and (3) withdrawals of excess IRA contributions.

Rollovers. A rollover is a tax-free transfer of cash or other assets from a qualified retirement plan to an eligible retirement plan. An eligible retirement plan is an IRA, a qualified employee retirement plan, or a qualified annuity plan. A rollover may also include a distribution from one IRA and a contribution to another.

The rollover must be completed not later than the 60th day following the day on which you receive the distribution. Generally, only one rollover is allowed per year for rollovers between IRAs. If you transfer funds directly between trustees of your IRAs and you never actually control or use the account assets, however, this is not considered a rollover and you may transfer your account as often as you like.

TaxSaver

Mandatory Withholding on Rollovers. *A mandatory withholding of 20% is imposed on distributions eligible for rollover unless the plan making the distribution directly transfers the payout to the IRA or other qualified plan that is designated to receive the rollover. Traditionally, distributions have been paid directly to retiring or terminating employees who in turn decided how much of the proceeds should be kept or rolled over.*

This new rule, however, sets a trap if the distribution check is made out to you. On a $100,000 distribution, for example, you would receive only $80,000 after withholding. If you plan to roll over the entire $100,000 to your IRA, you would have to come up with an additional $20,000 in order for the total amount deposited in the IRA within 60 days of receiving the $80,000 check to equal the original $100,000 distribution. Otherwise, the $20,000 withheld would be treated as a taxable distribution subject to ordinary income tax, and, if applicable, the 10% early distribution tax (discussed above). Note that the $20,000 withheld is refundable, but only after you file your Form 1040 after the close of the year. However, a check merely delivered to you will not present a problem, so long as it is not negotiable by you. For example, a check made payable to ''ABC Bank as trustee of the IRA of John Q. Smith'' is okay.

TAXSAVER

Because of the mandatory withholding rules, if you are going to receive a payment from a qualified plan that is to be rolled over to an IRA, make sure that the plan transfers the funds directly to the IRA through a trustee-to-trustee payment.

You can roll over the otherwise taxable portion of a distribution of any part of your account balance into a qualified retirement or annuity plan. A distribution that is required for an individual who is over age 70½ or that is part of a series of substantially equal periodic payments for life or a term of 10 or more years is ineligible for tax-free rollover.

TAXSAVER

If you need money for no longer than 60 days, consider withdrawing the money from your IRA if you are sure you will have the cash to put into another IRA within 60 days. You will not incur any tax or penalties, and you will have the cash for 60 days. You can do this only once in a 12-month period.

Simplified Employee Pensions

A simplified employee pension (SEP) is a written plan that allows an employer to make contributions toward an employee's retirement without becoming involved in more complex retirement plans. If you are self-employed, you can contribute to your own SEP.

The SEP rules permit an employer to contribute and deduct each year to each participating employee's SEP up to 15% of the employee's compensation or $30,000, whichever is less. If you are self-employed, special rules apply when figuring the maximum deduction for these contributions. In determining the percentage limit on contributions, compensation is net earnings from self-employment, taking into account the contributions to the SEP.

TaxSaver

Even if your employer makes contributions to a SEP for your account, you can make contributions to your own IRA. The IRA deduction rules, previously discussed, apply to any amounts you contribute to your IRA.

TaxSaver

A self-employed person can claim a deduction to a SEP as long as the plan is set up and the contribution made by the due date of the return, including extensions. Even if you failed to set up a Keogh plan by December 31, you can still establish a SEP after the end of the year and make a timely payment.

Keogh (HR 10) Plans

If you are self-employed and own your own business, you may set up a retirement plan, commonly known as a Keogh or an HR 10 plan. You must have earned income from the trade or business for which the plan was established to take a deduction for a contribution to the plan. A Keogh plan may be either a "defined contribution plan" or a "defined benefit plan."

Under a defined contribution plan, such as a profit-sharing plan or a money purchase pension plan, the benefit you eventually receive is based solely on the contributions credited to your account and the earning attributable to those contributions. Typically, contributions to a profit-sharing plan are made out of a company's profits, and therefore can vary from year to year. Contributions to a money purchase pension plan are usually calculated as a percentage of self-employed income and must be made whether the company had a profit or loss for the year.

Under a defined benefit plan, you are promised a fixed benefit and the annual contributions are based on the amount that is actuarially needed to provide you that benefit at a normal retirement age.

Deductible contributions to a profit-sharing plan are generally limited to the lesser of $30,000 or 13.043% of earned income for the year; deductible contributions to a money purchase pension plan are generally limited to the lesser of $30,000 or 20% of earned income for the year. If you maintain a combination of a profit-sharing Keogh plan and a money purchase Keogh plan, the maximum combined deductible contributions are limited to $30,000 or 25% of earned income per year.

The current maximum benefit that can be promised at retirement age under a defined benefit plan is generally the lesser of 100% of earned income (determined on a three-year average basis) or $118,000. This dollar limit is adjusted annually for cost-of-living increases. The $30,000 defined contribution plan limit will also be adjusted for cost-of-living increases once the defined benefit dollar limit reaches $120,000.

Note that, for purposes of these limitations, "earned income" must be reduced by an amount equal to one-half of your self-employment taxes for the year.

Here are a few more rules:

1. A Keogh plan must be established before the end of your tax year.
2. The plan must be written. Prototype plans can frequently be obtained from banks and other financial institutions.
3. A summary description of the plan must be provided to your employees. There are specific definitions of employees who must be covered. Also, there are specific rules on such items as discrimination and vesting.

Company Retirement Plans

For a discussion of how company retirement plan benefits are taxed, see Chapter 10, Retirement Planning.

5

Charitable Contributions

Introduction

Those who do good, should do well. So it is with the tax treatment of charitable contributions. You are entitled to a tax deduction for charitable contributions you make. How you make your contributions and even the type of property used—cash, stock, or whatever—can affect whether you get the maximum tax benefit from your contribution. This chapter discusses some of the tax strategies you can use so that the contributions you make can have the most impact on both the charities you're benefitting and the taxes you're paying.

A charitable contribution is a contribution or gift to, or for the use of, a qualified organization. Although contributions to tax-exempt organizations are generally made for charitable reasons, the potential tax benefits of the contributions should not be ignored. In many cases, the tax benefit can lower the cost of making a gift, perhaps enabling you to give an even more generous gift.

Making the most of your contributions will depend on:

- Who is the recipient—a public charity or a private foundation?
- When will you make the gift—now or later?
- What will you give—cash or property?
- How will you make the gift—outright or deferred?

Qualified Organizations

Only gifts to organizations recognized by the IRS as charities are deductible. You cannot assume that an organization to which you want to contribute is officially recognized as a charitable organization and that your contribution will be deductible for federal income tax purposes. Many tax-exempt organizations are not qualified to receive tax-deductible status. IRS Publication No. 78, which is periodically supplemented, contains a list of qualified organizations.

You may deduct a contribution you make to, or for the use of, the following organizations:

■ A state, a U.S. possession (including Puerto Rico), a political subdivision of a state or possession, the United States, or the District of Columbia, if the contribution is made only for public purposes

■ A community chest, corporation, trust fund, or foundation organized and operated only for charitable, religious, educational, scientific, or literary purposes, or for the prevention of cruelty to children or animals

■ War veterans' organizations, including posts, auxiliaries, trusts, or foundations organized in the United States or its possessions

■ Domestic fraternal societies operating under the lodge system, if the contribution is to be used only for charitable, religious, scientific, literary, or educational purposes, or for the prevention of cruelty to children or animals

■ Nonprofit cemetery companies, if the contribution can be used only for the perpetual care of the cemetery as a whole, and not for a particular lot or mausoleum crypt

Examples of Qualified Organizations. Qualified organizations include the following:

■ Nonprofit volunteer fire companies
■ Public parks and recreation facilities
■ Nonprofit hospitals and medical research organizations
■ Churches and other religious organizations
■ Most nonprofit educational organizations
■ Most nonprofit charitable organizations, such as the Boy Scouts, CARE, Gifts in Kind, Girls and Boys Clubs of America, Girl Scouts, Goodwill Industries, Red Cross, Salvation Army, United Way, and Volunteers of America.

Deductible Contributions. Only individuals who itemize deductions may deduct charitable contributions. Even then, deductions for charitable contributions are subject to the overall limit on itemized deductions for taxpayers with adjusted gross income in excess of $111,800. See discussion on page 68.

Your total deduction for charitable contributions is limited to 50% of your contribution base, an amount generally equal to your adjusted gross income, but in some cases you may be limited to 20% or 30% of your contribution base. See "Limits on Deductions" later in this chapter, especially the section on "When contributions are more than 20% of your income."

Benefits Received. If you contribute to a charitable organization and also receive a benefit from it, you may deduct only the amount that is more than the value of the benefit you receive. If you pay more than fair market value to a qualified organization for merchandise, goods, or services, the amount you pay that is more than the value of the item may be a charitable contribution.

Example: If you contribute $100 to a symphony orchestra and receive a pair of tickets worth $25, your deduction is limited to $75. Generally, the charity will advise you of the value of the benefit and how much you can deduct.

Dues, fees, or assessments are deductible if you pay them to qualified organizations. However, you may deduct only the amount that is more than the value of the benefits you receive. You may not deduct dues, fees, or assessments paid to country clubs and other social organizations.

Athletic Tickets. If you make a payment to or for the benefit of a college or university that would be deductible as a charitable contribution but for the fact that you receive (directly or indirectly) the right to purchase seating at an athletic event in the institution's athletic stadium, only 80% of such payment is treated as a charitable contribution. The 80% deduction rule does not apply if you receive tickets or seating (rather than merely the right to purchase tickets) in return for the payment. In that case, the deduction must be reduced by the value attributable to the tickets.

Out-of-Pocket Expenses. You may deduct certain amounts you pay in the course of providing volunteer services to a charitable organization. You may not, however, deduct the value of your time or services.

Car Expenses. You may deduct unreimbursed out-of-pocket expenses, such as the cost of gas and oil, that are directly related to the use of your car in giving services to a charitable organization. You may not deduct any part of general repair and maintenance expenses, depreciation, or insurance.

If you do not want to deduct your actual expense, you may use a standard rate of 12 cents a mile to figure your contribution deduction of the use of your car in providing services to the charitable organization.

Travel Expenses. You may deduct your transportation and other travel expenses while you are away from home performing services for a charitable organization. Deductible travel expenses include: air, rail, and bus transportation; out-of-pocket expenses for your car; taxi fares and other costs of transportation between the airport or station and your hotel; lodging cost; and the cost of meals. Travel expenses are only deductible if there is no significant element of personal pleasure, recreation, or vacation in the travel.

When Deductible. To deduct your contributions, you must make them in cash or other property before the close of your tax year. If you make a contribution with borrowed funds, a deduction is allowed in the year you make the contribution, regardless of when you repay the loan.

TAXSAVER

Contributions charged on your credit or charge card are deductible in the year you make the charge, not when you pay the bill.

Gifts of properly endorsed stock certificates are deductible in the year you mail or personally deliver the certificates to the charity or to the charity's representative. However, if you give the certificates to your broker or the issuing corporation for transfer to the charity, a deduction is not allowed until the stock is transferred on the corporation's books. If you plan to give stock to a charity, plan far enough in advance to assure yourself of having the certificates. A note or a pledge to a charity is not deductible until it is paid.

TAXSAVER

For most people, the simplest approach to gift-giving is to give an outright gift. Even then, proper planning can pay surprising dividends for you.

Consider your tax rates in planning charitable contributions. A $1,000 contribution reduces taxes by $150 for a taxpayer in the 15% bracket, $280 for a taxpayer in the 28% bracket, $310 for a taxpayer in the 31% tax bracket and so forth. The after-tax cost of a contribution decreases as tax rates increase. Thus, if you can control the timing of your charitable contributions, you should consider making larger contributions in years in which you are subject to high marginal tax rates.

Consider also when your contribution is made. A deductible contribution reduces the tax due April 15 of the year following the contribution. A contribution made on December 31 reduces the tax due by as much as the contribution made on the prior January 1, except you have the use of the money from January 2 to December 30. While it is not always practical to defer your giving until the last day of the year, when planning substantial gifts the time value of money should be considered.

Private Foundations

A private foundation is an entity which can be formed and controlled by you or your family to support your charitable activities or to make charitable grants according to your wishes. Once the foundation qualifies for tax-exempt status, your charitable contributions to it are deductible, subject to the limitations discussed later.

TaxSaver

You don't have to be inordinately rich to consider setting up your own private foundation. Private foundations afford you a good deal of flexibility in determining how your charitable contributions will be spent, may be controlled by a single individual or family, and provide some tax benefits, too. The foundation has to be set up according to specific IRS rules and you will need professional advice.

Example: Suppose you want to commit to making a contribution of $20,000 a year to a charity for the next five years. Assuming you are in the 39.6% tax bracket and can realize an 8% rate of return on your investments, (1) you could contribute about $80,000 to your private foundation, which would make the payments in each of the five years, or (2) you could make these contributions out of current income. Choosing the latter would cost you more. Your savings can be even greater if you fund the foundation with appreciated stock, because you will not have to pay any tax on the unrealized capital gain if your contribution is made by December 31, 1994.

TaxAlert

This favorable rule for donating long-term capital gain property to a private nonoperating foundation is scheduled to expire on December 31, 1994, based on current law.

TaxSaver

The tax benefits from creating a private foundation can also be achieved by contributing to a community trust. A community trust is a public charity in which you may establish a segregated account, thus avoiding the costs of setting up your own private foundation. However, because it is a public foundation, you will not have the same degree of control over the use of the contributed funds as you would with your own private foundation.

Nondeductible Contributions

Some organizations are not qualified to receive tax-deductible contributions. For example, contributions to the following organizations are not deductible:

- Chambers of commerce and other business leagues or organizations
- Civic leagues
- Communist organizations
- Country clubs and other social clubs
- Homeowners associations
- Political organizations (and candidates)

Contributions used to influence legislation are not deductible. Even if an organization is a qualified organization, no deduction is allowed for contributions to the organization that are earmarked for use in, or in connection with, attempting to influence the general public on legislative matters, elections, or referenda.

Direct contributions to needy or worthy individuals are not deductible. The contributions must be made to, or for the use of, a qualified organization and not earmarked by you for the use of a specific person.

Gifts of Property

If you donate property to a qualified organization, you generally may deduct the fair market value of the property at the time of the contribution. However, if the property increased in value while you owned it, you may have to make some adjustments. See Giving Property That Has Increased in Value, below.

Determining Fair Market Value. Fair market value is the price at which property would change hands between a willing buyer and willing seller, neither having to buy or sell, and both having reasonable knowledge of all the necessary facts.

Used Items. The fair market value of used items is ordinarily far less than their original cost. You should claim as the value the price that buyers of used items actually pay in stores where such property is for sale, such as consignment or thrift shops. (See IRS Publication 561, *Determining the Value of Donated Property.*)

Giving Property That Has Increased in Value.
If you donate property with a fair market value that is more than your basis in it, you will have to reduce the fair market value by the amount of appreciation (increase in value) when you figure your deduction, unless the property would produce a long-term capital gain if it were sold on the date of the contribution.

Ordinary Income and Short-Term Gain Property. If the donated property would have resulted in ordinary income or a short-term capital gain if it had been sold at its fair market value on the date it was contributed, your deduction is its fair market value minus the amount that would be ordinary income or short-term capital gain. Examples of ordinary income property include inventory and any property held for one year or less. Generally, your deduction is limited to your basis in the property.

Example: You donate stock that you held for five months to your church. The fair market value of the stock is $20,000, but you paid $16,000 (your basis). Because the $4000 of appreciation would be a short-term capital gain if you sold the stock, your deduction is limited to $16,000 (fair market value less the appreciation).

Long-Term Capital Gain Property. You usually may deduct a contribution of such capital gain property at its fair market value. Capital gain property is property that would have resulted in long-term capital gain if it had been sold at its fair market value on the date it was contributed. It also includes certain real property and depreciable property used in your trade or business and held for more than the required long-term holding period.

TAX*SAVER*

Tax preference treatment for purposes of determining the alternative minimum tax was eliminated for charitable contributions made after December 31, 1992, of any type of appreciated property, including, for example, appreciated real property or stock.

The change in the tax law regarding untaxed appreciation associated with a charitable contribution enables taxpayers to recognize a charitable contribution deduction for the full fair market value of appreciated property for both regular tax and AMT purposes. Taxpayers who previously made gifts that were not fully deductible due to the regular tax percentage limitations imposed on charitable contributions will still have preference items in future tax years when these amounts ultimately become deductible. Charitable remainder and charitable lead trusts funded with appreciated property now may be even more attractive as planning ideas.

TAX*SAVER*

If you donate appreciated securities that you have held for more than the required long-term holding period, you benefit in two ways. First, you are entitled to a deduction based on the fair market value of the securities. Second, you avoid paying tax on the appreciation. Consequently, the real cost to you of your contribution is reduced by the tax deduction you claim and the tax you avoided by not selling the appreciated property.

*   **Example:** *You have adjusted gross income of $190,000 and are in the 36% tax bracket. If you give stock that cost you $20,000 but is now worth $50,000 directly to a public charity, your taxable income will be reduced by $50,000 and you will have a tax savings of about $18,000 (provided you are not subject to the alternative minimum tax). If you sell the stock first and give the proceeds to the charity, you will still have a $50,000 deduction, but you will also pay tax on the entire $30,000 of capital gain, probably at the maximum capital gain rate of 28%—$8,400. This will reduce your overall tax savings to $9,600 ($18,000 less $8,400). Thus, the best approach in this example is to give the appreciated stock to charity. You get a $50,000 deduction and recognize no gain.*

*   *On the other hand, if the property value has decreased below your cost, it usually is better to sell the property and donate the proceeds. By selling it you will realize a capital loss that may be used to offset other capital gains or—within limits—other income.*

TaxSaver

To ensure that you get the maximum tax benefit from a contribution of appreciated property, be sure that the property qualifies for long-term capital gain treatment if sold.

Bargain Sales

A bargain sale of property to a qualified charitable organization—that is, a sale at less than the property's fair market value—is partly a charitable contribution and partly a sale. The part that is considered a charitable contribution is the difference between the fair market value at the time of sale and that amount realized. The part that is considered a sale is the amount realized. It may result in a taxable gain. To determine the amount of the gain, you must allocate your adjusted basis in the property between the part that is consdered a charitable contribution and the part sold. The adjusted basis of the part sold is figured as follows:

$$\text{Adjusted basis of entire property} \times \frac{\text{Amount realized}}{\text{Fair market value of entire property}}$$

TaxSaver

Suppose you want to make a $50,000 donation to a public charity but you have no cash. However, you have *stock in a publicly traded corporation that cost you $30,000 a few years ago and is now worth $75,000. You plan to sell the stock on the open market for $75,000 (less, of course, transaction costs) and give $50,000 in cash to charity, but that would mean paying a tax on the $45,000 of long-term capital gain. Capital gains can be taxed at a rate up to 28%. In this situation, a bargain sale may help.*

If you sell the stock to the charity for $25,000, you will provide it with a $50,000 benefit ($75,000 value — $25,000 cost = $50,000) and generate a $50,000 deductible charitable contribution for yourself. Because you have sold an asset, you do recognize some gain. However, under a special tax rule relating to bargain sales to charity (explained above), the gain realized on the $25,000 bargain sale price is $15,000—or $30,000 less than the taxable gain that would have resulted from your selling the stock and donating the cash. If the tax rate on your gain is at the top 28% capital gain rate, the tax attributable to the gain from the bargain sale ($4,200) would be much less than that of the out-right sale ($12,600).

Limits on Deductions

If your total contributions for the year are 20% or less of your adjusted gross income, they are fully deductible (provided they otherwise qualify), and it is not necessary to figure whether the limits discussed below apply.

Partial Interest in Property. Generally, no deduction is allowed for a charitable contribution of less than your entire interest in property. For example, the owner of property will not get a deduction for giving a "life estate interest" in the property to charity. (A life estate interest is an interest in property that terminates upon the death of the life estate's owner.) A contribution of the right to use property is a contribution of less than your entire interest in that property and is not deductible.

Exceptions: There are some situations in which you may claim a deduction for a charitable contribution that is less than your entire interest in the property:

1. *Undivided part of your entire interest.* A contribution of an undivided part of your entire interest in property must consist of a part of each and every substantial interest or right you own in the property. It must extend over the entire term of your interest in the property.
2. *Remainder interest in a personal residence or farm.* You may take a charitable deduction for a gift to a qualified organization of a remainder interest in a personal residence or in a farm, if the gift is irrevocable. A remainder

interest in an asset is an interest that takes effect after a specified period of time—often the lifetime of the person giving the interest.

TaxSaver

If you give a remainder interest in a personal residence (or a farm) to a qualified charity, the present value of the remainder interest is deductible as a charitable contribution. One significant advantage of such a gift is that you suffer no loss of income or increase in expense from the gift, but you still gain a current income tax deduction. The gift may be made without the use of a trust. In addition, you continue to use and enjoy the home for life.

To qualify for the deduction, the gift must be a gift of your personal *residence. The home does not have to be your principal residence. Thus, the gift may be your vacation home.*

The charity receives no immediate benefit; however, the opportunity for future benefits can be substantial.

Example: *Assume a 62-year-old individual owns a personal residence with a fair market value of $162,000. The land on which the residence is located is valued at $42,000. The residence has a remaining useful life of 35 years and an estimated salvage value of $30,000. According to IRS tables, the value of the remainder interest in the home and the land is approximately $40,000—which is currently deductible on a donation of the interest. Besides a substantial income tax deduction, the donor will receive an estate tax deduction for the value of the interest that passes to charity at his or her death.*

3. *Interest transferred in trust.* A charitable deduction is available for the transfer of an income or remainder interest in property if the property is held in a qualifying charitable trust.

TaxSaver

Because the cost of making an outright gift to charity may be too great, some people may hesitate to make such a gift. For example, assume you want to make a contribution to charity but you need all your income for current expenses. You can either leave the property to charity when you die or give the property to charity now, subject to a retained income interest. The latter technique is referred to as deferred giving, *which simply involves a present gift to charity of the future use and employment of property. One big advantage of making the gift during life rather than at death is that you can get an income tax deduction now. In addition, deferred giving allows you to satisfy your charitable goals now and continue to receive needed income. Moreover, you may even be able to enhance your cash flow in retirement years. Following are some deferred giving techniques:*

Charitable Remainder Trusts

You transfer cash or income-producing property into a charitable remainder trust. The trust provides that at least annual payments be made to you or any other designated beneficiary that is not a charity either over a term not exceeding 20 years or over the lifetime of the beneficiary or beneficiaries. When the term or lifetime interest ends, the charity will have full use of the entire property. And, although actual receipt of the charity's interest is deferred, you receive an *immediate* income tax deduction for the present value of the interest that passes to charity. Later, the trust assets will be included in your taxable estate, but you will also receive an estate tax charitable deduction of an equal amount.

The lifetime gift or the charitable bequest must be in the form of a charitable remainder annuity trust, a charitable remainder unitrust, or a pooled income fund. See explanations below.

Charitable Remainder Annuity Trust. A charitable remainder annuity trust must pay the income beneficiary a fixed *dollar amount* of at least 5% of the initial value of the assets placed in the trust.

Charitable Remainder Unitrust. The charitable remainder unitrust, another type of remainder trust, differs from the annuity trust in that it must pay the income beneficiary a fixed *percentage* of the fair market value of the trust's assets, valued annually. Payments from a unitrust can be limited to trust income with any unpaid amounts carried over to future years, when the trust has sufficient income to pay its current and past obligations. Thus, a charitable remainder unitrust may also be used as a retirement planning vehicle.

Example: Suppose a 55-year-old donor who intends to work for 10 more years transfers $100,000 of appreciated stock to the trust in exchange for annual payments for life equal to 7% of the trust's value. The donor would receive an immediate contribution deduction of about $24,000, the present value of the interest passing to charity. The trust could sell the stock tax-free and invest the proceeds to maximize growth. After 10 years of minimal or zero payout, the trust reinvests its assets to maximize yield. Payments to the donor could be made of the entire income of the trust until the trust has made up for the 10 years of missed payments. As an added benefit, the donor could take the $8,640 (36% × $24,000) of tax savings from the deduction and purchase life insurance that would be owned by and payable to his or her children. The insurance proceeds paid to the children would partially replace the stock transferred to the trust and, with appropriate planning, would not be taxed in the parent's estate.

Pooled Income Fund. A pooled income fund is a large trust maintained by a charity to which you may donate the remainder interest in property while retaining a life income interest. The amount of income you receive depends on the fund's rate of return. The tax consequences are similar to those for charitable remainder unitrusts.

Deferred charitable giving allows you to realize the many personal benefits of making charitable gifts currently without impairing your present financial condition. In fact, because you receive a current income tax deduction, your immediate financial position is generally improved.

The Charitable Lead Trust. A charitable lead trust can be viewed somewhat as the mirror image of a charitable remainder trust. In the charitable lead trust, the charity gets the *income* or *lead* interest, and the remainder interest returns to you or passes to beneficiaries of your choice.

If the remainder interest reverts to you, there may be a current charitable income tax deduction equal to the value of the income stream. However, the trust income will be included in your income as the charity receives it, and the remainder will be included in your estate. If the remainder interest passes to beneficiaries other than a charity, there may be no up-front charitable deduction, but usually (1) the income will not be included in you taxable income and (2) the remainder will not be included in your estate.

Future Interest in Tangible Personal Property. You may deduct the value of a charitable contribution of a future interest in tangible personal property only after all intervening interests and rights to the actual possession or enjoyment of the property have either expired or been turned over to someone other than yourself or a related party or organization.

A future interest is any interest that is to begin at some future time, regardless of whether it is designated as a future interest under state law. The amount of the deduction is the value of the future interest when you and a related person no longer have an interest in the tangible personal property. When these interests end, the deduction is allowed to you even if there are other outstanding interests that must end before the future interest is realized by the qualified organization.

Example: You transferred a sculpture in 1994 to your son to use and enjoy for life. When your son dies the sculpture will go to the local museum of art. If your son irrevocably transfers his life interest to a local college or any other unrelated person in a later year, you may take a charitable deduction in that year, but not sooner. The amount of your deduction is the value of the future interest in the sculpture at the time of the transfer to the unrelated person.

When Contributions Are More Than 20% of Your Income.

If your contributions are more than 20% of your adjusted gross income, the amount of your deduction may be limited to 20%, 30%, or 50% of your adjusted gross income.

How much you can deduct depends on three main factors: the type of the charity to which the contribution is given—a public charity or a nonoperating private foundation; the nature of the contribution—cash or property; and the manner of the contribution—to the charity or for the use of the charity. Sometimes the use to which the property will be put also needs to be considered. In addition to the percentage limitation, ordering rules apply. These may limit deductions if multiple contributions are made during the year. You should consult with your tax advisor.

Percentage Limitations

Contribution to a Public Charity

Cash	50%
Property	
Ordinary Income Property	50%
Short-Term Capital Gain Property	50%
Tangible Personal Property (unrelated to exempt purpose or function of donee)	50%
Tangible Personal Property (related to exempt purpose or function of donee)	30%
Appreciated Long-Term Capital Gain Property (taxpayer elects to forgo deducting amount attributable to gain)	50%
Appreciated Long-Term Capital Gain Property (taxpayer elects to claim fair market value deduction)	30%

*Contributions to a
Nonoperating Private Foundation*

Cash	30%
Property	
Ordinary Income Property	30%
Capital Gain Property	20%

*Contribution "for the Use of" a Public Charity
or a Nonoperating Private Foundation*

Contributions, whether in cash or property, for the use of a charity are contributions of an income interest or contributions in trust.	30%

Carryovers

You may carry over your contributions that cannot be deducted in the current year because they exceeded your adjusted gross income limit. You may deduct the excess in each of the next five years until it is used up, but not beyond that time. Contributions limited in the original contribution year will be similarly limited in the carryover years. Excess contributions cannot be carried back and deducted in previous tax years.

TAXSAVER

If a gift of long-term capital gain property subject to the 30% limitation is made and, for some unforeseen reason, cannot be used entirely in the current year or in carryover years, you may elect to reduce its value by 100% of the gain and deduct the lower basis on the gift under the 50% limitation.

Example: *John Walsh makes a contribution of long-term capital gain property that cost him $40,000 and now has a fair market value of $50,000. John dies during the taxable year. His adjusted gross income on his final return is $80,000.*

Without the election (mentioned above), John's deduction would be limited to $24,000 (30% × $80,000). However, if the value of the property is reduced by $10,000, the appreciation in the value of the property, the deduction is subject to the 50% limit (50% × $80,000) and is increased to $40,000, his basis in the property.

TAXSAVER

If you anticipate a decline in your future adjusted gross income and you are subject to the 30% limitation for long-term capital gain property, you may want to con-

sider electing to deduct the property's basis rather than its fair market value.

Record-Keeping and How to Report

You are required to keep records to prove the amount of the cash and noncash contributions you make during the year. The kind of records you must keep depends on the amount of your contributions and whether they are cash or noncash contributions.

Cash Contributions

If you make a cash charitable contribution, you must keep one of the following for each contribution:

1. A canceled check, evidencing the charitable contribution
2. A receipt (or a letter or other written communication) from the charitable organization showing the name of the organization, the date of the contribution, and the amount of the contribution, or
3. Other reliable written records that include the information described in (2). Records may be considered reliable if they are of a contemporaneous nature, if you regularly keep records, or if, in the case of small donations, you have items such as buttons, tokens, or emblems that have been given to contributors.

Substantiation Rules

The records you must keep and the forms you must file depend on whether your contribution is $250 or more in cash or your contribution is made in property other than money and is (1) $500 or less, (2) over $500 but not more than $5,000, or (3) over $5,000.

Starting in 1994, you must obtain a contemporaneous written acknowledgment from any charitable organization to which a contribution of $250 or more is made in order to deduct that contribution. *Contemporaneous* for this purpose means that the written acknowledgment must be obtained by you on or before the earlier of the date on which the return is actually filed for the year in which the contribution was made or the due date for the return, including extensions. A canceled check does not constitute adequate substantiation for a contribution of money. The written acknowledgment must state the amount of cash and a description (but not value) of any property other than cash contributed. It must also state whether the charitable organization provided any goods or services in consideration, in whole or in part, for the contribution and, if so, a description and good faith estimate of the value of goods or services provided. If the goods or services provided as consideration for the contribution consist solely of *intangible religious benefits,* a statement to that effect must be included in the written acknowledgment.

You are not required to obtain substantiation for a donation if the charitable organization files a return with the IRS which includes the same information otherwise required from the taxpayer. Note, however, that primary responsibility lies with you, not the charitable organization, to request and maintain in your records the required substantiation.

Furthermore, for any *quid pro quo* contribution over $75 (that is, any contribution for which the charity provides goods or services such as a charity dinner), the charity must provide a statement to the donor that reports the estimated value of the goods or services received by the donor in exchange for the contribution. As under prior law, a payment to a charity is deductible only to the extent that it exceeds the value of any goods or services received in return.

Deductions of $500 or Less. If you make a noncash contribution, you must get and keep a receipt from the charitable organization showing (1) the name of the organization, (2) the date and location of the contribution, and (3) a reasonably detailed description of the property.

Deductions Over $500 but Not More Than $5,000. Form 8283 must be attached to your return if noncash charitable contributions exceed $500. This form must contain the following information: name and address of the organization receiving the gift; description of the property contributed; date of the contribution; date the property was acquired; how you acquired the property (e.g., gift, purchase); and fair market value of the property and the method used to determine such value.

Deductions Over $5,000. Individuals are required to obtain independent qualified appraisals for donations of noncash property if the claimed value of the property exceeds $5,000 or if the claimed value of all similar items donated to one or more charitable organizations exceeds $5,000. Nonpublicly traded securities must be appraised if they are valued at over $10,000. Publicly traded securities are not subject to this requirement.

6

Capital Gains and Losses

Introduction

If you are looking for a tax break, generating capital gains could be one of your biggest opportunities. Since the 1993 Tax Act, the tax benefit of long-term capital gains has again become substantial. Under the new law, the top tax rate applicable to long-term capital gains is 28% while the rate applicable to ordinary income can go up to 39.6%. That's an 11.6% difference. If you can generate net capital gains, instead of ordinary income, you will save considerably on your taxes. Also with capital assets you usually have the flexibility to control when you recognize the income or loss, because in most cases you determine when to sell your assets.

How Capital Gains Are Taxed

Generally, capital gains are taxable, whether the underlying asset is held as an investment or for personal purposes. On the other hand, capital losses are only deductible if the assets were held for investment purposes. Consequently, if you sell your personal residence for a gain, the gain will be considered a capital gain. However, if you sell your residence at a loss, you will not be able to deduct the amount of the loss.

If you incur losses from the sale of capital assets, you can deduct those losses to the extent they equal your capital gains. But if your losses exceed your capital gains, you can only deduct up to $3,000 of those losses in a given tax year against ordinary income. Any excess will be carried over until it can be offset against future capital gains or be deducted as a loss against your ordinary income up to $3,000 a year. (See Deducting Capital Losses on page 118 for more details.)

Generally it is preferable to defer gains and accelerate losses for the simple reason that the later the taxes are paid, the longer time you have the use of the money. In addition, when you recognize a gain or loss it can also affect the tax benefits of your itemized deductions and exemptions. That's because capital gains and losses are included in figuring your adjusted gross income. That means your capital gains and losses affect the calculation of the phase-out of your itemized deductions and personal exemptions. Also miscellaneous itemized deductions are only deductible to the extent that they exceed 2% of your adjusted gross income. Medical expenses are only deductible to the extent that they exceed 7.5% of your adjusted gross income. Capital gains income has an impact on both these calculations, too. Depending on your itemized deductions, when you recognize a capital gain or loss can have a significant impact on your taxes.

Defining a Capital Asset

For the most part, everything you own and hold for personal or investment purposes is a capital asset. Examples of capital assets include stocks and bonds, your house or other residence, household furnishings, automobiles and boats, jewelry, and gold, silver, or other metals. Capital assets do not include inventory; notes and accounts receivable acquired in the ordinary course of a business for services rendered or from the sale of inventory; or, in certain cases, copyrights or literary, musical, or other artistic compositions. Letters and memorandums prepared by or for you also are not classified as capital assets. Gains on sales of certain assets used in a trade or business are taxed at capital gains rates, however, you may have to pay ordinary income tax rates on a portion of a gain resulting from the sale of such property.

Capital Gains Tax Rates

The top tax rate on net capital gains is 28%. The 39.6% tax rate for individuals does not apply to net capital gains—that is, the net long-term capital gain for the year over the net short-term capital loss for the year. A long-term capital gain or loss results from the sale of an asset help over one year. Sales or assets held one year or less produce a short-term capital gain or loss.

·TaxSaver

If you are a high-income individual, the widened tax rate differential between capital gains (28%) and the top rate on ordinary income (39.6%) may encourage you to favor investments geared toward appreciation that will be taxed at the lower capital gains rate when the investments are sold instead of investments that generate current interest and dividends, which would be taxed at ordinary income rates as high as 39.6%.

Some members of Congress continue to urge the reduction of the capital gains rate to less than 28%. Here are a few rules to follow while Congress ponders the matter:

- *Buy or sell a capital asset for reasons based on market factors, not solely for tax reasons.*
- *Take state and local taxes into consideration when trading capital assets, not just federal taxes.*
- *You can take a deduction for a net capital loss but only up to the $3,000 per year limit. The excess can be carried forward as long as necessary.*

Figuring a Gain or Loss

You figure the gain or loss on a sale or trade of property by comparing the amount you realize with the adjusted basis of the property. The adjusted basis of a property is your original cost or other basis such as "carryover basis" if the property was acquired by gift, or a "stepped up" basis, if the property was acquired by inheritance—properly increased or decreased for items such as purchase commissions, legal fees, capital improvements, and depreciation. "Carryover basis" is the basis of the donor whereas "stepped-up basis" generally is the fair market value of the property on the date the person from whom the property was inherited died. The amount you realize from a sale or trade is the total of all money you receive, plus the fair market value of all property or services you receive. An indebtedness against the property, or against you, that is paid off as a part of the transaction or that is assumed by the buyer must be included in the amount realized.

Deducting Capital Losses

Capital losses are deductible to the extent that they do not exceed certain limitations. If your capital losses are more than your capital gains, up to $3,000 ($1,500 if you are married and file a separate return) of losses may be deducted provided your taxable income is at least equivalent to the amount of the deduction.

Example: You have capital gains and losses for the year as follows:

	Short-Term	Long-Term
Gains	$700	$ 400
Losses	800	2,000

Your deductible capital loss is $1,700, calculated as follows:

Short-term capital losses	$800	
Minus: Short-term capital gains	700	
Net short-term capital loss		$100
Long-term capital losses	$2,000	
Minus: Long-term capital gains	400	
Net long-term capital loss		$1,600
Deductible capital loss		$1,700

Your deduction in this example (assuming you are not married, filing a separate return) is limited to this $1,700 or your taxable income, whichever is smaller.

If your capital loss is more than the yearly limit, you may carry over the unused part to the next tax year and treat it as if it occurred in that year. A net loss may be carried forward until it is exhausted or until you die. This carry-forward may be used to reduce your tax when you have a capital gain in the future. If you do not have future capital gains, you may nonetheless use the carryforward loss to offset taxable income up to $3,000 per year.

TaxSaver

You may save taxes by carefully planning major sales and exchanges. It may be better to wait until after the end of the year before finalizing a sale so that a gain may be deferred until the next year or so that more losses may be realized in the current year. Remember, too, capital gains increase your AGI. If your AGI is above $111,800, a portion of your itemized deductions is lost. Furthermore, if your AGI is above $167,700 (on a joint return), your personal exemptions are decreased.

TaxSaver

Qualified Small Business Stock. *An individual taxpayer who holds* qualified small business stock *(QSBS) for more than five years can exclude from gross income 50% of any gain realized from the sale or exchange of the stock. This exclusion is limited to the greater of:*
1. *10 times the taxpayer's basis in the stock; or*
2. *$10 million in gain from all of the taxpayer's transactions in stock of that corporation (held for more than five years).*

The new rules apply only to stock issued after August 10, 1993.

The rules for determining whether stock is "qualified small business stock" can be summarized as follows:
■ *The stock must be newly issued stock.*

- *The stock cannot be acquired in exchange for other stock.*
- *The issuing corporation must be a "C" corporation (i.e., not an "S" corporation that passes its income and losses directly on to the shareholders), but may not be a cooperative, Domestic International Sales Corporation (DISC), former DISC, Real Estate Investment Trust (REIT), Regulated Investment Company (RIC), Real Estate Mortgage Investment Conduit (REMIC), a corporation having a possessions tax credit election in effect and may not own a subsidiary who has a possessions tax credit election in effect.*
- *At least 80% of the corporation's assets must be used in the active conduct of a qualified trade or business, or in the start-up of a future qualified trade or business.*
- *A qualified or business is any business other than one involving the performance of services in the fields of health, law, engineering, architecture, accounting, actuarial science, performing arts, consulting, athletics, financial services, brokerage services, or any other trade or business where the principal asset of the business is the reputation or skill of one or more employees. A qualified trade or business also cannot involve the businesses of banking, insurance, financing, leasing, investing, or similar businesses, farming, or certain businesses involving natural resource extraction or production, and businesses operating a hotel, motel, restaurant, or similar business.*
- *The corporation may not have greater than $50 million in gross assets (i.e., sum of cash plus the aggregate fair market value of other corporate property) at the time the qualified small business stock is issued. If the corporation meets this test at the time of issuance of the stock, a subsequent event that violates this rule will not disqualify stock that previously qualified.*

Note: A new tax benefit allows the tax on the gain from the sale of publicly traded securities to be deferred if the proceeds from the sale are used to acquire common stock in a specialized small business investment company (SSBIC) within a 60-day period.

Strategies for Individuals Selling Securities

Specify Shares to be Sold

If your broker holds your securities that you purchased at different prices and dates, you must tell him or her which shares you are going to sell. If you don't, the shares you purchased first generally will be considered the shares sold. This rule can result in a different gain or loss than you intended. See Chapter 9, Investment Planning, for further discussion.

TaxSaver

Selling Shares in Mutual Funds. This can be tricky because shares are often bought at different times, or bought with reinvested dividends, or both. Remember to keep good records and to add to your basis all regular and capital gains distributions that are reinvested in the fund for more shares. You want to avoid paying tax again on the reinvested dividends.

Also remember that an exchange of shares from one fund to another even within a family of funds is a taxable exchange (i.e., it is treated as a sale of the first fund and a purchase of the second fund).

Put Options

Acquiring a put option means buying an option contract to sell 100 shares of stock at a set price (the "strike price") during a specific time period. Put options can be used as a means of protecting and deferring your capital gain. While deferring a sale to a subsequent year, put options protect against a fall in value. Investors who own appreciated securities that they are not yet ready to sell because of tax reasons can buy put options as a way of protecting their gains against possible price declines. If the price of the stock goes above the strike price, you get the benefit of the increased price less the cost of the put, which you let expire. If the stock price declines, you may either sell your shares at the strike price or sell the put option separately. Either way, the sale and your capital gain have been deferred to next year. However, the premium you pay for the option contract must be factored into your consideration for using this planning technique.

Selling Short Against the Box

Selling short is not a hedge but rather a bet that the security price will drop. Selling short against the box means selling borrowed securities while owning substantially identical securities that you later deliver to close the short sale. That allows you to lock in a profit while delaying the recognition of a gain. Many investors with unrealized profits may want to consider a short sale against the box to postpone recognizing a gain until a later tax year.

Other Strategies

If you have excess gains over losses, you should sell the property on which you have losses to offset your gains and eliminate the tax on them.

If you have already realized more than $3,000 of capital losses over and above your realized capital gains, and you want to sell an appreciated asset that you think has gone up as far as it will go, sell that asset and use your accumulated losses to offset the gain.

Wash Sales

Suppose your objective is to take a tax loss this year while preserving your investment position. It can be done as long as you don't run afoul of the wash sale rule. A wash sale occurs when you sell stock or securities and within 30 days before or after the sale you buy, acquire in a taxable exchange, or acquire a contract or option to buy substantially the same stock or security. To the extent that the same number of stocks or securities sold are replaced in a wash sale, the loss will not be recognized for tax purposes.

The easiest way to maintain your investment position in a security, recognize a loss, and avoid the wash sale rule is to buy identical securities 31 days before you sell your old securities at a loss. Another possibility is to reinvest in a similar security that would not be considered "substantially identical" and therefore would not violate the wash rule. For example, if you sold your investment in a mutual fund that invests in bonds, you could reinvest in another fund that owned bonds of a similar grade and yield.

Installment Sales

You can defer recognition of a gain from the current year by structuring the sale of the investments on an installment basis. In an installment sale, only part of your gain will be recognized at the time of the sale. The rest of the gain will be recognized as subsequent installments are received. Such sales need to be carefully evaluated. Stock or securities traded on established markets cannot be reported for tax purposes on an installment basis.

Like-Kind Exchanges

Generally, the tax on the gain from any real estate held for investment or business reasons can be deferred if the property is traded for similar real estate. However, if you received "boot" (that is, cash or unlike property) in addition to the like-kind property, you may have to recognize a gain equal to the value of the money or property received. The rules for like-kind exchanges are complicated, and you should consult with your tax advisor in order to properly structure this transaction.

Other Opportunities for Individuals

Qualified Small Business Stock

The law provides that an individual taxpayer who holds qualified small business stock (QSBS) for more than five years can exclude from gross income 50% of any gain realized from the sale or exchange of the stock. This exclusion is limited to the greater of:

1. 10 times the taxpayer's basis in the stock; or
2. $10 million in gain from all of the taxpayer's transactions in stock of that corporation (held for more than five years).

The new rules apply to stock issued after August 10, 1993.

The rules for determining whether stock is "qualified small business stock" are summarized on page 119.

TaxSaver

The lawmakers who have supported the new capital gains provision believe that by targeting the provision to smaller businesses it will provide more effective incentives for long-term equity investments in those businesses. By limiting the preferential capital gains treatment to stock that is newly issued, the provision is designed to respond to concerns that an across-the-board capital gains provision would provide a windfall to wealthy investors who already own appreciated investments.

This new provision could benefit the shareholders of corporations that are engaged in retail sales, manufacturing, or production of high-technology products.

Start-up companies are routinely faced with the question of when their trade or business begins. This provision eases such determinations by permitting assets used in certain start-up activities, research and experimental activities or in-house research activities, to be treated as used in an active conduct of a qualified trade or business for purposes of the 80% test described on page 120.

Rolling Gain Over into a Specialized Small Business Investment Company

Under certain circumstances, gain on the sale of publicly traded securities will not be taxed if the proceeds from the sale are used to acquire common stock in a specialized small business investment company.

Special Treatment for Lump-Sum Distributions

If you were at least age 50 on January 1, 1986, you may be able to elect to treat a portion of the taxable part of a lump-sum distribution as a long-term capital gain taxable at a 20% rate. This treatment applies to the portion you receive relating to your participation in the qualified plan before 1974. Capital gains treatment is not available for lump-sum distributions received after 1991 by individuals who were less than 50 years old on January 1, 1986.

Gifting Appreciated Assets

When making a charitable contribution, it may be tax-wise to donate appreciated marketable securities instead of cash. You may be able to avoid the capital gains tax on the property, and the charity generally sells the stock or securities, receiving cash but not paying any tax due to their tax-exempt status. If you want the stock or securities you donated in your portfolio, take the cash you were planning to give to charity and repurchase the identical investment. Your investment now has a new, increased cost basis.

If you plan to make a charitable contribution of an investment asset, follow these two rules:

Rule 1

If you have appreciated property that you have held for more than a year, donate it—don't sell it and donate the cash. The following example explains why.

Example: Let's assume that you are going to donate $30,000 to your favorite charity. You have stock that you bought for $6,000 several years ago; it now has a market value of $30,000.

If you give the stock directly to the charity you don't report any capital gain and you can deduct $30,000 as a charitable contribution. Assuming you are in the 39.6% tax bracket, the charitable contribution would reduce your taxes by $11,880.

Here's what happens when you sell the stock and give the proceeds to charity. First, you have a gain of $24,000 on which you pay a 28% capital gains tax of $6,720. You would, however, be able to claim a charitable contribution deduction of $30,000 that would normally reduce your taxes by $11,880, assuming you were in the 39.6% tax bracket.

Adding the taxes you pay on the gain to the taxes you save from the deduction, your net tax benefit is $5,160.
Rule 2

If you have property that has depreciated in value, sell it and give cash—don't donate the property directly. Here's why.

Example: Let's suppose that you own stock that cost $33,000 a few years ago. The stock is currently worth $30,000. If you donate it to a charity, you will get a deduction of $30,000, its fair market value. If you sell it you will have $30,000 in cash. You can give the cash to a charity and claim a charitable deduction. You will also have a capital loss on the sale of your stock of $3,000. The capital loss is also deductible.

Stock Options

The wide gap between the top tax rates on ordinary income and capital gains (11.6%) is likely to enhance the attractiveness of incentive stock options (ISOs) to executives compared to nonqualified stock options (NSOs). ISOs generally do not trigger taxable income until the stock received from exercising the option is sold. Exercising an ISO does, however, result in income for alternative minimum tax purposes and, therefore, may trigger the alternative minimum tax (see discussion on page 138). Careful planning should be undertaken in this regard. Further, if ISO stock is sold at least one year after the date of exercise and two years following the date the ISO was granted, the difference between the sale price and exercise price is taxed as a long-term capital gain at the 28% rate. By contrast, the recipient of an NSO generally will recognize income when the NSO is exercised, which could be taxed at a rate of as much as 39.6%. See Chapter 1 for more about stock option as an employee benefit.

Concerns Regarding Community Property

Community property is most often property acquired by spouses while they are married and domiciled in a community property state. But not *all* property acquired during the marriage is community property. If one spouse individually receives a gift or inheritance, it is not community property but rather is "separate property" owned solely by the recipient. Property acquired or otherwise owned by each spouse prior to marriage is also considered separate property.

Community property and marital property are treated differently from noncommunity property when someone dies. In a noncommunity property state, the basis of the decedent's property is increased or decreased for tax purposes to fair market value as of the date of the decedent's death. However, when one spouse in a community property state dies, the basis of *both* spouses' interest in *every* piece of community property is stepped up or down, that is, increased or decreased to the fair market value at date of death.

7

Filing Status and How To Calculate Your Tax

Introduction

This chapter explains the basics of filing status issues and how to calculate your tax. The actual calculation you will have to make is straightforward:

If your allowable standard deduction exceeds your allowable itemized deductions, your taxable income is your adjusted gross income minus your standard deduction and personal and dependency exemptions.

If the sum of your allowable deductions exceeds your allowable standard deduction, you can itemize those deductions. Your taxable income will be your adjusted gross income, minus your itemized deductions and personal and dependency exemptions.

You can determine your income tax liability by using the tax tables supplied by the IRS with your tax return form booklet if your taxable income does not exceed $100,000. If your taxable income exceeds $100,000, the tax rate schedules (reproduced in the Appendix of this book) are used to compute your tax.

This chapter also discusses special situations that could affect your tax liability, including investment income of children under age 14, the alternative minimum tax, and tax credits. Filing rules, estimated taxes, and withholding taxes are also explained.

Who Must File

In general, if you are a citizen or resident of the United States, you must file an income tax return by April 15 for the previous taxable year. For the taxable year 1994, income tax returns are due on April 17, 1995. (April 15, 1995, is a Saturday.) You can gain additional time to file if you apply for an extension. (See discussion on page 129.) You must file a tax return if your gross income for the year is at least as much as the amounts shown in Table 7.1.

(See the discussion below for persons claimed by another taxpayer as a dependent.)

In addition, if married persons filing jointly do not live in the same household at the end of the taxable year, or if either of them can be claimed as a dependent by a third person, the limit for a married person filing separately usually applies.

The following persons must also file a return even if their income is less than the amounts shown above:

1. Persons claimed as dependents on another's return who have unearned income and the total of their unearned income and earned income exceeds $600 (See below for an exception applying to children under age 14.)

Note: The following amounts do not include the additional standard deductions for blind individuals. Such individuals are entitled to an additional $750 standard deduction if married, and $950 if their filing status is single or head of household. These amounts are revised annually by a cost-of-living adjustment. (See page 40 for further discussion.)

TABLE 7.1 1994 Filing Requirements

Filing Status*	Required to file return if gross income exceeds**
Single	
Under 65	$ 6,250
65 or over	$ 7,150
Head of household	
Under 65	$ 8,050
65 or over	$ 8,950
Married filing jointly	
Both under 65	$11,250
One 65 or over	$11,950
Both 65 or over	$12,650
Surviving spouse***	
Under 65	$ 8,800
65 or over	$ 9,500
Married filing separately****	$ 5,625

*For details on determining your filing status, see discussion on page 132.
**These amounts are adjusted annually by a cost-of-living adjustment.
***You must meet the "surviving spouse" requirements; otherwise you will be treated as single or head of household. (See page 134.)
****Assuming at least one spouse itemizes deductions.

2. Persons with earnings from self-employment of $400 or more
3. Persons receiving any advanced earned income credit payments
4. Persons with a liability for the alternative minimum tax, recapture of investment tax credit, tax due on an early withdrawal from an individual retirement account (IRA), or social security tax on tip income
5. Persons with wages of $108.28 or more from a church or qualified church-controlled organization that is exempt from employer FICA contributions
6. Persons who owe any taxes

Parents may elect to include on their return the unearned income of a child who is under age 14 at the end of the tax year if that child's unearned gross income is between $500 and $5,000, and consists only of interest and dividends. If the parents make this election, the child will not be required to file a separate return. (See page 136 for a discussion of how children under 14 are taxed.)

To obtain a refund for tax that has been withheld, a return should also be filed even if it is not required.

Special rules for filing requirements applicable to non-resident aliens and certain other individuals with special status are not discussed in this book.

How to Get an Extension of Time to File

If you need more time to file your income tax return, you can easily apply for an automatic four-month extension. All you need to do is complete an application (IRS Form 4868, *Extension to File U.S. Individual Income Tax Return*) and send it in by the original due date of your income tax return. Additional extensions beyond the four-month period are granted only for good reason. Under normal circumstances, an extension of more than six months will not be granted unless you are outside of the United States. If an extension is granted, no penalty for late payment of tax will be imposed if at least 90% of the tax liability shown on the return is paid on or before the original due date.

An automatic extension of two months is also granted to U.S. citizens and U.S. residents whose tax home is outside the United States and Puerto Rico on the date the return is due. Unlike the automatic extension for other individuals, no application is required for such automatic two months' extension and there is no minimum payment required to avoid a late payment penalty.

Even though the due date for filing a return is extended, any unpaid portion of the final tax will accrue interest from the original due date to the date paid.

Interest rates for underpayments are equal to the short-term federal rate plus three percentage points. (The short-term federal rate is announced by the Treasury Department in the Federal Register.) These interest rates are adjusted quarterly and become effective during the first calendar quarter following the adjustment. Interest is compounded daily.

Which Form You Should Use

All individual taxpayers resident in the United States are required to file their returns on Form 1040, Form 1040A, or Form 1040EZ. Most taxpayers who use this book will probably find that they are required to use Form 1040.

TaxORGANIZER

Although Form 1040EZ or Form 1040A may be easier to use, you should review your tax information before deciding which form to use. You may have deductions that can be itemized, which can only be claimed if you file Form 1040. You may therefore be overpaying your taxes if you use one of the easier forms that does not allow you to claim these deductions.

TaxSAVER

Electronic Filing. *If you are due a refund, you should consider filing your return electronically with the IRS instead of mailing in the paper forms. Electronic filing can shrink the time for receiving your refund down to three weeks. Remember, however, that most tax return preparers and other firms authorized to make electronic filings will charge a separate fee for the service—generally about $30 to $40. If you need the refund money right away, it may make sense to pay for filing electronically.*

Every individual (other than a nonresident alien) with net earnings of $400 or more from self-employment must file a report of self-employment income and compute the self-employment tax on Schedule SE (Form 1040), even if the filing of an income tax return is not otherwise required. The FICA tax calculation is composed of two parts. Part one, for old-age, survivors, and disability insurance (OASDI), is calculated at a rate of 6.2% applied to wages and 12.4% on net self-employment income up to $60,600 in 1994. Part two, for Medicare insurance, is assessed at a rate of 1.45% on wages and 2.9% on net self-employment income in 1994.

TaxALERT

The dollar limit on wages and self-employment income subject to Medicare taxes for wages and other earned income received after 1993 has been eliminated. Thus, the 1.45% rate for employees (2.9% for self-employed individuals) will apply to all wages and earned income beginning in 1994.

TAXORGANIZER

You should be aware that you are not excused from filing a return because the IRS did not send you the necessary forms. You can usually obtain the forms from your local IRS office, post office or bank, or The Ernst & Young Tax Guide, published annually. Copies of forms may be used.

TAXORGANIZER

Even if you are not required to do so, you should still file a return if:
(1) You had income tax withheld from your pay. Even if you are entitled to a refund, you cannot claim it unless a return is filed.
(2) You qualify for the refundable earned income credit. (See page 142.)

Accounting Periods and Methods

You must determine your taxable income for a fixed period of time for each tax year. This is defined as an "accounting period." Most individual income tax returns cover a calendar year based on a 12-month accounting period from January 1 through December 31, unless permission is granted in advance by the IRS to use a different 12-month period.

In addition, you must also account for your income and deductions in a consistent way that clearly reflects your taxable income. This is defined as an "accounting method." The two accounting methods most often used are the cash method and the accrual method. Individuals who do not own and operate their own business are required to use the cash method only. The cash method reports all items of income in the year in which you actually or "constructively" receive them. You have "constructively" received income when it is credited to your account or is set apart in any way that makes it available to you. You do not have to physically possess the funds. For example, interest credited to your bank account on December 31, 1994 is constructively received and taxable to you in 1994 if you could have withdrawn the funds in 1994—even if the amount is not entered in your passbook or actually withdrawn until 1995. On the other hand, you generally can deduct expenses only in the year you actually pay them.

If you are qualified to use the accrual method, you generally report income when you earn it, regardless of when you receive the money. You also generally deduct expenses as they are incurred and not when you pay them.

Filing Status

Your filing status will determine your filing requirements, standard deduction, eligibility to claim certain deductions and credits, and correct tax. Your filing status is determined by your status on the last day of the tax year, which for individuals is almost always December 31. So, if you got married on December 31, you are treated for tax purposes as being married for the entire tax year. Generally, the effective tax rate for single taxpayers is higher than for married taxpayers filing jointly or unmarried individuals filing as head of household. That is because the amount of taxable income that qualifies for the 15% tax rate is lower for single filers ($22,750) than for married taxpayers filing jointly ($38,000) or heads of household ($30,500). (See the tax table in the Appendix.)

Single Taxpayers

Your filing status is *single* if you are unmarried or you are legally separated from your spouse and you do not qualify to file as head of household or qualifying widow(er) with dependent child. (See page 133.) Children under age 14 whose unearned income (interest, dividends, capital gains, etc.) is $600 or over are taxed under special rules. (See page 136.)

Married Taxpayers

You and your spouse may agree to file either a joint return or separate returns. A joint return may be filed by a married couple even though only one person has gross income or deductions. A joint return, however, may not be filed if (1) the individuals have different taxable years, or (2) either spouse was a nonresident alien at any time during the taxable year unless an election to file a joint return is in effect. (The catch is that a joint return requires that the worldwide income of both spouses for the entire year be included in taxable income.)

TaxSaver

If you and your spouse each have income, you may want to calculate your tax two ways: filing jointly and filing separately. You can file your returns based on the method that yields the lower tax.

If one spouse dies, the survivor, if not remarried at year-end, may file a joint return for the year of death. A joint return is filed in the name of both spouses and includes the total income and deductions of the surviving spouse and the income and deductions up to the date of death of the other spouse. (See also Surviving Spouse, page 134.)

If a taxpayer and spouse file separate returns, the original election to file separately may normally be changed as long as an amended joint return is filed within three years of the return's original due date. However, if a joint return is filed, an amended separate return may not be filed for that particular taxable year after the due date of the return, unless the executor of a deceased spouse's estate disaffirms the joint return.

TaxSaver

When to get married: If one of you has much less income than the other, consider getting married in December rather than January. You will generally be taxed less on the same income if you are married filing jointly than you would be if each of you filed single returns. If both of you have similar levels of income, choose January. Marriage partners who earn approximately the same income may pay more tax if they file a joint return or file separate married returns than they would if they could file two single returns. This is known as "the marriage tax penalty."

When to get divorced: If you both have similar levels of income, choose December since the marriage tax penalty may be avoided. If one has more income than the other and both want to save taxes, choose January.

Individuals legally separated under a decree of divorce or separate maintenance agreement are not considered married. Although there may be a tax incentive to do so, the IRS maintains that couples who divorce immediately before year-end and remarry immediately after the start of the new year are considered married at year-end for tax purposes.

Head of Household

A separate, lower tax rate schedule can be used if you are unmarried and can qualify as head of household. In general, an unmarried taxpayer at the close of the tax year, other than a surviving spouse or a nonresident alien, qualifies as a head of household if the individual furnished over one half of the maintenance cost of:

1. His or her personal residence, which, except for temporary absences, is lived in during more than one half

of the taxable year by a relative who qualifies as a dependent. You do not qualify as a head of household if you can only claim a relative (other than an unmarried child, grandchild, stepchild or adopted child; or a parent who does not live with you) as a dependent under a multiple support agreement. The residence can also be lived in by an unmarried son, daughter, grandchild, or stepchild even though not qualified for the dependency deduction, or

2. A household (even if separate) for a parent who qualifies as a dependent other than through a multiple support agreement.

In determining head-of-household status, a taxpayer whose spouse is a nonresident alien at any time during a taxable year is not considered married if an election to file jointly is not made. In addition, a married individual who otherwise qualifies for head-of-household status but for his/her marital status can file using head-of-household status if his/her spouse is not a member of the household for the last six months of the tax year.

TaxOrganizer

You should keep track of your support payments to establish your qualifications for head-of-household status.

Surviving Spouse (Qualifying Widows and Widowers)

If your spouse died in 1994, you may use married filing jointly as your filing status for 1994 if you would otherwise qualify.

If your spouse died during either of the two years immediately preceding this current tax year and you meet all the following tests, you may be able to use *surviving spouse* as your filing status if:

1. During the current year, you furnished more than one half of the cost of maintaining your home which also constitutes the principal place of residence of your son, stepson, daughter, or stepdaughter;
2. You did not remarry before the end of the year; and
3. You were entitled to file a joint return with your spouse for the year your spouse died.

The return of a surviving spouse is accorded the same benefits as a joint return. This means that you are entitled to a lower tax rate schedule and a higher standard deduction amount if you do not itemize your deductions.

Citizens Living Abroad

If you are a U.S. citizen or resident alien (a green-card holder) living overseas, you are subject to U.S. tax on your worldwide income regardless of where such income is earned, paid, or received. However, you can elect to exclude up to $70,000 of your foreign earned income and certain foreign housing costs, and you may also claim a credit against U.S. tax for foreign income taxes you paid.

To qualify for the exclusions, you must meet one of two tests: (1) the bona fide foreign residence test or (2) the physical presence test.

The Foreign Residence Test. The bona fide foreign residence test applies to U.S. citizens only. It requires you to be a resident in a foreign country (or countries) for an uninterrupted period including an entire taxable year.

The Physical Presence Test. The physical presence test applies to both U.S. citizens and resident aliens. It will be met if you are physically present in a foreign country (or countries) for 330 full days during any consecutive 12-month period.

Housing Costs. You may also elect to exclude from your U.S. taxable income the excess of reasonable overseas housing expenses over a base housing amount—which is $9,443 in 1994—multiplied by a fraction: the numerator of which is the number of qualifying days of residence or physical presence and the denominator of which is the number of days in the tax year. Interest and real estate taxes are excluded from housing costs for the purpose of calculating the foreign housing exclusion. The exclusion applies only to employer-provided housing costs.

If you are a self-employed individual, you can deduct your foreign housing costs in computing your adjusted gross income, but the deduction is limited to the excess of foreign earned income over the foreign earned income exclusion. Any nondeductible amounts can be carried forward to the following year to the extent that you receive foreign income in the succeeding year.

Expenses, including moving expenses (which are subject to special rules), and foreign tax credits that are attributable to excluded amounts cannot be deducted or credited against your U.S. tax bill.

TAXSAVER

If you are living in a foreign country with a higher tax rate than the United States' tax rate, you may be better off foregoing the foreign earned income and housing exclusions and claiming the foreign tax credits instead. Excess foreign tax credits may be carried back to prior tax years or carried forward.

The foreign earned income and housing exclusions are elected separately. The total of the earned income exclusion and the housing cost exclusion, however, cannot exceed your total foreign earned income. The exclusion amount of up to $70,000 is prorated on a daily basis based on the number of days in the taxable year that you meet either test. Once made, an exclusion election remains in effect for future years until revoked. If the election is revoked without the approval of the IRS, a new election may not be made until the sixth taxable year following the year of revocation.

Ordinarily, you are allowed a two-year replacement period when you sell your home, which enables you to defer paying tax on any gain from the sale. (See page 71.) However, this replacement period is suspended during the time you maintain a tax home outside the United States. The replacement period in such a case may not exceed four years from the date of the sale of your home.

Foreign Tax Credit

You may also elect to claim a credit for foreign income taxes paid or accrued during the tax year or you may claim the taxes paid as an itemized deduction.

As discussed above, if you elect to take either the foreign earned income exclusion or the foreign housing exclusion, or both, the amount of foreign taxes that you may receive credit for will be reduced accordingly. See page 144 for more about the Foreign Tax Credit.

Children Under Age 14

If your child was under 14 at the end of the taxable year and received more than $1,200 of unearned income, such as interest and dividends, your child's unearned income in excess of $1,200 will be taxed at your marginal tax rate.

Example: A child who does not itemize his or her deductions has $800 of earned income and $2,100 of unearned income. He or she would be taxed on $1,200 of unearned income at his or her rate. The remaining $900 would be taxed at his or her parents' marginal rate. The child's standard deduction is limited to $800 (based on the greater of $600 or the child's earned income).

TAXSAVER

If your child is under age 14 and you are in the top income tax bracket, income-producing property that earns up to $600 should be transferred to your child because it will escape tax completely. The next $600 is taxed at only 15%. Furthermore, you may want to tailor the child's investment strategy so that any of the child's annual unearned income over $1,200 is generated from tax-exempt or from tax-deferred instru-

ments, such as U.S. savings bonds that will mature after the child reaches age 14.

If you are divorced, your child's tax liability is determined by using the custodial parent's tax rate. If you are a married individual filing separately, your child's tax rate is the same as the tax rate of the parent with the greater amount of taxable income.

Any child who is subject to these rules must include the parents' Social Security numbers on his or her tax return.

Including Your Child's Income on Your Return.

Parents may elect to include the unearned income of any of their children under age 14 on their own return instead of filing separate returns for each child. This election may be made only if (1) your child's gross income consists solely of interest and dividends totaling no more than $5,000, (2) your child makes no estimated tax payments for the year under his or her own name and Social Security number, and (3) your child is not subject to backup withholding.

TAXORGANIZER

If you elect to include the unearned income of any of your children under age 14 on your return, you may save paperwork, but your family could end up paying more taxes. Including your child's unearned income on your return could increase the amount of state income taxes you pay—if your state's tax is based on federal income and your child would not otherwise owe state tax. Your child would also forfeit the ability to claim itemized deductions and to deduct any penalty on the early withdrawal of savings.

TAXSAVER

If your children are at least age 14, you should consider taking advantage of their 15% tax bracket, which applies to the extent their taxable income is below $22,750. Here are a few ideas to consider:
- *Convert EE bonds to HH bonds, which pay interest currently, or redeem the bonds and invest in something else, like CDs, which generally produce a greater return with little additional risk.*
- *Convert growth stocks to dividend-paying stocks and mutual funds.*

Tax Rates for Individuals

The 1994 tax schedule contains five rates for individuals—15%, 28%, 31%, 36% and 39.6%. The top tax rate on net capital gains—the excess of net long-term capital gains over net short-term capital losses—is capped at 28%.

Alternative Minimum Tax

The tax law gives special treatment to some kinds of income and allows special deductions and credits for certain expenses. Taxpayers who benefit from these laws have to pay at least a minimum amount through a special tax. This special tax is called the "alternative minimum tax."

Individuals, trusts, and estates must pay the alternative minimum tax (AMT) if it exceeds their regular tax liability for the year. The amount subject to the AMT will be determined by adding a number of preference items to your taxable income and making various adjustments to your regular taxable income. This amount is reduced by the exemption amounts, shown in Table 7.2, and the balance is subject to the AMT rate. Your tax advisor can help you with the calculation.

The AMT rate is 26% on alternative minimum tax income (AMTI) of $175,000 in excess of the exemption amount, and 28% on AMTI more than $175,000 above the exemption amount. For married taxpayers filing separately, the 28% AMT rate applies to the extent that AMTI is more than $87,500 above the exemption amount. Furthermore, the base exemption amounts are $33,750 for single individuals and heads of household, $45,000 for married taxpayers filing jointly, and $22,500 for married taxpayers filing separately, trusts, and estates.

TABLE 7.2   Exemption Amount

Filing Status	Base Amount	Less 25% of the Amount by Which AMT Exceeds Income
Single	$33,750	$112,500
Married filing jointly, surviving spouses	45,000	150,000
Married filing separately, estates and trusts	22,500	75,000

Tax Preference Items

Tax preference items are income and expense items that receive special treatment under the tax laws. They must be added back to the taxable income shown on your return in figuring your alternative minimum taxable income. The AMT preference items are:

1. Allowable depletion, to the extent that it exceeds the adjusted basis of the property involved
2. The amount by which excess intangible drilling costs exceed 65% of the net income from oil, gas, and geothermal properties for the taxable year

TaxSaver

To avoid treating excess intangible drilling costs as a tax preference item, you may elect to capitalize and amortize these expenses over a 10-year period in your regular tax calculation.

3. Interest on specified tax-exempt private activity bonds issued after August 7, 1986, reduced by deductions that would be allowable if such income could be included in regular taxable income
4. Accelerated depreciation on certain property bought and put into use before 1987 (Depreciation methods are described on pages 222–226.)
   (a) Allowable depreciation in excess of straight-line depreciation on real property and leased personal property that was placed in service before 1981. (Straight-line depreciation is calculated by dividing the cost of the property by its useful life.)
   (b) Accelerated cost recovery allowances in excess of the allowance that would be available on real property placed in service after 1980 and before 1987, using the straight-line method of depreciation over 15 years (18 years for most property placed in service after March 15, 1984, and 19 years for property placed in service after May 8, 1985). (*Note:* Straight-line depreciation is computed without considering salvage value); and
   (c) Accelerated cost recovery allowances in excess of the allowance that would be available on leased personal property placed in service after 1980 and before 1987, using the straight-line method, no salvage value, the half-year convention, and an extended recovery period. The half-year convention discussed on page 225, assumes the property was placed in service during the mid-point of the year for depreciation purposes.
5. The excess of the rapid amortization of pre-1987 certified pollution-control facilities over the depreciation that would be allowable.

Adjustments

Besides accounting for tax preference items, certain adjustments (increases or decreases) must be made to taxable income to arrive at alternative minimum taxable income. The adjustments are:

1. An alternative depreciation deduction (using less accelerated methods and longer depreciable lives) is substituted for the regular tax depreciation deduction for real and personal property and certified pollution-control facilities placed in service after 1986. Recomputations are done in the aggregate—that is, the amount of the adjustment is not determined on a property-by-property basis. *Note:* This adjustment does not apply if you have elected to apply the alternative depreciation system (ADS) for regular tax purposes. (See page 225 for details.)

2. Mining exploration and development costs must be amortized over 10 years using the straight-line method.

3. The percentage-of-completion method of accounting must be used for long-term contracts entered into on or after March 1, 1986. Certain small construction contracts entered into on or after June 21, 1988, must use new simplified procedures for cost allocations in the percentage-of-completion calculation.

4. An alternative tax net operating loss deduction replaces the regular net operating loss deduction.

5. The installment method of accounting is disallowed for certain installment sales occurring after March 1, 1986.

6. The treatment of itemized deductions is modified as follows:

- Medical expenses are deductible only to the extent that they exceed 10% of the taxpayer's adjusted gross income.
- State, local, and foreign real property and income taxes and state and local personal property taxes are deductible for alternative minimum tax (AMT) purposes only if they are deductible for regular tax purposes in computing adjusted gross income.

Note: These are taxes related to business, rental property, and farming that are deducted on Schedules C, E, or F.

- Investment interest is deductible to the extent of net investment income that is adjusted for amounts relating to tax-exempt interest earned on certain private activity bonds.
- Home mortgage interest is allowed as a deduction for AMT purposes. However, the definition of such interest is narrower than that of "qualified residence interest" for regular tax purposes. Refinanced home mortgage interest that is applicable to any mortgage in excess of the outstanding mortgage before refinancing is not deductible for AMT purposes. (See page 51 for further discussion.)

- No deduction is allowed for miscellaneous itemized deductions which are subject to the 2% of adjusted gross income limit for the regular tax computation.

7. No deduction is allowed for the standard deduction.

8. Circulation expenditures and research/experimental costs must be amortized over 3- and 10-year periods, respectively.

9. Deductions for passive farm losses are denied except to the extent that the taxpayer is insolvent or the activity is disposed of during the year.

10. Rules limiting passive loss deductions also apply to the AMT, except that (a) otherwise disallowed losses are reduced by the amount by which the taxpayer is insolvent, and (b) all AMT adjustments and preferences are taken into consideration in computing income and/or losses from passive activities.

11. For beneficiaries of estates and trusts, the difference between a distribution included in income for regular tax and the AMT income shown on Schedule K-1 must be taken into account.

12. For property disposed of during the year, the gain or loss is refigured to take into consideration the impact that AMT adjustments, such as depreciation, have on the taxpayer's basis in the property.

13. For partners in partnerships and shareholders in S corporations, the income or loss is refigured to take into account AMT adjustments.

14. If exercising an incentive stock option (ISO), the taxpayer needs to adjust for the difference between the option price and the fair market value at the time the option is exercised. (For corporate "insiders" who exercise an ISO within six months of when the option was granted, the adjustment between the option price and its fair market value is made six months after the option is granted.) In calculating the AMT gain or loss on the subsequent sale of the ISO stock, the AMT basis in the stock is the sum of the option price paid and the AMT adjustment included in alternative minimum taxable income when the stock became substantially vested.

You will only pay the alternative minimum tax if it is higher than your regular tax. You may, however, offset your AMT liability by using any foreign tax credit, as computed under the AMT rules, that you are allowed to claim. Other nonrefundable credits cannot, under any circumstances, reduce your AMT liability. To the extent that no tax benefit is obtained for these nonrefundable credits for the year the AMT applies, such credits are generally carried back or forward to other taxable years.

AMT Credit. The law provides a credit against the regular tax for all or a portion of the AMT you paid in previous years. The credit is the AMT attributable to deferral, rather than exclusion, items. Deferral items, such as accelerated depreciation, are those that have the effect of reducing your regular taxable income relative to alternative minimum taxable income in early years but the situation reverses over time. When you pay AMT as a result of deferral preferences, the law gives you a credit that can be used to reduce your regular tax liability in the future. This credit helps you avoid double taxation on the same income. Exclusion preferences, such as certain tax-exempt interest income, reduce your regular taxable income permanently. Since these preferences never reverse in the future, no AMT credit is provided for exclusion preferences. The AMT credit is carried forward indefinitely from the year of payment and cannot be carried back.

TaxSaver

If you know you will be subject to exclusion-item-generated AMT in a given year, you should consider accelerating income into that year to be taxed at 26% or 28% rather than a possibly higher regular tax rate in the future. Likewise, consider deferring deductions, especially those that are not deductible for AMT purposes and will give you no benefit. For example, state income taxes are not deductible for AMT purposes. Therefore, you should not pre-pay your state income taxes in an AMT year. Many people ordinarily do pre-pay those taxes before year-end in order to claim that deduction for the current tax year. Another approach would be to elect to depreciate assets using the straight-line method of depreciation for regular tax purposes rather than an accelerated method.

Credits that Reduce Your Tax

The credits discussed below may be used to offset your current income tax liability. For this purpose, income tax does not include certain other taxes, such as the alternative minimum tax and the additional taxes resulting from a premature distribution from certain retirement plans or an annuity contract.

Earned Income Credit

The earned income tax credit (EITC) is a refundable credit available to lower-income workers. For more information, see *The Ernst & Young Tax Guide 1995.*

Credit for Dependent Care Expenses

If you have dependent care expenses and your adjusted gross income is $10,000 or less, an income tax credit is available equal to 30% of certain employment-related expenses incurred for such care. The amount of the credit will decrease by 1% (but not below 20%) for each $2,000 (or part thereof) of your adjusted gross income in excess of $10,000. The maximum amount of employment-related expenses that can be taken into account for the credit is $2,400 for one qualifying individual and $4,800 for two or more qualifying individuals.

A qualifying individual is a dependent under the age of 13 for whom you are entitled to claim a dependency deduction, or a dependent or spouse who is physically or mentally incapable of caring for himself or herself.

For married taxpayers, expenses are limited to the lesser of the two earned incomes. However, the credit is available to married couples who file jointly when one spouse is physically or mentally incapable of caring for himself or herself or is a full-time student at an educational institution for five months during the year. Certain payments to relatives and to children over 19 who are not claimed as dependents will be considered qualified expenses. Married taxpayers must file a joint return in order to claim the credit.

Employment-related expenses are ordinarily expenses for household services and for the care of a qualifying individual that are incurred to enable you to be gainfully employed. Eligible expenses must be reduced by the amount excluded from your income for employer-provided dependent care assistance, including benefits received from cafeteria plans to which you have contributed. (See page 37.)

Credit for the Elderly and the Permanently and Totally Disabled

If you or your spouse is 65 years old or older, you may be entitled to a credit of as much as $1,125 against your tax. Furthermore, taxpayers under 65 years of age who are permanently and totally disabled may also be eligible for the credit. You are permanently and totally disabled if you cannot engage in any substantial gainful activity because of your physical or mental condition. A physician must certify that the condition has lasted or can be expected to last continuously for 12 months or more, or that the condition can be expected to result in death. Disabled veterans may file a VA Form 21-0172, "Certification of Permanent Total Disability," instead of the physician's statement.

In general, if you file as a single individual, you do not qualify for the tax credit if you are 65 years old or over and (1) you receive nontaxable Social Security or other nontaxable pensions of $5,000 or more, (2) your adjusted gross income is $17,500 or more, or (3) your tax is zero. Generally, the credit is not available to a nonresident alien.

Other Credits

Investment Tax Credit. The regular investment tax credit is generally no longer available for property placed in service after 1985, with certain exceptions.

Expenditures to rehabilitate certified historic structures and other qualified buildings that are to be used for nonresidential purposes are still eligible for the investment tax credit. For qualified buildings placed in service after 1986, the credit is equal to 10% of qualified expenditures for nonresidential buildings first placed in service prior to 1936 and 20% for certified historic structures. The 20% credit is available for both residential and nonresidential buildings. The regular investment tax credit and the business energy credit do not apply to any portion of the basis in the property that qualifies for the rehabilitation credit.

Transitional rules apply to property placed in service before 1994 and qualifying under additional transition rules.

General Business Credit. The investment credit is combined with the targeted jobs credit (page 247), the alcohol fuel credit (page 247), and the research credit (page 247) into one general business credit. This credit can be claimed against 100% of the first $25,000 of tax liability net of all other nonrefundable credits and 75% of the remaining tax liability. Excess credits can be carried back for 3 years or carried forward for a 15-year period. Excess credit carryovers generally are used on an earliest-year-first basis, followed by current-year credits and credit carrybacks.

If property on which the investment credit was previously taken is disposed of before the end of the period used in initially determining the credit, the credit must be recomputed, and the unearned portion may have to be recaptured as additional tax in the year of disposal. For ACRS property (see page 223), a portion (33% for three-year property, 20% for other property) of the credit amount is earned for each full year subsequent to being placed in service. If the property disposed of was subject to the limitation applied to used property, you may reselect used property on which no investment credit was taken in the year of acquisition to take the place of the property disposed.

Foreign Tax Credit

An individual may elect to claim a credit instead of a deduction for foreign income taxes. The foreign tax credit that may offset your U.S. tax liability is limited to the ratio of foreign-source taxable income to worldwide taxable income times the U.S. tax. To the extent that you use the foreign earned income exclusion (page 134), the foreign tax available for credit must be scaled down. To be able to use the credit in an earlier year, a taxpayer may make a binding election to take the credit for foreign taxes on the accrual method.

Excess credits may be carried back two years and forward five years. The foreign tax credit must be recomputed to determine the foreign tax credit you are allowed to use against any alternative minimum tax liability.

> **TAXSAVER**
>
> *Because $1 of tax credit reduces your tax liability by $1, whereas $1 of deduction will only reduce your federal tax liability by at most 39.6 cents, it is generally a good idea to elect to take a credit for foreign taxes paid rather than a deduction.*

Credit for Excise Taxes Paid on the Use of Gasoline and Special Fuels

A credit or refund is available for the federal excise tax paid on gasoline for nonhighway business use, qualified bus and taxicab use, and certain aviation use. A boat must be used as a commercial fishing vessel for the fuel use to qualify for the credit. A credit or refund is also available for special fuels used for certain nontaxable purposes or resold during the tax year. The credit claimed must be included in income if the cost of the product was deducted as a business expense according to your method of accounting.

Estimated Tax Payments and Withholding

The IRS requires that taxpayers pay their anticipated tax liability as it accrues through withholding and/or the payment of estimated taxes in quarterly installments.

Individuals are automatically exempt from estimated tax payments if they fall into one of two categories:

(1) Those whose tax for the current year, after credit for withheld taxes, Social Security tax refunds, and backup withholding is less than $500, and

(2) Those who had no tax liability for the preceding tax year and were U.S. citizens throughout such year. This rule does not apply if the preceding tax year consisted of less than 12 months or if a return was not filed for the preceding year.

Withholding Tax From Your Wages. Income tax is generally withheld from your wages and salaries based on the amount you earned and the withholding information you have supplied your employer on Form W-4, *Employee's Withholding Allowance Certificate*. If you have significant income from other sources such as self-employment, alimony, interest, dividends, and rent, or the amount of tax withheld from your wages and salaries is not enough, you may have to make estimated tax payments.

Estimated Tax Payments. Estimated tax may be paid in full when the taxpayer determines he or she is liable for such tax or in equal installments. Estimated tax payments for a calendar-year taxpayer are due on April 15, June 15, and September 15, and January 15, of the following year. If a filing or payment due date falls on a Saturday, Sunday, or legal holiday, the next working day is substituted. You can make your estimated payments either through crediting an overpayment from your prior year's return to the current year or by sending in your payment with a payment voucher, Form 1040-ES.

If conditions requiring estimated tax payments do not arise until after March 31, a calendar-year taxpayer must make payments on the due dates shown in Table 7.3.

The amount of estimated tax you pay may be amended on or before any subsequent installment date.

A complete return may be filed by January 31, with payment of the balance of tax due for the calendar year, in lieu of a January 15 payment of estimated tax.

TaxSaver

It is generally not a good idea to file your tax return by January 31 if you owe tax with the return. You will be better off keeping any additional tax you owe in an interest-generating bank account for two and a half months rather than paying your tax bill early with no tax or economic benefit.

The IRS does not issue reminder statements for installments due on estimated taxes. It is the taxpayer's responsibility to remit each installment on a timely basis. (See below for information on waiver of the underpayment penalty for certain taxpayers.)

TABLE 7.3   Estimated Tax Payment Deadlines

Date Requirement Met	Date Payments Due*
After March 31 and before June 1	June 15, and September 15, 1994, and January 17, 1995
After May 31 and before September 1	September 15, 1994 and January 17, 1995
After August 31	January 17, 1995

*Corresponding dates apply to fiscal-year taxpayers for payments and returns.

Any unpaid tax is generally due by the original due date of the tax return, which is April 17, 1995, for a calendar-year 1994 taxpayer. If you have overpaid your tax, you may elect to have the overpayment refunded or applied against next year's tax liability.

TaxSaver

If it appears during the year that you will have underpaid your current year's taxes because previous estimated payments and/or withholding prove insufficient in meeting your actual tax liability, you can correct the situation by instructing your employer to withhold greater amounts from your wages for the rest of the year.

Underpayment Penalties. You may be penalized for not paying enough tax for a particular installment period. The amount subject to the penalty is the amount by which the required installment, defined as the lesser of items 1 or 2 below, exceeds the amount paid for the quarterly period:

1. 90% of the tax shown on the return (after certain adjustments), allocated evenly to each of the quarterly periods; or
2. 100% (or 110% for certain high-income taxpayers, see below) of the prior year's tax, allocated evenly to each of the quarterly periods (provided the prior year comprised 12 months and a return was filed for such year); if your previous year's adjusted gross income exceeds $150,000, you must pay 110% of last year's liability to be certain of avoiding any underpayment penalties.
   Example: Ms. Green's 1995 income tax liability is $55,000. Her adjusted gross income in 1994 was $175,000, while her 1994 tax liability was $40,000. Ms. Green will avoid an underpayment penalty in 1995 if the total amount of tax withheld and estimated tax payments exceeds 110% of her 1994 tax liability, or $44,000, because her 1994 adjusted gross income exceeded $150,000.

The underpayment penalty may also be avoided by using a special rule based on your annualized income. Under the special rule, no penalty is imposed for a quarter if the cumulative amount paid by the installment date equals or exceeds 90% of the cumulative estimated tax as computed on annualized income.

In general, the annualized method allows you to calculate your quarterly payment based on taxable income received up to the end of the latest quarter, annualized to a 12-month period. You can usually benefit from the annualized method if you do not receive your taxable income evenly throughout the year (for example, if you are the owner of a ski shop that receives most of its revenue during the winter months).

The use of the methods for determining the underpaid amount, described above, may vary from quarter to quarter to provide the minimum underpayment amount by quarter. Remember, however, that if you pay the annualized income installment, you must add the difference between the amount you pay and the required installment to the required installment for the next period if the annualized income method is not used for the next period.

The tax computed for purposes of determining the quarterly payments required to avoid the underpayment penalty includes the self-employment tax and all other taxes (including the alternative minimum tax), minus any allowable credits.

If the amount paid for a quarterly period is greater than the amount required to avoid penalty, the excess is applied first against underpayments in prior quarters, and then against subsequent underpayments. Any penalty is assessed from the installment due date to the date paid or the original due date of the return, whichever is earlier. The rate of the penalty is the same as the rate of interest for underpayments of tax. However, the penalty is not compounded daily, whereas the interest is.

Special requirements and exceptions are provided for farmers, fishermen, and nonresident aliens.

Penalties

The penalty imposed for late filing is 5% of the unpaid amount for each month or part of a month that it remains unpaid up to a maximum of 25% of the unpaid tax. If you fail to file for more than 60 days, the penalty may not be less than the smaller of either $100 or 100% of the tax required to be shown on the return. If the return is filed on time but is not accompanied by payment of the balance due as shown on the return, the penalty is one half of 1% of the balance due for each month or part of a month of delinquency (up to a maximum of 25% of the unpaid tax). The penalties apply unless the taxpayer can show reasonable cause for the delay. Additional penalties are also imposed on underpayments of tax due to negligence or fraud, and on substantial understatements of tax liability.

8

Year-End Planning for Individuals

Introduction

This chapter takes a look at the future direction of the tax law and suggests some strategies that you might adopt to better cope with increased tax rates. Even if the year has already ended, there are steps that you can still take to minimize your future taxes.

In 1993, Congress increased the top tax rate on ordinary income to 39.6%—an increase of 8.6 percentage points over the top 1992 tax bracket. Long-term capital gains remain taxed at a maximum rate of 28%. Although Congress still has to face health care reform and possible tax increases connected with it, we do not believe that income tax rates will be increased again in the near future.

What kind of tax strategies does that suggest? Generally, when tax rates are stable, you would be wise to defer as much income as possible from one year to a later year and to accelerate deductions so that you can postpone the payment of the tax. And there is an added benefit of deferring your tax: you have the use of more money for a longer period of time, although you need to take care to have enough cash on hand to pay the tax when it is due. On the other hand, if you expect to be in a higher tax bracket next year, you might consider accelerating income into the current year and deferring deductions.

In theory, the strategy is simple: realize income when your tax rate is low and pay expenses when it is high. Marriage, divorce, promotions, retirement, illness, death, or sales of major assets can cause your taxable income to change from one year to another. All of these life-cycle events require special tax planning. The following discussion highlights several strategies that can help you save money on your 1994 taxes and beyond.

The first step in your year-end planning will be for you to estimate your 1994 and 1995 taxable income. The worksheets provided on pages 163–164 will help you do this.

149

Shifting Income

By boosting the top income tax rate 8.6 percentage points above the 31% maximum rate that existed under prior law, and by creating a 24.6% spread between the highest (39.6%) and lowest (15%) marginal tax rates, the 1993 Tax Act enhances the tax savings that can potentially be realized by shifting income among family members, especially to children. Higher-income parents should consider transferring assets that generate ordinary income, such as dividends and interest, to children age 14 or older in order to take advantage of their lower tax bracket. For example, shifting $10,000 of investment income from a parent in the 39.6% tax bracket to a child over 14 who is in the 15% bracket (which currently applies to taxable income up to $22,750) can save the family $2,460 in taxes per year. Even greater tax savings may be achieved by spreading ordinary income among all of the taxpayer's children to take advantage of each child's lower tax bracket. Finally, since children under age 14 pay only $90 in tax on the first $1,200 of unearned income they receive (unearned income above $1,200 is taxed at their parents' highest marginal tax bracket . . . the so-called *kiddie tax*), shifting income-producing property that earns $1,200 to a child under 14 can save the family as much as $385 in taxes each year [($1,200 × 39.6%) (parents' rate) − $90 (tax paid by the child)].

Accelerating deductions to the current year would be potentially beneficial if the deduction will not be lost or substantially diminished by the 3% of adjusted gross income floor on certain itemized deductions or other limitations on deducting itemized deductions. The 3% floor is explained on page 68.

Limits on Certain Itemized Deductions

Given the limits on certain itemized deductions and exemptions for certain high-income taxpayers (explained in Chapter 2), your best planning move, if possible, would be to exercise some control over the amount of your adjusted gross income. If you can keep your income below the level at which deductions become subject to certain limitations in one year, you would be able to deduct the full amount of personal exemptions and deductions. Obviously, you would want to take as many deductions as possible in such a year.

The Alternative Minimum Tax Rate

As discussed in Chapter 7, the Alternative Minimum Tax (AMT) is a tax system imposed on the regular tax system to prevent taxpayers from taking too great an advantage of special tax breaks such as accelerated depreciation, interest on certain tax-exempt bonds, etc. Taxpayers who do not use these tax preferences to lower their regular income tax will not be subject to the AMT. Taxpayers who do avail themselves of tax preferences may still escape the AMT because their Alternative Minimum Taxable Income is reduced by exemptions:

Filing Status	Exemption Amount	Phased out by 25% of amount in excess of	Fully phased out at
Married filing jointly	$45,000	$150,000	$330,000
Single	33,750	112,500	247,500
Married filing separately	22,500	75,000	165,000

High-income taxpayers who do avail themselves of tax preferences may be subject to the tax if they do not plan carefully.

Taxpayers subject to the AMT will pay tax at the following rates for 1994:

Rate	Married Filing Separately	All Other Filers
26%	Up to $87,500 over exemption amount	Up to $175,000 over exemption amount
28%	Greater than $87,500 over exemption amount	Greater than $175,000 over exemption amount

Taxpayers subject to the alternative minimum tax may find that accelerating income and deferring deductions may be the most effective planning approach. For further discussion of the AMT, see Chapter 7.

Filing Status

In general, the effective tax rates on total family income for married taxpayers filing jointly and heads of households are lower than for a taxpayer who files individually (see Filing Status in Chapter 7 and the tax tables in the Appendix for more information.) Thus, if you are eligible to file a joint return for the year, you probably should. For a married person filing jointly in 1994, the 15% tax bracket applies to income ranging from $0 to $38,000; filing separately $0 to $22,750. Not only can you save on your taxes, but for most people, it's simpler to complete a joint return. Since a husband and wife are treated as one taxpayer, you won't have to sort out which deductions are his and which are hers.

Effects of Filing Status.

There are circumstances where single individuals will find that their combined tax is higher after they marry. This is commonly known as the "marriage penalty."

Example 1: Bob Jones and Mary Smith each have taxable income of $50,000. As single individuals, they are each in the 28% bracket. But if they marry they will have a joint income of $100,000 and part of their income will be in the 31% bracket.

> **TAXSAVER**
>
> *If your filing status will change before the end of the year, you should decide whether to defer income and accelerate deductions or the opposite, depending on whether or not you will be subject to the marriage penalty. You also should consider whether you would be better off filing separate returns.*

Example 2: Two people are married and one spouse has medical expenses of $10,000; the other has none. Both have adjusted gross income of $50,000. They are allowed a medical deduction for amounts in excess of 7.5% of AGI. If they file a joint return, the medical deduction would be $2,500 ($10,000 − [7.5% × $100,000]). If they file separate returns, all other things being equal, the medical deduction would be $6,250 ($10,000 − [7.5% × $50,000]).

> **TAXSAVER**
>
> *You should figure your tax both jointly and separately to see which produces the best result.*
>
> *Your filing status may also affect the new limitations on itemized deductions. All taxpayers, whether filing as individuals, heads of household, or joint, have their itemized deductions reduced by an amount that is equal to 3% of the excess of their adjusted gross income over $111,800. Medical expenses, casualty and theft losses, and investment interest expense are not subject to this limitation. A working couple with a combined AGI over $131,800 is subject to a floor of $600 (3% of $20,000). However, two single individuals each with AGI of $65,900 are both beneath the $111,800 limitation.*

When to File as a Head of Household. If you are unmarried at the end of the year, you might save money by filing as a head of household, instead of a single return. To qualify, in addition to being unmarried, you must maintain a household that was the principal home for the year of a child, grandchild, or other relative who qualifies as your dependent.

If you are still married but have lived apart from your spouse for at least six months of the year, and you have custody of your child, you may be able to file as head of household instead of married filing separately. You will benefit from lower tax rates and you also may be able to claim the standard deduction even if your spouse itemizes deductions. If your income is high enough that some of your exemptions may be phased out, you should consider letting your spouse claim dependents.

If Your Spouse Died During the Year. If your spouse died during 1994, leaving you with one or more dependent children, you may continue to file jointly for the two years following your spouse's death and take advantage of the more favorable married filing jointly rates. You may claim an exemption for your deceased spouse in the year of death, but not in subsequent years.

Income

Compensation

The higher tax rates first imposed in 1993 may enhance the benefits of deferred compensation plans and other tax-deferral arrangements, particularly if you anticipate being in a lower tax bracket when the income is eventually received. For example, 401(k) plans, individual retirement accounts, Keogh plans, other retirement plans, and life insurance policies that build up cash surrender value benefits over a period of years may now be more attractive to you.

Bonuses. Just like weekly or monthly wages, bonuses generally are income to you when you receive them, not when earned. But they are also deductible by your employer when paid. If you want to defer income, you may be able to arrange with your employer before the amount of the bonus is determined that you will not be paid your bonus until next year. Although it keeps your employer's cash flow higher than it would have been had he or she paid the bonus currently, it will increase his taxable income. So it is a matter of negotiation. But remember to do it early in the year. You can't wait until your employer is passing out the checks and say "I'd like mine next year."

Deferred Compensation. Another way to defer income from one year to the next is to use a deferred compensation plan. These plans are designed for executives who can afford to defer a portion of their income until a future date. Under these plans the executive makes an election to defer some portion of his or her income until a stated time and is taxed on the deferred income only when it is received.

Deferrals can be made from regular salary or from bonuses. To be effective, however, an election to defer income must be made before that income is earned. Further, the executive and the employer must enter into a *written* deferral agreement. Be aware, however, that the IRS may be suspicious of short-term deferrals, say, from December 1994 to January 1995. One problem with deferred compensation plans is that they must be subject to the claims of general creditors and may be subject to the whims of future management.

TaxSaver

An acceptable way to fund deferred compensation— generally over a relatively long period—is to use a "rabbi trust." A rabbi trust is generally an irrevocable trust established by the employer to pay deferred compensation to the employee. Although the trust's assets must remain subject to claims of the employer's creditors, the trust arrangement protects the individual from the whims of the employer and from a change in control of the company. The employee is not protected if the employer becomes insolvent or goes into bankruptcy.

Even more secure than a "rabbi trust" is a "secular trust." Funds held in a secular trust are not accessible by an employer's creditors. However, the price for the added security is that you must pay tax currently on any amounts contributed to the trust. In turn, the company is allowed a current tax deduction when funds are transferred to the trust.

401(k) Plans. If your employer has a 401(k) plan, you can elect to defer into the plan a certain amount of your salary on a pretax basis. These amounts are withheld from your salary and are not reported as taxable income until withdrawn from the plan. Before the end of the tax year, it is usually a good idea to make sure you have made as large a contribution to your 401(k) plan as possible. You can elect to defer up to 20% of your wages up to a maximum of $9,240 in 1994. Also see the discussion of 401(k) plans in Chapter 4, IRAs, 401(k) Plans, and Other Retirement Plans.

Taxation of Social Security Benefits

For tax years starting in 1994, the law taxes up to 85% (up from 50%) of Social Security benefits received. This represents a significant tax increase for middle-income retirees. The added tax burden means that certain Social Security recipients would benefit from shifting some of their investments from income-producing assets to investments that favor capital appreciation. You may defer recognition of income by investing, for example, in U.S. Savings Bonds. If you never cash in the bonds, your heirs will recognize the income. Alternatively, you may stagger the recognition of U.S. bond (or other) income so that you create alternating years of high and low income. Under the right circumstances, an individual may reduce the amount of Social Security benefits taxed in the *low-income* years without increasing the amount of benefits that otherwise would have been taxed in the *high-income* years.

Interest Income

Taxable Interest. One way to defer interest income from now until next year is to purchase short-term (one year or less) certificates of deposit before the end of the year. Not just any CD will do: it must be the type on which interest is not made available, without substantial penalty, before the 1995 maturity date. The advantage is that you can postpone interest income accruing in 1994 from the date of purchase until 1995.

Treasury bills offer a similar opportunity. T-bills do not pay interest, but are sold at a discount and mature at their face value. The difference represents interest. It is not taxable to you until the T-bill matures if you hold it until that time. By buying a T-bill that matures next year, you can defer reporting interest from the date of purchase until the following year.

Example: Suppose you have $25,000 in a savings account that credits you with interest on the last day of each month. If, on November 1, 1994, you purchase a six-month CD or a three-month T-bill, you will be able to defer the November and December interest until next year.

Tax-Exempt Interest. The higher income tax rates under the 1993 Tax Act should increase the appeal of tax-exempt bonds and bond funds, especially for taxpayers in the 39.6% top marginal tax bracket. As tax rates rise, taxable securities must provide higher yields in order to match the yield offered by tax-exempt bonds of similar quality and time to maturity.

Example: If you are in the 31% tax bracket, a taxable bond yielding 8.69% is comparable to a municipal bond with a 6.0% tax-exempt yield. However, if you are in the new 39.6% bracket, you would need almost a 10% yield on a taxable bond to match the municipal bond's 6.0% return. In addition, consider the fact that some states have income tax rates over 10%. Consequently, your combined federal and state marginal tax rate—factoring in the phaseout of deductions and exemptions for higher income taxpayers and other "back door" tax increases—can exceed 50%. An investor living in such a high tax state would need a 12% taxable bond to achieve the same after-tax return as a 6% municipal bond.

Here's a chart showing the equivalent taxable investment yields for tax-exempt yields ranging from 5%–8% at various individual tax rates.

Your Tax Bracket	Tax-exempt Equivalent Yields			
	5%	6%	7%	8%
15%	5.88	7.06	8.24	9.41
28%	6.94	8.33	9.72	11.11
31%	7.25	8.69	10.14	11.59
36.0%	7.81	9.37	10.93	12.50
39.6%	8.28	9.93	11.59	13.25

If you are in the 36% bracket, a 7% yield on a tax-exempt investment provides you with the equivalent after-tax return as a taxable investment yielding 10.93%.

Alimony

Alimony received is income to the recipient and a deduction for the payor. The tax law allows a great deal of discretion to both the payor and payee of the alimony about how to set up payments that will provide the maximum tax benefit to both parties. Therefore, there are a variety of year-end planning opportunities to consider.

Example: Individuals finalizing a divorce or separation agreement in the final months of 1994 can negotiate a disproportionately large deductible payment for 1994 as long as it does not exceed the average of the total payments for 1995 and 1996 plus $15,000.

This is a very complex area of the law. You should consult with your tax advisor. Be sure your records are in good order. See Chapter 2.

Business Expenses

Business Travel. The IRS allows employers to reimburse employees for business automobile travel at the rate of 29 cents per mile. However, actual expenses will frequently exceed the allowable reimbursement. In many cases you will be entitled to larger deduction for automobile expenses if you use your actual automobile expense figures rather than the IRS per-mile allowance.

Unreimbursed Business Expenses. Many self-employed taxpayers don't realize that they are entitled to deduct the cost of unreimbursed items such as business gifts up to $25 per recipient. These unreimbursed business expenses should be treated as trade or business expenses, not as miscellaneous itemized deductions subject to the 2% of adjusted gross income floor. An employed executive who buys an attaché case and is not reimbursed would treat the expense deduction as a miscellaneous itemized deduction, subject to the 2% floor. However, if a self-employed individual makes a similar purchase, it is a trade or business expense, fully deductible on Schedule C.

Vacation Homes
Review your personal use before the year ends to avoid the loss of your deduction for interest and taxes (see Chapter 3).

Capital Assets
Stock. Since it is unlikely that tax rates on capital gains will be increased next year, you should consider deferring the recognition of capital gains from 1994 to 1995. Several strategies can be used to defer the gain on the sale of stock until the following year (see the discussion of capital gains and losses in Chapter 6):

Passive Activity Losses. You can recognize suspended losses from a "passive activity" when you dispose of your entire interest in it. Year-end may be a particularly opportune time to recognize such losses. These passive activity losses can offset active or passive activity income or portfolio income. "Passive activities" are discussed on page 18. You should consult your tax advisor before recognizing passive activity losses.

Business Property
Selling property at a loss this year can keep your adjusted gross income down. This not only reduces your taxable income but can also—if your adjusted gross income is above a certain level—actually increase the amount of your exemptions and itemized deductions.

The sale of certain business property qualifies for special tax treatment. If you sell it at a loss the loss is an ordinary income loss. If you sell it at a gain the gain is treated as long-term capital gain. It's one of the few win-win situations left in the tax law—sole proprietors should pay special attention.

Giving Business Property to Charity. If you are a self-employed individual and are thinking about giving business property to charity, make sure that you won't be better off from a tax standpoint selling the property and making an outright contribution to the charity from your personal funds.

Adjustments and Deductions

These days, reducing your adjusted gross income (AGI) can be as important as reducing your taxable income. Your personal exemptions are phased out if your AGI is above a certain amount. Furthermore, your itemized deductions are limited if your AGI exceeds $111,800.

Adjustments

You may be able to reduce your adjusted gross income through various adjustments:

- Your IRA deduction and your spouse's deduction, if applicable;
- One-half of self-employment tax;
- Health insurance for self-employed individuals;
- Keogh and Simplified Employee Pension (SEP);
- Alimony.

All of these items, except alimony (see page 45), are discussed below.

Self-Employment Tax and Health Insurance for Self-Employed Individuals

If you pay self-employment tax, half of it is deductible. Since you are going to have to pay it anyway, you may want to consider paying it this year.

Self-employed individuals and employee-owners of 2% or more of the stock in an S corporation used to be able to deduct (as an adjustment to gross income) 25% of the premiums paid for health insurance coverage of the individual and his or her spouse and dependents. But this provision of the tax law expired on December 31, 1993. Congress intends to restore this provision in the health care reform bill on a retroactive basis. Consequently, this deduction will likely be available to you in calculating your 1994 taxes. If, however, the health care bill or other legislation is not enacted until later, you may file an amended return to claim the deduction. Further, it appears that the provision will be expanded to allow self-employed individuals and employee-owners a higher percentage deduction, instead of only a 25% deduction.

TAXSAVER

If you have already filed income tax returns treating the deduction as having expired on June 30, 1992, you may wish to file amended returns reflecting the reinstatement of the deduction. This deduction may be extended further if a health care reform bill is passed by Congress. If not, Congress once again may need to enact other legislation to extend the health insurance deduction for self-employed individuals.

IRAs, Keoghs, and SEPs

IRAs. Contributions can be made up to the due date of your tax return not including any extensions and still be deductible on your previous year's tax return. Thus, you have until April 15, 1995, to make an IRA contribution and claim it on your 1994 return. By contributing pretax dollars to an IRA, you can accumulate savings while reducing your taxable income. For a further discussion of IRAs, see Chapter 4.

Keogh Plans. Individuals with self-employment income may establish a retirement plan known as a Keogh plan, to which they may make tax deductible contributions. (For details, see Chapter 2.) Although a plan must be established by year-end, unlike an IRA, you have until the due date of your return, including extensions, to make the maximum allowable contributions. A Keogh plan is a qualified retirement plan. Participation in a Keogh plan limits IRA deductions. Before establishing one you should consult your tax advisor. A rule of thumb is that a start-up business should produce at least $15,000 in self-employment income before a Keogh plan becomes as cost effective as an IRA.

SEPs. A Simplified Employee Pension (SEP), like an IRA, can be established after the end of the taxable year for which the deduction is being claimed. The plan must be established prior to the due date of the *employer's* tax return including any extensions. For further details about SEPs, see Chapter 4.

Itemized Deductions

To receive the maximum tax benefit when itemizing your deductions, you should generally try to bunch your deductible payments in years in which they exceed the amount of your standard deduction and also exceed the floors based on adjusted gross income for medical expenses and miscellaneous deductions.

Your first decision is to choose between itemizing deductions or taking the standard deduction amount ($6,350 in 1994 for married taxpayers filing jointly; $3,800 in 1994 for a single filer). You should choose whichever alternative yields the higher deduction. (See Chapter 2 for a further discussion of itemized deductions and the standard deduction.) If it is likely that you will opt to itemize your deductions, you'd be well advised before the end of the tax year to review them and see if there are ways you can slide some into whatever tax year might yield a more favorable result.

Casualty and theft losses cannot be planned. It's also usually difficult to plan deductible moving expenses related to your job. So, for practical purposes, you should focus your review on the following four types of expenditures:

- Medical and dental expenses in excess of 7.5% of your adjusted gross income
- Certain state and local taxes
- Interest
- Contributions to charity.

Each of these types of expenses is discussed below.

Medical and Dental Expenses

Your medical expenses, including certain health insurance premiums, are deductible only to the extent that they exceed 7.5% of your adjusted gross income (AGI) (10% if you fall prey to the alternative minimum tax, AMT). Since you do not have control over medical emergencies, elective medical procedures should be bunched in years when your AGI is lower. That way your medical expenses are more likely to exceed the 7.5% floor. You may be better off still if you participate in your employer's cafeteria plan (see page 27, Cafeteria Plans, for further explanation).

Taxes You Paid

State and local income and property taxes generally are itemized deductions. For the most part you will have paid your state income taxes, and in some instances your local income taxes, through withholding. However, before year-end you may wish to pay those taxes that you would normally pay early next year because your liability was not fully satisfied through withholding. Taxpayers with large state and local tax liabilities, however, may be subject to the AMT, since these taxes are not deductible for AMT purposes.

Interest You Paid

Qualified Home Mortgage Interest. Typically, homeowners make monthly mortgage payments throughout the year. The mortgage interest on those payments generally is deductible subject to the rules and limits explained in Chapter 2.

Personal or Consumer Interest. Since 1991, personal or consumer interest has not been deductible. But home equity loans still provide deductible interest. So, one way to increase your interest deduction is to consolidate your nonbusiness loans into a home equity loan. Many banks are now structuring what used to be personal and auto loans as home equity loans. You should discuss this with your tax advisor. (There is a further discussion of home-equity loans in Chapter 3.)

Contributions to Charity

Most taxpayers make many of their charitable contributions at the end of the tax year. The reason is simple: you can have use of the money for the entire year and, at the same time, you can take the tax deduction for that year. If you made your contribution in January, you would be entitled to the same tax deduction but would not have use of the money for the rest of the year. Charitable contributions are available only if you itemize your deductions. You'll find a comprehensive discussion of charitable contributions in Chapter 5.

> ### *TaxSaver*
>
> *Two points to consider, especially at year-end:*
> 1. *If cash is not readily available, you can use a credit card to charge donations to charity. They will be deductible in 1994 even though you don't pay the charge until 1995.*
> 2. *If you are going to give publicly traded stock to a charity, check with your stock broker to ensure that you have readily transferable title to the property that you want to donate to charity.*

Deferred Giving. There are ways to make deferred contributions to a charity and claim a deduction, too: (1) A charitable "remainder" trust lets a donor retain an interest in the property's current income stream and to claim a current charitable deduction for the present value of the remainder interest given to charity. (2) A charitable "lead" trust pays income to a charity for a term of years (the lead), at the end of which the principal of the trust reverts to the grantor or other noncharitable beneficiary. This technique can result in a current deduction equal to the present value of the income the trust will pay to the charity. You would include income on your return as the trust earns it. If the trust is funded with tax-free bonds, the interest you receive in future years is treated as tax free. If you want to establish a charitable remainder or lead trust, you should do so before year-end and with the assistance of a professional advisor. Also, see Chapter 2 for details.

Miscellaneous Deductions

Generally, only the amount of miscellaneous deductions that, considered as a group, exceed 2% of your adjusted gross income is deductible. Therefore, you should bunch these expenses as much as possible so that the total will exceed the 2% floor. If it appears that you will not exceed the floor this year, defer these expenses until next year if you can. Alternatively, accelerate expenses to this year if that will enable you to exceed the 2% floor. Married persons who customarily file jointly should consider filing separately to maximize miscellaneous deductions. Note, however, that miscellaneous itemized deductions are not allowable for the alternative minimum tax.

Exemptions

Review the amount of support you have provided so far this year to your dependents, children and parents, so you meet the support test that allows you to claim an exemption for them as dependents. Also be aware of the rules that phase out the tax benefits of exemptions if your adjusted gross income exceeds certain levels. See Chapter 2.

Paying Your Taxes

An important aspect of tax planning, particularly year-end tax planning, is how and when you pay your tax liability. This affects your cash flow and may result in real savings for you.

You should review not only your expected tax liability but also when that tax is paid. Significant overpayments are essentially interest-free loans to the government, but underpayments may result in a nondeductible penalty. See page 147.

TaxSaver

If you have not paid enough up to this point, consider increasing your federal and state withholdings from salary or wages for the remainder of the year. Taxes withheld are considered paid evenly throughout the year. Therefore, increased withholdings at the end of the year could eliminate an underpayment in the beginning of the year. In addition, itemized deductions would increase as a result of the additional state taxes withheld. However, taxpayers claiming large state tax deductions may subject themselves to the AMT.

If you project a significant overpayment, reduce your tax payments for the balance of 1994 by at least the amount of your overpayment. This step should be done only when estimates are considered fairly accurate, or when you are certain not to have an underpayment penalty. Reducing current payments below your tax bill for the year will cause a larger amount to be due with your return. That balance due, unlike the return itself, generally cannot be extended beyond the original due date of the return (i.e., April 15, 1995, for 1994 calendar-year taxpayers).

Worksheet to Estimate 1994 and 1995 Federal Income Tax*

Gross income	1993 (actual)	1994	1995
Wages and salaries	$_____	$_____	$_____
Interest income	_____	_____	_____
Dividends	_____	_____	_____
Income or loss from trade or business	_____	_____	_____
Net capital gains or losses	_____	_____	_____
Rents and royalties	_____	_____	_____
Income or loss from partnerships, trusts, estates, and S corporations (1)	_____	_____	_____
Pensions and annuities	_____	_____	_____
Taxable social security benefits	_____	_____	_____
Other	_____	_____	_____

Less: Deductions for adjusted gross income (AGI)

	1993 (actual)	1994	1995
Alimony paid	(_____)	(_____)	(_____)
Payments to an IRA or Keogh plan (2)	(_____)	(_____)	(_____)
Other	(_____)	(_____)	(_____)
Equals: AGI	$_____	$_____	$_____

Itemized deductions

	1993 (actual)	1994	1995
Medical and dental (in excess of 7.5% of AGI)	$_____	$_____	$_____
State and local income taxes, property taxes (3)	_____	_____	_____
Qualified residential interest	_____	_____	_____
Investment interest expense (4)	_____	_____	_____
Charitable contributions	_____	_____	_____
Casualty and theft loss (in excess of 10% of AGI)	_____	_____	_____
Moving expenses	_____	_____	_____

Other: Tax preparation fees, investment fees, and employee business expenses (5)	———	———	———
Total itemized deductions	———	———	———
Less: 3% of AGI adjustment (6)	(———)	(———)	(———)
Adjusted itemized deductions	———	———	———
Standard deduction	———	———	———
AGI less the higher, of adjusted itemized deduction or the standard deduction (7)	———	———	———
Less: Number of exemptions × $2,450 (8)	(———)	(———)	(———)
Equals: Taxable income	———	———	———
Regular tax (from tax rate schedule, see page 269) (9)	———	———	———

*Does not include the Alternative Minimum Tax (AMT) computation (see the discussion of the AMT on page 138).

1. Except for rental losses allowed up to certain AGI limits, passive activity losses in excess of passive activity income from each activity are disallowed.
2. If you or your spouse are participants in an employer-maintained retirement plan, your IRA deduction may be limited.
3. If you have unusually large deductions for state and local taxes and/or substantial tax preference items, page 138, you may be subject to the alternative minimum tax.
4. Investment interest expense deductions are limited to the amount of the taxpayer's net investment income.
5. Most miscellaneous itemized deductions are deductible only to the extent they exceed 2% of AGI. Employee business expenses in excess of reimbursement are miscellaneous itemized deductions.
6. See page 68 if your AGI is in excess of $111,800.
7. See page 68 for more about 1994 standard deductions and page 39 for personal exemptions. To estimate your 1995 income, use 1994 amounts.
8. In 1995, the exemption amount will be adjusted for inflation. At this printing, the amount is not known. To estimate your income, assume it will be the 1994 amount of $2,450. These should be adjusted for the phase-out of exemptions as described on page 40.
9. If you have net capital gains the maximum rate is 28%.

II

How to Improve Your Financial Future

Everyone hopes for or dreams about a bright financial future. Yet, few Americans are doing much to secure it. Consider the fact, for example, that although Americans are richer per capita than individuals in most other countries, they save or invest a smaller percentage of their income than the Japanese, Swiss, Portuguese, Turks, Greeks, Italians, and Norwegians, to mention just a few. Now there are more and more reasons for Americans to be concerned. Many corporate pension plans are not as generous as they once were, and while many Americans are working well past age 65, they are living longer, too.

Taxes are not the only consideration in planning your financial future, but they are an important one. Savvy investors can defer taxes so that they have more of their money building their nest egg. At some point, depending on your age and need for income, you may want to consider investments that are tax-free. Now—not later—is when you need to plan how you are going to afford to retire. And, as unwelcome a task as it may be, you need to consider planning your estate and how you want to provide for your heirs. In fact, in some important respects, you can enhance the quality of your life by giving serious consideration to how you want your assets handled after your death.

9

Investment Planning

Introduction

The best way to achieve your financial goals and objectives is to plan. The planning process needs to take into account your personal investment biases and your tolerance for risk. Generally, the more risk you are willing to take, the higher the potential returns. But, are you comfortable trading stocks and bonds? Or, would you feel better putting your money in fixed-income government securities? You also have to set realistic goals for the rate-of-return you expect to earn on your portfolio.

The purpose of this chapter is *not* to suggest where you should and should not invest. That task is something you, and perhaps your investment advisor, have to tackle.

But tax-saving strategies enable you to keep more of your investment profits and improve your financial future. This chapter, among other things, will provide you with brief descriptions of various popular investment products, their tax consequences, and tax strategies you should be aware of when establishing your financial plans and investment portfolio. Table 9.1 briefly describes various types of investments and the tax treatments of the income generated from these investments. You can use it as a quick reference when considering different investment options.

Where to Start. Investment planning can't take place in a vacuum. In coming up with your investment strategy, you need to take account of your current and future cash needs. You need to think about saving money—and investing it prudently—for your retirement. You should also give some thought to estate planning. Will your estate be liquid enough to pay debts and estate administration expenses due after you die, or will assets have to be sold to cover these expenses? (See Chapter 11 for more information about estate planning.)

And, of course, there are taxes. An investment strategy, an estate plan, or almost anything else can't be developed

167

properly without giving thought and consideration to tax consequences.

But we urge that you keep two important principles very much in mind:

1. You should adopt a systematic and disciplined saving program.
2. You should diversify your investment portfolio among different types of assets—cash and cash equivalents, fixed-income securities, equities, and real estate.

Diversification can moderate the effects that market fluctuations can have on your portfolio. It does not eliminate risk or guarantee that you will meet your financial goals, but it is the most prudent way to reduce risk. Also, when purchasing specific stocks or mutual funds, you should consider "dollar cost averaging" i.e., the systematic purchase of a specific dollar amount at regular intervals regardless of the price level of the stock or the market in general. Dollar cost averaging is based on the assumption that the market rises in the long-term and fluctuates in the short-term. As a result of using this technique, you will purchase more shares when the market value of the investment has declined and fewer shares when the value has increased, resulting in a lower average cost per share than you might otherwise obtain. In addition, dollar cost averaging offers a regular and disciplined approach to investing in equities.

Capital Gains and Losses

The top tax rate on ordinary income in 1994 is 39.6% for taxpayers with taxable income over $250,000, while the maximum tax rate on net long-term capital gain is 28%. The 11.6 percentage-point differential encourages high-income taxpayers to favor investments that offer capital appreciation, which are taxed at the lower capital gain rate when the investment is sold, over investments that generate current income and dividends, which can be taxed at a rate as high as 39.6%.

Gains on property will be treated as long-term only if the property is held for more than one year. Because ordinary income and capital gains are included in your adjusted gross income for purposes of figuring the limitation on itemized deductions and the phaseout of personal exemptions, the effective rates on ordinary income and capital gains actually exceed 39.6% or 28%, respectively. (For more information on how to figure a capital gain or loss, see Chapter 6.)

TaxSaver

There are a number of planning techniques you can use to save or defer taxes if you sell securities or other capital assets. The advantage you have is that you generally control the timing of a transaction so you can recognize the capital gain or loss in the year of your choice. A cautionary note: Your decision to buy or sell should be based on sound economic and investment criteria and not solely on the tax effect of the transaction. Here's a list of some techniques you can use that can influence how and when you pay taxes:

Sell the Shares You Bought for the Highest Price First.

If you bought shares in one company at different times, you may want to identify the specific shares you sell. This will enable you to sell the shares with the highest cost first and may produce, depending on the sales price, a loss or a lower capital gain. If you don't specify what shares you are selling, it will be assumed that the first-in were the first-out.

Sell Now, Buy Back Later.

If your objective is to generate a tax loss this year while preserving your investment position, you can sell the securities and repurchase them later. However, you cannot deduct any losses you sustain on the sale if you or your spouse repurchases (or enters into a contract or option to repurchase) within 30 days before or after the sale. Such a repurchase would violate the wash sale rules, which are explained on page 122.

Purchasing Put Options.

You can use a put to lock in your gain without paying tax in the current year. The use of put options is explained on page 157.

Selling Short Against the Box.

This is another way to defer capital gains tax until a later year and at the same time lock in your gain. See page 121 for further details.

Installment Sales.

You can postpone the gain on the sale of assets such as real estate or stock of a closely held business—but not the stock of a publicly traded company—by using the installment sale method. As a seller, you may be able to report your gain only as you receive payments. For information on how to qualify a sale and report your gain under the installment sale method, see page 122. Installment sales can also be an effective year-end planning tool. See page 157 for details.

Charitable Remainder Trust.

The use of a charitable remainder trust may provide (1) for the deferral or elimination of tax on capital gains, (2) a current income stream, and (3) a future gift to charity. Establishing such trusts requires careful analysis, involves additional costs, and should be done only after consulting with an experienced tax and financial planning consultant. See Chapter 5, Charitable Contributions, for further details.

Selling Your Home. Any gain on the sale of your home is taxable. However, if certain conditions are met the tax can be postponed. If you're over age 55 when you sell your principal residence, you may be entitled to elect a one-time exclusion of up to $125,000 of your profit. See pages 72–73 for details.

TAXSAVER

You can use capital losses to offset your capital gains, thus lowering your taxes. If you have capital losses greater than your capital gains in any year, you may use the net losses to offset up to $3,000 of ordinary income. For a further explanation, see Chapter 6.

Annuities

Annuities are arrangements in which an investor pays one or more premiums to an insurance company in exchange for the promise of distributions at some future date. Whether structured as a single premium, annual premium, or flexible premium contract, annuities fall into two categories: fixed and variable. With a fixed annuity, the investor pays the premium to the insurance company and the company credits a specified rate of interest on the cash value of the annuity. That rate is generally guaranteed for a term of one or more years.

With a variable annuity, the premium is allocated by the investor among one or more mutual fund-type accounts. The investor can typically choose among stock funds, bond funds, and money market funds.

At some point, the investor can decide to withdraw the funds from the annuity. A variety of payment terms is available, including payments over the investor's lifetime or the joint lives of the investor and another person. The amount of the payments will depend upon a number of factors, including the amount of premiums paid and the earnings over the years.

Interest or gains earned from a tax-deferred annuity are not taxed until withdrawn. When distributed, they are taxed at ordinary income rates. In addition, the tax law provides that certain distributions that are not in the form of regular period payments, made before age 59½, are subject to a penalty of 10% of the taxable portion of the distribution.

E&Y FOCUS: Annuities

While taxes are of obvious concern to an investor considering a deferred annuity, the costs associated with using deferred annuities as tax-advantaged investments should also be considered.

Typically, the insurance company will allow the investor to withdraw, without charge, a certain percentage (e.g., 10%) of the cumulative premium paid or the actual value of the account each year. Amounts withdrawn in excess of stipulated percentages will be assessed a surrender charge. These charges vary among companies and products, but generally are between 5% and 10% of the amount withdrawn and phase down and out over a period of five to ten years. Variable annuities may also be subject to additional annual charges that can total 0.5% to 2.25% of the value of the account. These charges potentially lower the annual yield of the annuity.

As a general rule, to make the investment worthwhile, an investor should plan to let his or her money accumulate in the annuity for at least ten years, and not begin to withdraw funds until after age 59½.

An investor should also consider whether deferring tax is a worthwhile objective. Since the earnings and gains of the annuity will be taxed as ordinary income when distributed, the deferral might not be advantageous if ordinary income tax rates are higher at the time of withdrawal. Also, capital gains that might have been taxed at preferential rates are taxed when distributed at ordinary rates. On the other hand, the deferral will have allowed the money in the annuity to compound tax-free until withdrawal.

Here are some points to consider when selecting an annuity:

1. Since you could be "doing business" with the insurer for decades, it pays to buy from strong, quality insurers.
2. The fixed-annuity investor should examine whether the current interest rate is competitive and for how long a period the rate is guaranteed. An investor should ask for data on how the company has credited rates *after* the guarantee period.
3. The variable annuity investor should look at the breadth of investment choices within the annuity and the track record of *all* the funds.
4. For both fixed and variable annuities, consider the applicable surrender charges for withdrawals. Also, be sure you understand what the fees, expenses, and charges are and how they work.

Dividend Income

Most, but not all, dividends you receive are taxable, and that can make a world of difference when contemplating your investment options—and your tax return.

Ordinary dividends are taxable income and must be reported on your Form 1040. See pages 13–16 for details. The corporation making the distribution will inform you about whether the dividends are taxable or not.

Nontaxable corporate distributions include the following:

- Stock received in a stock split.
- Mutual fund dividends which represent tax-exempt interest.
- Return of capital.
- Dividends on insurance policies (unless they exceed your net premiums).
- Dividends on veterans' insurance.
- Stock dividends or stock rights. If you receive a nontaxable distribution of stock or stock rights—in effect, a certificate entitling you to buy additional stock—your adjusted basis of the old stock must be apportioned between the old stock and the new, based on their proportionate market values. You will not pay any tax until the stock is sold. Also see page 16.

Exceptions: If a corporation offers you a choice between a cash dividend or a stock dividend, can you choose between a taxable and nontaxable dividend? Unfortunately not. The previously nontaxable stock dividend will now be considered taxable income because you could receive taxable cash in its place. Therefore, is it better to take cash? Not necessarily. If you believe in the company's potential, you might choose the stock dividend with the hope that the price of the shares will rise. You must include in your taxable income the market value of the additional shares on the date the dividend is paid. The new shares will have their own basis, equal to the market value you include in your taxable income.

Other instances in which stock dividends may be taxable include the following:

1. When preferred stock is issued to some shareholders and common stock to others;
2. When the dividends are on preferred stock;
3. When convertible preferred stock is issued and the same result in (4) occurs;
4. When there is an unequal distribution in which some shareholders receive cash and you receive a stock dividend that increases your percentage of ownership in the corporation; and
5. When there is an increase in a shareholder's proportionate interest in the company even if no shares are physically issued.

Should you participate in a dividend reinvestment plan? Many companies now offer dividend reinvestment plans, which let you use your dividend to buy more shares of stock rather than receive cash and with some companies purchase additional shares directly from the company. This can be an effective approach to saving money and buying additional shares at regular intervals without a brokerage commission. Of course, how good an idea this is depends on how the stock performs. It's not a way, however, to save or defer taxes.

You have to include your reinvested dividend in income. If the company allows you to buy stock at less than its fair market value under a reinvestment plan, you must report the difference between the fair market value of the stock and the amount you invest as taxable income to you. The fair market value of the stock is its price on the date the dividend is paid.

Individual Retirement Arrangements (IRAs)

IRAs represent an attractive investment vehicle for two reasons. First, earnings and appreciation on the funds you invest in your IRA accumulate "tax-free" until you begin withdrawals. Second, your contributions may also qualify for a deduction from your gross income. Pages 44–47 describe IRAs in general. You'll find specific year-end planning strategies for IRAs and other retirement plans in Chapter 8, page 159.

Interest Income

Investors are always looking for interest income at attractive yields. Interest you receive from U.S. Government obligations, bank accounts, corporate bonds, or loans you made to others, to name a few sources, is taxable at ordinary income tax rates. However, interest received from obligations of a state, U.S. territory or possession, or one of its political subdivisions, is excluded from gross income for federal income tax purposes; consequently, the interest paid is generally lower. The savvy investor should focus on the after-tax yield of an investment. A table comparing the equivalent taxable yields for various tax-exempt rates of return for different tax brackets appears on page 33.

Tax-free bonds, including tax-free zero coupon bonds, are one of the few remaining tax shelters available. But you should proceed with caution. Since the mid-1980s, municipal bond prices have been extremely volatile.

Before purchasing a portfolio of municipal bonds, you may want to consult closely with an investment advisor. Also remember that the interest from certain municipal bonds is subject to the alternative minimum tax.

Series EE Bonds. Though subject to federal income tax, Series EE bonds offer an attractive "tax-sheltered investment." If you do not elect to pay taxes on interest each year, the interest on the bonds can be deferred and taxed when the bonds are either redeemed or reach final maturity, thereby allowing you to select the most desirable taxable year to recognize the income. For further information, see pages 13–14. If EE bonds are used for educational purposes, the interest, for many taxpayers, is not just deferred, it is tax-free. For more details, see page 13.

TAXSAVER

If you do not qualify for the tax break on Series EE bonds used for educational purposes because your income is too high, consider buying the bonds in your child's name. When the child reaches age 14, he or she may cash them in and will be taxed at his or her rate, rather than yours, which presumably is higher.

Investment Expenses
You may deduct certain expenses as miscellaneous itemized deductions if the total amount of the deductions exceeds 2% of your adjusted gross income. There are specific limits on what constitutes an investment expense and how much you can deduct. See page 66.

Investment Interest Expense
Investment interest expense is interest paid on indebtedness allocable to property held for investment. However, interest paid on money borrowed to purchase or carry tax-exempt securities is not deductible. See pages 52–54.

Rental Property
Rental income includes any payment you receive for the use of property. You may deduct expenditures that you incur in renting the property. If the property is not rented, you can still deduct expenses you incur in trying to rent it. Special rules apply to vacation homes that you rent out. See Rental Income and Expenses, page 17.

Tax Shelters
The 1986 Tax Reform Act eliminated most tax shelters, largely prohibiting investors from claiming what are now called "passive losses."

Municipal Bonds. Municipal bonds are among the last, true tax shelters left. Interest income from "munis" can be tax-free—at the federal, state, and city level. Compared to a municipal bond yielding 5.75%, a taxable investment would have to pay nearly 8% in order to throw off as much income for someone whose marginal tax rate is 28 percent. With the federal maximum tax rate approaching 40%, residents of high-tax states like California or New York may find that the combination of federal, state and local levies can push the overall marginal rate to around 50 percent. That means that current tax-free yields on qualifying state and local bonds that are exempt from all three levels of taxes can approach 11.5% on a tax-equivalent basis.

Still, municipal bonds are not without risks. As noted in the TaxSaver on page 173, bond prices have fluctuated sharply over the last few years. And now there is a new danger on the horizon. Just as home mortgages can be refinanced when interest rates fall, most long-term municipal bonds can be redeemed at the discretion of the issuer. January 1 and July 1 are the usual call dates.

Other Shelters to Consider. "Working interests" in oil and gas partnerships still enjoy some tax breaks. While Congress has cracked down on real estate limited partnerships, investors in low-income housing and active landlords may still be entitled to claim some tax benefits. See discussion regarding business credits in Chapter 13 and active real estate participation in Chapter 1.

All tax shelters need to be evaluated carefully. Generally, you should make an investment when it satisfies your investment criteria, not because of the potential tax breaks you might receive.

TaxSaver

Many people haven't explored legitimate ways to shelter income—either by deferring taxes or earning tax-free income. Here's a list of questions you might ask yourself to see if there are any tax-saving opportunities you may have overlooked:

- *Am I maximizing my contribution to my 401(k) account?*
- *Do I have a Keogh plan or a Simplified Employee Pension in which I can make a contribution based on my self-employment income?*
- *Would my company set up a deferred compensation plan for me?*
- *Have I considered whether having more tax-exempt municipal bond interest is appropriate for my situation?*

- *Am I managing my investment income in a way that allows me to deduct all the interest I pay on my margin account?*
- *Should I make IRA contributions even if I don't qualify for a tax deduction?*
- *Will shifting income to a child who's in a lower tax bracket help reduce the family tax bill?*
- *Do I have appreciated stocks, art, or other assets to donate to charity?*
- *Have I looked into how trusts could fit into my estate plan?*
- *Have I considered a home-equity loan with deductible interest to replace nondeductible interest on car loans and credit cards?*

Table 9.1 Tax Attributes of Various Investments

Security	Description	Tax Attributes
Cash, CDs, and Savings Accounts	Money in bank, government insured up to certain limits.	Annual interest taxed.
Treasury Bills	Short-term (up to 1 year) debt obligation of U.S. Treasury.	Interest earned taxed at maturity or earlier if bills are sold. Interest exempt from state and local taxes.
Treasury Notes	Medium-term (2 year to 10 year maturity) debt obligation of U.S. Treasury.	Annual interest taxed. Interest exempt from state and local taxes.
Treasury Bonds	Long-term (more than 10 years' maturity) debt obligation of U.S. Treasury.	Annual interest taxed. Interest exempt from state and local taxes.
Ginnie Mae—GNMA	A security representing a share in a pool of mortgages in which the timely payment of interest and principal is guaranteed by the Government National Mortgage Association.	Annual interest is subject to federal, state, and local tax. The principal, which can be paid off sooner or later than expected, is not taxable.
U.S. Savings Bonds	Debt obligation of U.S. Treasury. When held 5 years or longer, pays variable interest rate equivalent to 85% of average yield on Treasury securities with 5 years remaining to their maturity, or 4%, whichever is greater.	Interest exempt from state and local taxes. Federal tax is deferred on Series E and EE bonds. Can be exempt from federal tax if bonds are used to fund higher education, but income limits and other restrictions apply.

Table 9.1 Tax Attributes of Various Investments (continued)

Security	Description	Tax Attributes
Municipal Bonds	Debt obligations of states, cities, or towns or their agencies.	Interest exempt from federal tax and in state where issued. Interest on certain private activity bonds can be subject to AMT.
Corporate Bonds	Debt obligations of corporations.	Annual interest taxed. Special rules for bond premium and discount: the amount paid above or below a bond's face value.
Zero Coupon Bonds	Fixed rate debt obligations of U.S. Government, state or corporation. No annual interest paid. All earned interest paid at maturity.	U.S. Government and corporate interest taxable each year as though it had been received. State obligation interest is tax exempt.
Stock, Common and Preferred	Security denoting units of equity ownership in a corporation.	Dividends, when paid, generally taxable. Appreciation, if any, taxed when stock sold, generally at a favorable tax rate. Losses are deductible but subject to limitations.
Mutual Fund Shares	Shares in a company that invests money from many investors to buy stocks, or bonds, or both, in many corporations. Some funds invest in government bonds only.	The fund's earnings paid to shareholders are treated as dividends or capital gains. Dividends may be taxable or exempt depending upon their source.

10

Retirement Planning

Introduction

A major concern for most middle-aged individuals is the accumulation of sufficient funds to ensure a secure retirement. However, retirement planning is probably one of the most neglected aspects of personal financial planning. This chapter offers ideas to help you develop your retirement strategies and objectives. To formulate a sound retirement plan, you need to answer two questions: How much will I need? And where will it come from? This chapter can help you get started.

If you begin at an early enough age, retirement planning can help ensure that you and your spouse will be provided for adequately. Retirement planning is closely allied with investment planning and the cash flow analysis process described in this chapter.

A retirement planning timetable depends on your personal circumstances and goals. Two guidelines exist, though. First, it's never too soon to plan for retirement, and second, it's never too late. Late-in-life planning doesn't mean that you won't be able to retire on your timetable. Rather, it's simply more difficult to accumulate the necessary funds.

Planning for Retirement Expenditures

As with any phase of personal financial planning, the starting point is identifying your objectives. When considering how much money you will need to accumulate to meet your retirement objectives, three factors predominate:

1. **Your Current Standard of Living and the Amount of Cash Flow Needed to Maintain this Standard.** A cash flow analysis for the current year should be prepared. This involves determining your annual cash re-

179

ceipts from all sources, including compensation and income from investments, and comparing that total to your annual expenditures including housing, food, transportation, and entertainment. From this analysis, you can develop a projection for your first year of retirement of how much income you will need on an annual basis. If possible, factor in the costs based on where you think you would like to live when you retire. There can be substantial differences between the cost of living in different parts of the country—Manhattan versus parts of Florida, for example. (See Chapter 3 for a discussion about domicile.)

2. **Medical Expenses and Medical Insurance Costs.** Because the medical expenses associated with a serious illness can destroy the best-made retirement plan, medical insurance coverage must be carefully evaluated.

3. **The Level of Discretionary Expenditures You Want (or Need).** A review of the discretionary expenditures you plan to make for items such as a new or second home or to assist children or grandchildren with educational costs will help determine how much in additional funds you will have to set aside to meet your objectives.

Retirement Cash Flow and Inflation

When planning for retirement expenditures, one especially important consideration is the effect of inflation.

Because you probably don't plan to work during retirement, your income will in large part be fixed. As a result, inflation is of particular concern. Inflation robs you of buying power and can erode the best retirement plan.

Thus, your retirement plans need to consider inflation. As a general rule, this requires investments in assets that have historically been good inflation hedges, such as common stocks and quality real estate. The income streams from these types of assets tend to increase with inflation (as corporate earnings and rents rise). Note, however, that these types of investments increase your exposure to the risks of the market. If you invest in fixed income securities it is important not to invest all of your assets in securities of a single maturity. By purchasing fixed income investments of varying maturities, both short-term and long-term, you retain flexibility to deal with changing interest rates which usually rise as inflation rises.

Sources of Retirement Income

The three main sources of retirement income are company retirement plans, your own retirement savings, and Social

Security. For many individuals, the absence of any one of these can cripple a secure retirement.

Company Retirement Plans

The most important aspect of any company retirement plan is understanding the benefits provided by the plan and the payment options available.

There are two basic choices on how benefits will be paid from a plan:

Joint and Survivor Annuities.

In most instances, benefits will be paid in the form of an annuity, meaning that the employee (and spouse, if married) will receive monthly payments for as long as they live. Generally, a joint and survivor annuity is offered under which an annuity is paid for the joint lives of the employee and spouse. If the employee dies before his or her spouse, a reduced amount (as elected by the spouse but usually equal to one-half of the initial payment amount) is paid for the remainder of the survivor's life.

Lump-Sum Payments.

Some plans may offer a "lump-sum" option, meaning that the entire retirement amount allocated to an employee is paid in a single sum. All pension plans and most other retirement plans require that *both* spouses waive the right to a joint and survivor annuity in order for a lump-sum distribution to be made.

Tax Treatment of Annuities and Lump-sum Payments.

In general, the entire amount of an annuity received each month will be taxable as ordinary income. If you contributed on an after-tax basis to your annuity retirement program, a special rule allows you to recover tax-free the amount of your contribution, spread out over the length of the annuity. This is accomplished through the use of an "exclusion ratio," which compares your contributions in the annuity to the total amount expected to be received.

Unlike the ordinary income treatment applicable to annuities, qualified lump-sum distributions may be entitled to special tax treatment. (See discussion under Pensions or Annuities, pages 24–27 in Chapter 1.)

> ### TaxSaver
>
> **Which Plan To Choose.** *If your employer's qualified retirement plans offer the choice, should you select annuity payments or a lump-sum payout?*
>
> *Your choice depends on various factors, including the amount of the distribution, your marginal tax bracket during retirement, the pretax yield that can be earned on investments, your expected distribution pe-*

riod, and the degree of control you want over your investments.

Since annuities generally provide for monthly payments over the lifetime of a retired employee and his or her spouse, recipients can expect a steady stream of payments each and every month no matter how long they live. A lump-sum fund, however, could be prematurely exhausted if a retired couple were to outlive their life expectancies.

On the other hand, if you choose annuity payments and you or your spouse dies prematurely, any unpaid portion of your account balance could be forfeited. With a lump-sum distribution, the retiree gets possession of the full amount of his or her account balance up front. Whatever is left over at the retiree's death is available to pass on to heirs.

Some retirees welcome the discipline imposed by receiving a monthly annuity check. It forces you to stick to a monthly budget, which may be similar to how you were used to managing money during your working years. Receiving a large lump sum up front may present too much of a temptation to overspend or may make it difficult to manage a budget.

However, being locked into monthly annuity payments prevents you from pulling out extra funds if needed for an emergency or taking advantage of an opportunity. Lump-sum recipients have full access to their account assets, as needed.

Moreover, unless annuity payments are indexed or variable, inflation will steadily erode your purchasing power. Lump-sum proceeds, on the other hand, can be invested in assets that provide a hedge against inflation.

Recipients of a lump-sum distribution have complete flexibility to invest and manage their account assets as they choose. Of course, they also face the risk that poor investment results may leave them with insufficient retirement income. If you select an annuity, the promise of a predictable level of monthly payments relieves you of any investment burden.

To figure out the best payment scheme for you, you need to consider both the income tax ramifications of each type of distribution and your personal objectives for the use of the funds. If you are comfortable about directly managing your retirement funds, the investment flexibility and tax-planning opportunities available with a lump-sum distribution normally are better suited to your personal financial objectives.

IRAs, Keogh Plans, and Simplified Employee Pensions (SEPs)

An important source of retirement savings can be an IRA, a Keogh plan, or a Simplified Employee Pension (SEP). An individual retirement arrangement (IRA) is a personal retirement saving plan where the earnings and appreciation on funds you invest compound "tax-free" until you begin withdrawals. If you are self-employed and own your own business, you may have a retirement plan commonly known as a Keogh plan. SEPs are usually set up by employers to make contributions toward their own (if self-employed) and their employees' retirement. All three plans, as well as tax strategies related to each of them, are discussed in Chapter 4.

Retirement Investment Strategy

There are many other ways to save for retirement; in some cases an investment can meet both your current lifetime objectives and your retirement objectives. For example, buying a vacation home *might* be appropriate both as a purchase you can enjoy currently and as an investment consistent with your retirement goals. You needn't be concerned about simply putting money away if your investment strategies are consistent with your long-range retirement goals. Nearly any investment can be used toward funding your retirement. However, as you near retirement a few changes in your investment strategies are frequently appropriate.

Investment Risk. The amount of investment risk assumed should probably be reduced—especially if you have already built up a retirement fund that meets your objectives. Should risky investments fail while retirement is decades away, you'll have time to regroup. But if investments sour at, say, age 62, you may not have enough time to recoup the losses.

Liquid Assets. Your need for liquidity should be matched to your investments. A carefully planned strategy of converting illiquid assets (which served you well during your earning years) into more liquid assets that you can consume during retirement years should be pursued. The idea is to avoid forced sales of illiquid assets at inopportune times causing, among other things, unplanned tax liabilities.

Cash Flow. If you need current cash flow for living expenses, you should generally choose steady income over potential appreciation.

Diversification. Diversification—that is, not putting all your eggs in one basket—enables you to reduce the impact that an underperforming or failed investment could have over your entire portfolio. Diversification entails spreading your investment dollars across different asset categories, like stocks, bonds, and real estate, and among different investments within each category. Determining how much and in what assets and asset categories to invest depends upon your attitude toward risk and your financial objectives. However, even as you approach retirement and begin to shift your portfolio toward more conservative and liquid assets, it is important to keep your investments diversified.

Social Security

Social Security is an essential ingredient of many personal retirement plans.

Figuring Your Benefit. The calculation of your probable monthly benefit is complicated. To save time and headaches, you can request an estimate of your tentative benefits by filing Form SSA-7004-PC, "Request for Earnings and Benefit Estimate Statement." The form is simple to complete and the information could be invaluable to your personal planning. Copies of the form can be obtained from your local Social Security office or by calling (800) 772-1213.

The maximum monthly benefit for a 65-year-old worker retiring in 1994 is $1,147. For each year short of the current normal retirement age of 65 that you retire, the maximum entitlement is reduced. The earliest age at which you're eligible to receive retirement checks is 62, with a 20% reduction in benefits. For those born after 1937, the normal retirement age is scheduled to increase gradually to age 67. Retirement benefits will still be available to these workers at age 62, but will be further reduced.

Working Beyond Age 65. Regardless of your age, if you work, your wages or self-employment income are subject to Social Security and Medicare taxes. On the other hand, there's a reward for working past normal retirement age. For each month you postpone collecting your Social Security benefits beyond age 65 (and before age 70) your retirement benefit is increased by what's called a "delayed retirement credit." The table below shows the monthly and maximum yearly delayed retirement credit for individuals who will reach 65 by 2003.

Delayed Retirement Credit

Turn 65 in	Monthly Credit	Maximum Yearly Credit*
1994 or 1995	3/8 of 1%	4.5%
1996 or 1997	5/12 of 1%	5.0%
1998 or 1999	11/24 of 1%	5.5%
2000 or 2001	1/2 of 1%	6.0%
2002 or 2003	13/24 of 1%	6.5%

*The maximum yearly credit increases by ½ of 1% every other year up to a ceiling of 8% for those turning 65 in 2008 or beyond.

How to Lose Benefits. You can be penalized if you take Social Security benefits and continue to work. For 1994, retirees between ages 65 and 69 lose $1 in benefits for every $3 earned above $11,160. Recipients under 65 forfeit $1 of benefits for each $2 earned over $8,040. At age 70 or over, there are no limits on how much you may earn.

Note that this rule is limited to *earned* income. So, for example, dividends and interest income don't jeopardize benefits, no matter what their amount.

Your spouse can receive either one-half your monthly benefit (scaled back if benefits begin before age 65) or his or her own individual entitlement based on personal earnings, if higher. As long as you were married for at least ten years, your former spouse remains entitled to a benefit equal to half your monthly benefit even after a divorce.

Income Tax on Benefits. Starting in 1994, up to 85 percent of Social Security benefits may be subject to federal (and perhaps state) income taxes. See section on Social Security benefits in Chapter 1.

Early vs. Late Retirement. Generally, you'll come out ahead by withdrawing your Social Security benefits early—e.g., at age 62—rather than waiting to age 65, even though the monthly benefit may be 20% less. That's because you'll have received three additional years of benefits. Mathematically, it would take about 12 years—until age 77—for the higher benefits available based on retirement at age 65 to catch up. And this is calculated before taking into account earnings on the investment of the benefits during the intervening years. However, if you are going to continue to work after age 62, there is the possibility of your losing some of your benefits.

Taxes on Wages and Self-Employment Income. The Social Security program and the Medicare program are financed by a payroll tax on both the employee and the employer and by a self-employment tax. See the appendices for tax rate information.

11

Estate and Gift Planning

Introduction

Although it is not possible to take it with you, with careful thought and astute planning it is possible to provide your heirs, loved ones and friends with a significant portion of your wealth. This chapter discusses the estate tax, the gift tax, and the generation-skipping tax. The chapter also contains some ideas and techniques in estate planning that may aid you in making your plans for the future.

Frequent tax law changes continue to have a significant impact on estate planning. This makes it more difficult to protect your assets from the ravages of time unless you have planned effectively. Because of these changes, and because as you go through life your goals and expectations are also constantly changing, you should periodically review the impact of these changes on your estate and gift tax plan. This review will help you: (1) discover how your objectives may have changed; (2) assess whether your plan can still achieve your objectives; and (3) determine how recent legislative changes may have affected existing plans and whether you can accomplish your goals more advantageously.

This chapter is intended as an introduction to estate planning. You should seek professional advice especially if your financial or family situation is complicated; if you own interests in closely-held corporations or other illiquid assets; or if your spouse is not a U.S. citizen.

Getting Started

A periodic review of your personal financial plan makes sense. Filing an annual income tax return forces most taxpayers to look over their situation. Yet many—perhaps most—individuals allow years to go by without adequately considering possible changes in property holdings or key provisions in wills and trusts. To be on the safe side, you should periodically reappraise the following six basic tax and financial considerations:

1. Have there been any changes in the tax laws or rulings that might adversely affect your present estate plan?
2. Does your estate have sufficient cash or other liquid assets to take care of debts, taxes, funeral expenses, and estate administration expenses?
3. Have there been any changes in your family's circumstances—births, adoptions, deaths, marriages, illness or disability, special schooling needs, etc.—that might call for revisions in your estate plan?
4. Should you initiate a plan to give away some of your assets as gifts to your children, to other family members, or to charitable institutions? If you have already been giving gifts, should you continue to do so? Which assets are most appropriate for such a gift program?
5. Is the current form of ownership of your family assets appropriate for saving taxes and expenses and providing you the flexibility you need to deal with unexpected situations?
6. Have you properly designated a beneficiary for, and decided on the form of, payment of distributions from qualified employee benefit programs?

Do You Need A Will?

A will is a legal document that specifies who receives what at your death and who will manage your estate.

Even if you die without a will, you already have an estate plan of sorts. Generally, assets you own jointly with another person—a bank account, stock, personal residence, or business interest, or where you have designated a particular beneficiary as under an insurance policy—will be passed on to the joint tenant or designated beneficiary. But, assets you own in your name alone will be passed on in accordance with your state's intestacy laws.

If you die without a will (i.e., intestate), state laws detail how your estate is divided up among your surviving spouse, children, and parents and what happens when there is no surviving spouse. It is rare for intestate distribution to conform with the wishes of the decedent.

The biggest problem for many dying without a will is not the distribution of the property, but rather the guardianship of minor children. If both parents die without a will that directs who will be guardian of a minor child, the court and the state social welfare department will make the decision. So, even if you do not have enough assets to have to pay federal estate tax, a will might be very desirable, if only for nontax reasons.

Estate Tax Fundamentals

Who Has to Pay Federal Estate Tax?

The law provides two major exemptions from federal estate tax:

1. For estates under $10 million, there is no federal tax on the first $600,000 of assets.
2. There is an unlimited marital deduction. Any amount given or left at death to a surviving spouse, whether given outright or in certain types of trusts, is exempt from federal estate tax. For more information, see the discussion later in this chapter.

These exemptions certainly make planning easier for most Americans, but they shouldn't lull you into thinking that estate planning is unnecessary. You may be worth more than you think. Many middle-class families now own homes that are worth several times what they cost. Moreover, stock prices have tripled over the last 20 years, even though in constant dollar terms they have remained practically flat. If the future continues to mirror the past, inflationary trends will continue to inflate values. Even if your assets currently do not exceed $600,000, at the time of your death they might.

How to Value Your Estate

Assets Subject to Estate Tax. Federal estate tax is a levy on the transfer of property at death. Your gross estate will include the value of all property to the extent of your interest in it at the time of death. Following are types of property included in your gross estate by law:

Tangible Personal Property, Real Estate, and Other Assets. This category includes property you own that is transmitted at death according to provisions of a will or state intestacy laws. Such property is commonly referred to as the probate estate. Examples: real estate, stocks, bonds, furniture, personal effects, jewelry, works of art, an interest in a partnership, an interest in a sole proprietorship, a bank account, and a promissory note or other evidence of indebtedness you hold.

Jointly Owned Property. Only one-half of the value of property owned by a husband and wife as joint tenants with right of survivorship will be included in the estate of the first spouse to die. The unlimited marital deduction prevents the transfer of the property from the deceased to the surviving spouse from being subject to federal estate tax. Upon the survivor's death, however, the entire property will be subject to tax (assuming it is still held at the time of death).

If the joint tenants are not married, the entire value of the property is included in the gross estate of the first to die unless the estate can prove that all or part of the payment for acquiring the property was actually furnished by the other joint owner. If you and another joint owner acquired property by gift or inheritance, only your fractional share of the property is included.

Life Insurance. Your gross estate will include life insurance proceeds that are received (1) by your estate or (2) by other beneficiaries if you own all or part of the policies at the time of your death. "Ownership" includes the power to change the beneficiary of the policy, the right to cancel the policy and receive the cash value, the right to borrow against the policy, and the right to assign the policy.

TAXSAVER

You can transfer a life insurance policy and ownership of the policy to your spouse or children or to a trust for your family's benefit and reap significant tax advantages. To be effective in keeping the proceeds out of your estate, the gift must be made more than three years before death. The three-year waiting period can be avoided for a newly purchased policy if proper steps are taken to have someone else (e.g., a trustee of an irrevocable trust) apply for the policy. These types of irrevocable life insurance trusts can be structured so that you contribute money each year to the trust for paying premiums, with the transfers often qualifying for the annual gift tax exclusion (explained on page 195). The trust therefore can be viewed as a way to get insurance proceeds to your heirs without gift or estate tax.

Employee Benefits. The value of payments from qualified pension plans and other retirement plans payable to surviving beneficiaries of an employee (or the owner, in the case of a Keogh/HR 10 plan) generally is included in your gross estate.

Certain Gifts and Gift Tax Paid Within Three Years of Death. Gifts of property made during your lifetime are generally not included in your gross estate, but must be figured in the estate tax calculation if they exceed the $10,000 annual gift tax exclusion (discussed later). However, as discussed above, life insurance proceeds are included if the policies or ownership of the policies were given away within three years of your death (see Tax Saver, above). Also included is any gift tax you have paid within three years of your death. Lifetime gifts that a decedent retains some interest in (e.g., a life income interest) or control over (e.g., voting rights in stock given as a gift) will be included in the decedent's gross estate.

Allowable Deductions. Deductions are allowed for funeral and administration expenses of the estate, and debts, unpaid mortgages, and other indebtedness on property included in the gross estate. Also allowed are such special deductions as the marital deduction and the charitable deduction. (See later sections for more details on these special deductions.)

Funeral and Administration Expenses. Deductible funeral expenses include burial costs, costs for a burial lot, costs for future care of a gravesite, etc. Deductible administration costs include executor's commissions, attorney's fees, accounting fees, appraisal fees, and court costs.

Other Deductible Estate Expenses. To be deductible, debts must be enforceable personal obligations of the decedent, such as outstanding mortgages or personal bank loans, auto loans, credit card balances, utility bills, etc. The deductible amount also includes any interest accrued on such debt at the date of death. Transfers made under a marital property settlement incident to a divorce may be treated as estate expenses. Taxes are also deductible debts if they are accrued and unpaid at date of death. Deductible taxes include accrued property taxes, gift taxes unpaid at death, and income taxes.

Valuing Estate Property. Property is included in an estate at its "fair market value," which is the price at which property would change hands between a willing buyer and a willing seller. Property that trades on an established market may be valued easily. For example, publicly traded stocks and bonds are valued based on the average of the high and low selling price on the date of death (or, if elected, the date six months after death). However, interests in closely held businesses or partnerships must generally be appraised taking into account the business's assets, earning capacity, and other factors. An accountant can assist you in appraising business interests for estate or gift tax valuation purposes.

Your gross estate is valued as of the date of your death or six months later (also known as the alternative valuation date), whichever your personal representative elects. An election to value the estate six months after date of death will apply to all assets in the estate, but is available only if the election results in a decrease in your estate tax liability. The amount remaining after subtracting any allowable deductions is your taxable estate. The federal estate tax is computed on this amount.

Basis to Beneficiaries

Property acquired from a decedent generally gets a new basis. In most cases, the new basis is the fair market value at date of death or alternative valuation date, whichever is used for estate tax purposes.

How Your Estate is Taxed

Tax Rates. The federal estate tax is progressive, ranging from a marginal rate of 18% to 55%. The 55% top rate applies to estates larger than $3 million. (See the table of rates in the Appendix.)

As noted previously, the first $600,000 of gifts and transfers at death are exempt from estate tax because of the unified credit (see below). A surcharge of 5% is imposed on taxable estates in excess of $10 million to phase out the unified credit and the benefit of the graduated rates.

Credits. Your estate can claim certain credits before figuring the amount of federal estate tax owed. The credits include:

Unified Estate and Gift Tax Credit. Each individual is entitled to a so-called "unified credit" of $192,800. This is the amount of tax generated by a transfer of $600,000. In other words, no federal estate or gift taxes will be assessed on the first $600,000 of an individual's combined taxable gifts and transfers at death. To the extent that the credit has been used to offset lifetime gifts, the credit against the estate tax is reduced.

If the amount you give away during your lifetime and in your estate exceeds $10 million, an additional 5% tax is imposed to effectively phase out the benefit of the unified credit and progressive estate tax rates. This phaseout means that a taxable estate of $21,040,000 or more pays tax at a rate of 55% on every dollar.

State Death Tax Credit. A credit is allowed for estate or inheritance taxes paid to any state or the District of Columbia. The tax must actually be paid on property included in the gross estate. The credit is limited to an amount computed under a graduated rate table based on the amount of the taxable estate, reduced by $60,000. (See the table in the Appendix.)

Foreign Death Tax Credit. A credit is allowed against the federal estate tax for any death taxes actually paid to a foreign country, Puerto Rico, or the Virgin Islands on property that is also subject to the federal estate tax. The credit is limited to the U.S. tax attributable to the property taxed by the foreign country.

Credit for Tax on Prior Transfers. Under certain circumstances a credit is allowed against the federal estate tax for part or all of any estate tax paid on property transferred to the present decedent.

State Tax Considerations. All states impose some kind of inheritance or estate tax. In many states, the estate tax is simply the amount of the federal credit for state death taxes. Consequently, in these states, if there is no federal tax, due to the unified credit, there is also no state tax. However, some states have estate or inheritance taxes which are not tied to the federal credit. Furthermore, some states do not allow an unlimited marital deduction, as the federal government does. In these states, state death tax considerations may influence how your estate plan should be structured.

The Marital Deduction. One of the most significant tax-saving provisions of the law is the marital deduction. As its name implies, it is a special deduction available only to married persons. An estate is allowed an unlimited deduction for the value of property transferred to the spouse of the deceased. Thus, in effect, the marital deduction permits a couple to postpone paying any estate tax until the surviving spouse dies.

TAXSAVER

An important feature of the marital deduction is that by placing property in a special trust it can be arranged for your spouse to receive a lifetime income interest in the property, with you determining who eventually receives the property.

TAXSAVER

Most married individuals will want to take advantage of both the unified credit and the unlimited marital deduction to reduce the federal estate tax to zero in the estate of the first spouse to die. (See the following examples about several ways this can be done.)

The marital deduction is unavailable for property transferred by gift or at death to a surviving spouse who is not a U.S. citizen at the time the transfer is made. Instead, the law provides that tax-free gifts to a non-U.S. citizen spouse can only total $100,000 per year. There is, however, no lifetime limit to the total value of gifts you can give tax-free to a spouse who is not a U.S. citizen.

TAXSAVER

Your will can be drafted so that your property is placed in a special type of trust that benefits a spouse who is not a U.S. citizen. The trust enables estate tax on the property to be postponed until the property is distributed out of the trust or the surviving spouse dies. This type of trust is called a Qualified Domestic Trust. It permits property to qualify for the marital deduction if certain requirements—which provide that the property will eventually be subject to estate tax—are met.

Examples: Here are three examples for computing the gross estate, the taxable estate, and the estate tax due for three different size estates of married individuals, each of whom was the first of the two spouses to die.

At his death, Tom had $3,000 in savings and checking accounts, 100 shares of marketable securities worth $70 each, and a residence worth $175,000. Tom's personal property consisted largely of a collection of rare coins valued at $80,000. The rest of his property included his car, clothing, and other personal effects. In addition, Tom accumulated $105,000 in his employer's deferred bonus and 401(k) plans, and his estate was the beneficiary of a whole-life insurance policy and an employer-maintained group-term policy.

Harriet's and Dick's gross estates were larger than Tom's. And there were other differences, as well. Harriet was the sole proprietor of a consulting business valued at $450,000 at the time of her death. Dick was a law firm partner whose interest in the firm was valued at $525,000 when he died. Dick also owned a beach house, which his father had willed to him outright.

Step 1: Computing the gross estate.

	Computing the gross estate of		
	Tom	Harriet	Dick
Assets			
Cash	$3,000	$15,000	$60,000
Marketable securities	7,000	20,000	50,000
Business equity	0	450,000	525,000
Residence	175,000	235,000	185,000
Vacation residence	0	0	90,000
Personal property	95,000	25,000	40,000
Deferred compensation	105,000	25,000	75,000
Ordinary life insurance	10,000	80,000	570,000
Group-term insurance	50,000	50,000	75,000
Gross estate	$445,000	$900,000	$1,670,000

Step 2: Computing your taxable estate.

The executor of your estate will subtract from the total value of your gross estate all those deductions allowable under the tax law, including the marital deduction.

Tom's will provided that his wife was to receive his total estate after payment of debts, thereby reducing the taxable value of the estate to zero. Tom could do this because of the unlimited marital deduction (discussed above).

In Harriet's case, the size of her estate's marital deduction was the product of some planning. The deduction was designed to dovetail with the $600,000 unified credit equivalent in order to eliminate any estate tax liability.

Dick's estate planned to use less than the full amount of the marital deduction that could have been used. He and his wife, Elaine, decided that with his bequest and her separate assets, she would not require ownership of all of Dick's estate. Thus, because of their children's needs, a decision was made to give more than $600,000 of his assets to them, even though taxes would be paid by his estate. The plan could have been structured to pay no taxes at the time of Dick's death if he were to leave only $600,000 to the children with the rest going to Elaine. The children could have then received the additional assets from Elaine as gifts or from her estate, and depending on the size of her estate, the amount of taxes she would pay may be more or less than in their original plan.

	Tom	*Harriet*	*Dick*
Gross estate	$445,000	$900,000	$1,670,000
Deductions			
Funeral expenses	3,000	4,000	6,000
Estate administration expenses	2,000	15,000	44,000
Debts	2,000	1,000	2,000
Mortgages	38,000	28,000	48,000
Marital deduction	400,000	250,000	550,000
Charitable deductions	0	2,000	20,000
Total deduction	$445,000	$300,000	$ 670,000
Taxable estate	$ 0	$600,000	$1,000,000

Step 3: Computing the federal estate tax.

Computing federal estate tax is straightforward. A "tentative" tax is computed using the tax rate tables. Then, the unified credit ($192,800 maximum) and any allowable credit for state death taxes paid are applied as direct, dollar-for-dollar offsets against the tentative tax specified in the federal estate tax tables for your taxable estate. Estates over $10 million must add back the 5% surtax discussed previously.

	Tom	Harriet	Dick
Gross estate	$445,000	$900,000	$1,670,000
Deductions	445,000	300,000	670,000
Taxable estate	0	600,000	1,000,000
Tentative tax	0	192,800	345,800
Unified credit	0	192,800	192,800
State tax credit	0	0	33,200
Estate tax	$ 0	$ 0	$ 119,800

Gift Tax Fundamentals

You might think that the government would make it easy to give money away to non-charitable donees. In some respects it does. You can give up to $10,000 ($20,000 if you file a joint return and your spouse consents) annually to as many individuals as you want without paying any gift tax. But, above that amount, gift tax is imposed. The reason is that without such a tax people could escape death taxes—assuming they were willing to give away a large portion of their property before death.

Any gifts you give above the annual amount that is exempt from tax is, in effect, included in your estate when you die. The value of the gift is not the value at the date of your death but the value at the time you gave the gift. In addition, there are some special rules. A gift of life insurance, for example, made within three years of your death will be included in your gross estate at its full face value. Any gift tax you pay on gifts made within three years of your death is also added to the value of your taxable estate. Nevertheless, giving gifts can substantially reduce your overall gift and estate transfer taxes as well as fulfilling other desires. But gift-giving does require careful planning—and the commitment to make the gifts before it is too late.

Basis to the Recipient of a Gift

In general, the basis of appreciated property acquired by gift is the donor's basis for tax purposes. If a gift tax return was filed, the donee should examine it for information regarding the donor's basis, the holding period, and depreciation recapture. The basis of gifts received after 1976 is increased by the amount of the federal gift tax attributable to the difference between the donor's basis and the gift's fair market value, if higher as of the date of gift.

How to Give Tax-Free Gifts
The Gift Tax Annual Exclusion. You may give up to $10,000 each year to as many individuals as you want without incurring any gift tax. And, if your spouse joins in making the gift (by signing a consent on a gift tax return),

you may give $20,000 to each person annually without paying any tax. But this annual gift tax exclusion applies only to gifts of "present interests"—items that can be used, possessed, and enjoyed presently. Examples of a gift of a present interest include gifts of money, holiday presents, etc.

Gifts of "future interests" do not qualify for the annual exclusion. Gifts of future interests include remainder interests, reversions, or any other interest that won't give the recipient the right to possess, enjoy or profit from the gift until some future date or time. An exception: gifts in trust to minors are subject to special rules that may allow an otherwise future interest to qualify for the annual exclusion.

Gifts to Pay Medical or Educational Expenses.
In addition to the annual exclusion, an unlimited gift tax exclusion is available to pay someone's medical or educational expenses. The beneficiary does not have to be your dependent or even related to you, although payment of a grandchild's expenses is perhaps the most common use of the exclusion.

TaxSaver

In order for a gift to be exempt from taxes, you must make the payment directly to the medical or educational institution providing the service. The beneficiary of the gift should not actually receive the payment. In addition, educational expenses include only tuition. Room and board, books, and other fees will not qualify for the unlimited exclusion, although they can, of course, qualify for the annual gift tax exclusion.

TaxSaver

You can reduce your taxable estate substantially through a planned annual program of $10,000 (or $20,000 if you are married) gifts. All gifts within the exclusion limits are exempt from federal estate taxes. In addition, outright gifts that qualify for the annual exclusion are also protected from generation-skipping transfer taxes (see page 201). Obviously, you cannot hope to significantly reduce the tax your estate will pay by making gifts in a single year. But, the estate tax savings can be substantial if you embark upon a carefully planned gift-giving program that extends for a number of years before your death.

TaxSaver

Another major tax advantage of making a gift is that future appreciation in the gift's value and after-tax in-

come earned on the property are not included in your estate.

Example: Suppose you give stocks worth $50,000 to your children now. If you die in 10 years and the stock is worth $130,000, the $80,000 of appreciation will not be included in your estate. Nor will you (or your estate) include any dividends paid on the stock after the gift.

Gift Tax Charitable Contribution Deduction.
An unlimited gift tax charitable deduction is available for gifts to certain charitable organizations.

The Gift Tax Marital Deduction.
The gift tax marital deduction allows you to transfer unlimited amounts of property during your lifetime to your spouse without gift tax. Property can be transferred outright or in trust. Also, a gift of a lifetime income interest in property to your spouse can qualify for the marital deduction, if it is structured properly. You should consult with your tax advisor.

TAXSAVER

The gift tax marital deduction can help you lower the taxes on your estate. Consider: In order for one spouse to make full use of his or her unified credit, it may be desirable to make gifts to that spouse so that he or she will have an estate at least equal to $600,000— the amount of assets required to make full use of the unified credit. Since the gift tax marital deduction allows you to make unlimited tax-free transfers to your spouse, you can build up his or her assets without worrying that your gifts will be taxable.

Some words of caution: The marital deduction is not allowed for gifts to a spouse who is not a U.S. citizen. (See section on the marital deduction under estate tax fundamentals earlier in this chapter.) Furthermore, the amount of the gift tax marital deduction for a particular state may differ from the federal amount. It is therefore vital to get professional advice before making any significant gifts.

Example: Giving Gifts Without Paying Gift Tax.
This example illustrates how you can set up a substantial gift program and avoid paying any gift tax. Note, however, that part of the unified credit is being used. (The unified credit is discussed earlier in this chapter.)

During the course of one year, James made outright gifts of $100,000 to his wife Helen, and $40,000 to each of his three children, for a total of $220,000.

James incurred no gift tax on Helen's gift because of the $10,000 annual exclusion and the unlimited marital deduction. James and Helen were entitled to a total of $60,000 in annual exclusions (based on $20,000 for each child) because they elected to treat one-half of those gifts as made by Helen. That still leaves, however, a taxable gift of $60,000 to the three children. By applying a portion of their unified credits, James and Helen can entirely eliminate paying gift tax. Assuming that this was their first gift using their unified credits they will have reduced the remaining assets in their estates that will be considered tax-free from $600,000 to $570,000 respectively.

E&Y FOCUS: How Paying Gift Tax Can Reduce Your Overall Taxes

Most of us have a natural aversion to paying taxes—and gift taxes are no exception. However, if you have a sizable estate that is well in excess of what you feel you need to live on, it might be worthwhile to consider how paying gift taxes *now* can save on estate taxes *later*. The end result is that more of your assets bypass the IRS and reach your heirs.

Example: Here's a simple example to show how paying gift tax can put more money in your heirs' hands. Assume Chris and Mimi have each survived their spouses and now have $2.5 million of liquid assets. Chris holds on to the full $2.5 million until death, while Mimi makes a gift of $1 million to her children (in addition to annual gifts that are excluded from tax). Assuming neither had previously made taxable gifts and Mimi lives for three years after the gift, this is how their taxes would compare:

	Chris	
Taxable estate		$2,500,000
Federal estate tax		833,000
Net estate to heirs		$1,667,000

	Mimi	
Pre-gift estate		$2,500,000
Taxable gift	$1,000,000	
Gift tax paid	153,000	
Estate reduction		1,153,000
Taxable estate		$1,347,000
Federal estate tax		605,030
Net estate to heirs		$ 741,970
Plus gift		1,000,000
Total to heirs		$1,741,970

By making the gift and paying gift taxes, the gift tax of $153,000 was removed from Mimi's estate.

This resulted in $74,970 more of Mimi's estate actually getting to Mimi's children. That doesn't even take into account the benefit of keeping the post-gift appreciation and after-tax income on the $1 million out of Mimi's taxable estate! The one catch is that the gift must be made more than three years before death, or the gift taxes will be brought back into your estate. Of course, you must be comfortable with the non-tax consequences of making a large gift that will deplete your estate.

Giving Gifts to Minors

Before a parent or grandparent gives a gift to a minor child, certain legal and practical matters need to be considered. Because a child typically cannot manage his or her own affairs and because parents usually do not want to give young children unfettered control over gift property, some special arrangements need to be made. The tax law, too, poses some challenges since only gifts of "present interest"—property for the beneficiary's immediate enjoyment—qualify for the $10,000 annual gift tax exclusion. Furthermore, state laws frequently discourage outright gifts to minors. Many states commonly prohibit or discourage the registration of securities in the name of a minor and impose supervisory restrictions upon the sale of a minor's property. Consequently, gifts to minors can take different forms and have different tax consequences.

Outright Gifts. The $10,000 annual gift tax exclusion is available for these gifts unless the property being given as a gift is a "future interest." Income from the property is taxed to the minor, and the property is included in the minor's estate if he or she should die. However, because of the "kiddie tax," which requires that a child's income be taxed at the parent's rate until the child reaches age 14, your child may actually be taxed at your rates on any income he or she receives from the property.

Guardianship. A guardianship is an arrangement where property is under a guardian's legal control subject to formal (and possibly burdensome) accounting to a court. The gift, income, and estate tax consequences are the same as for outright gifts. Thus, such gifts also qualify for the $10,000 gift tax exclusion.

Custodial Arrangements. To overcome the legal disability minors have in owning property outright, all 50 states, the District of Columbia, and the Virgin Islands have adopted the Uniform Gifts (or Transfers) to Minors Act. Under this act, a custodian may hold both cash and securities for a minor until he or she reaches adulthood. Securities may be registered in the name of any bank, trust company, or adult as custodian for the minor. Custodial gifts to minors are considered completed gifts for gift tax purposes, and such gifts are eligible for the annual gift tax exclusion. The income from the gift property during the custodial period is taxable to the minor (subject to kiddie tax provisions). However, income used for your minor child's maintenance and support is taxable to you as the person legally obligated to support the minor whether or not you are the donor of a gift or the child's custodian.

TAXSAVER

Generally, you should not act as custodian of your own gifts to your minor child. If you do and if you die before your child becomes an adult, the value of your gift will be included in your estate. Instead, your spouse may be the custodian. If you and your spouse both make gifts to your minor child, in essence splitting your gifts to take advantage of the annual gift tax exclusion, you should consider making a third party the custodian for the child.

Present Interest Trust. Special rules enacted by Congress provide a method of making gifts to minors that qualify for the annual exclusion. A gift to a qualifying trust established for an individual under the age of 21 will be considered a gift of a present interest and qualify for the $10,000 annual gift tax exclusion. The trust instrument must provide that the gift property and its income:

- May be expended for the benefit of the beneficiary before reaching age 21, and
- To the extent not so expended, will pass to the beneficiary upon becoming age 21.

If the child dies before reaching age 21, the funds must be payable to the child's estate or as the child may designate under a general power of appointment. This rule applies to trusts for children under the age of 21, even if a state law has reduced the age of majority to age 19 or 18.

Crummey Trust. This is a different type of trust to which you can transfer property and have the gift qualify for the annual gift tax exclusion. The distinguishing characteristic of a Crummey trust (which takes its name from a court case) is that it gives the beneficiary the annual right to demand distributions from the trust equal to the lesser of the amount of the contributions to the trust during the year or some specified amount (e.g., $5,000 or 5% of the trusts's value). The beneficiary (or legal guardian) must be notified of the power to withdraw the body of the trust, although the power is permitted to lapse or terminate after a short period of time, such as 30 days. If the beneficiary fails to make a demand during the window period, after being notified that a contribution was made, the right lapses for that year's contributions. To the extent the beneficiary (or guardian) has the right to demand distribution of the year's contribution, that contribution is considered a "present interest" and, therefore, qualifies for the annual gift tax exclusion.

In all other respects, the Crummey trust is very flexible. The trustee can be required to accumulate income until the child reaches a specified age above age 21. The trustee also can be restricted to using trust assets and income for specific purposes (e.g., college expenses). The trust is useful as a vehicle for permanently removing assets from the parents' gross estates.

Totten Trust. An "In Trust For" or so-called "Totten Trust" is created when a donor deposits his own money into a bank account for the benefit of a minor, and names himself as trustee. Under the laws of certain states, this is an informal and revocable arrangement. Upon the donor-trustee's death, the funds avoid probate and pass directly to the minor. However, the trust is not considered a separate entity for tax purposes because the donor retains complete control over any property in the trust. Accordingly, the donor will be taxed on the income as if the trust were not in existence. Also, assets in the trust account will be included in the donor's estate.

Coping with the Generation-Skipping Tax

An additional tax may apply to gifts or bequests that skip a generation. For example, a gift of property directly from a grandparent to a grandchild (which effectively "skips" the intervening generation) would be subject to the generation-skipping tax.

The reason for the tax is simple. It's designed to impose the equivalent of the gift or estate tax that would have been paid if the intervening generation had received the gift or bequest. So for a direct gift from a grandparent to a grandchild, the generation-skipping tax represents the amount of tax that would have been paid if the property had first been transferred to the child, who then died leaving the property to the grandchild.

The Generation-Skipping Tax is Stiff. It is imposed at the maximum estate and gift tax rate of 55%. It is payable in addition to any estate or gift tax otherwise payable as a result of the transfer. Fortunately, most individuals will escape paying it. First, $10,000 outright gifts from a grandparent to grandchildren that qualify for the annual exclusion are exempt from this tax. Furthermore, each individual is entitled to an aggregate $1 million exemption from the tax for lifetime gifts and transfers at death. Since a married couple can "gift-split," they can make up to $2 million in generation-skipping transfers without incurring the tax. In addition, any subsequent appreciation on the transferred property after it is given will escape generation-skipping tax.

TaxSaver

A wealthy individual can maximize his opportunity to avoid the imposition of the generation-skipping tax on transfers to his grandchildren and later generations by allocating his $1 million exemption for gifts during his lifetime.

If your living descendants are already well-provided for, you may want to consider establishing a "dynasty trust." As its name implies, the trust can benefit future descendants by sheltering assets from estate, gift, and generation-skipping taxes for several generations.

How to Use Trusts

A trust is possibly the most useful personal financial planning tool available—aside from a written plan itself. A trust is an arrangement under which one person or institution holds legal title to real or personal property for the benefit of another person or persons, usually under the terms of a written document setting forth the rights and responsibilities of all parties. Its primary virtue is that it can hold property for the benefit of other persons, now or in the future, and often avoid some taxes that otherwise would have to be paid.

Irrevocable Trusts. An irrevocable trust may not be changed or revoked after its creation. It is usually created to remove property and its future income and appreciation from the estate of the creator of the trust. A present interest trust and a Crummey trust, both of which have just been discussed, are irrevocable trusts. You might also use an irrevocable trust if you want to make a gift to someone but want to prevent the assets from being spent too quickly. An irrevocable trust also can be used to protect assets you give from your beneficiary's creditors.

However, property placed in an irrevocable trust will not be removed from your estate if you retain certain interests or powers in the trust—such as an interest that entitles you to receive the income from the trust for the rest of your life or the power to determine which beneficiaries will receive distributions. In addition, any transfer to an irrevocable trust will be subject to gift tax to the extent you relinquish control over the property. If someone else will receive the current income from the trust, or if it is a present income trust, the $10,000 annual gift tax exclusion can shield at least part of the property transfer to the trust from gift tax.

Besides saving you estate tax, irrevocable trusts created for your children can cut your income taxes. The amount of income tax savings depends on how much other income your children already receive and whether the kiddie tax applies to them. Also, there are very strict rules which limit the amount of control you or your spouse may keep over the trust in order for you not to include the trust's income on your tax return. The income from the trust will be taxed to you if the trust is used to pay for an item that you are legally obligated to provide as support for the beneficiary.

Revocable Trusts. A revocable trust (also known as a "living trust") is created during your lifetime, and you may amend or revoke it at any time. The trust instrument stipulates how the assets held by the trust are to be managed during your lifetime. This type of trust can also act very much like a will; the trust instrument can include instructions about how the assets in the trust should be distributed after your death.

What distinguishes a revocable trust from other kinds of trust arrangements is that you keep the power to reclaim the trust assets or contribute additional property to the trust at any time and for any reason. Thus, in effect, if you set up a revocable trust you really have not committed yourself to anything—at least until you die and the trust becomes irrevocable. For all practical purposes, you continue to own the trust property; the trust merely gets legal title. Since you keep complete control over the trust and its assets, the property held in it will be included in your gross estate for estate tax purposes. Also, all income and deductions attributable to the property in the trust will be included on your income tax return. On the other hand, you will not be liable for any gift tax when you contribute assets to the trust. This is the case even though the trust names the beneficiaries who will inherit the property upon your death. However, a gift will occur if you give up your power to revoke or amend the trust; or if income or principal is actually paid to someone else.

Essentially, there are no tax advantages gained by establishing a revocable trust. But there can be some real financial and administrative advantages, including:

Avoiding Probate. Revocable trust assets pass to the beneficiaries you name in the trust document and are not controlled by your will. This cuts out the costs and delays arising from the probate process. And, unlike probate, the identity and instructions for distributing estate property are not part of the public record.

Avoiding Legal Guardianship. If you become incapacitated, the assets kept in your living trust would be managed by a trustee you named in the trust document. Otherwise, the determination of whether and to what extent you are disabled or incompetent and who is going to handle your affairs could be left to public, and potentially costly, guardianship proceedings. A durable power of attorney can also be an effective tool for prearranging the management of your affairs in the event you become incapacitated.

Relief from Financial Responsibility. If desired, an independent trustee can be used immediately to relieve you of the details of managing your property and investments, record-keeping chores, and the preparation and filing of income tax returns.

Living trusts have some drawbacks and are not suited for everyone:

■ Expect to pay legal fees and other expenses, such as recording fees, to set up the trust and transfer property to it. You will also owe recurring trustee and administrative charges if you use a corporate trustee rather than managing the trust yourself.

■ You will not necessarily save on other legal, accounting, and executor's fees paid to handle your estate. Whether you assets are held in a living trust or pass through probate, the same sort of work will generally be needed to value your assets, prepare federal and state tax returns, settle creditors' claims, and resolve disputes among beneficiaries.

TaxSaver

Two reminders. If you establish a living trust, be sure that any property covered by the trust is legally titled in the trustee's name. This is a straightforward, but often overlooked, point. Also, after setting up a living trust, you must remember to conduct your personal business affairs through the trust. This is not difficult but can be a burden. Property held outside the trust at your death will be subject to probate—except for life insurance proceeds and property held jointly with right of survivorship, which by law would avoid probate.

How to Raise Cash to Pay Estate Taxes

In many instances, the estate of an owner of a closely held business—or for that matter, any estate—may not have sufficient cash to pay all the estate's obligations, including estate taxes. Without sufficient liquidity, the estate may be forced to sell a portion of the business to raise the necessary cash. But there are special rules for the estates of owners of closely held businesses. The techniques described below can help alleviate liquidity problems.

Stock Redemptions to Pay Death Taxes

A special provision (Section 303 of the Internal Revenue Code) allows certain redemptions or partial redemptions of closely held stock to be treated as a capital gain, not as a dividend. (Dividends would normally be treated as ordinary income and be taxed at a higher rate.) Since the estate's basis in the decedent's stock will be the stock's fair market value at the date of death, only post-death appreciation will be taxed upon the redemption and only up to the maximum capital gains tax rate of 28%. To qualify for what is called a Section 303 redemption, the value of all the stock of the corporation included in the decedent's gross estate must exceed 35% of the decedent's adjusted gross estate. The adjusted gross estate is the gross estate less the allowable deductions for funeral and administration expenses, debts, and certain losses (but before any charitable deduction or marital deduction). A qualifying redemption under Section 303 is limited in amount to the sum of the following items:

- Federal and state death taxes,
- Funeral expenses, and
- Estate administration expenses.

TaxSaver

An estate does not actually have to be illiquid in order to qualify for this special redemption. The estate may redeem stock up to the maximum amount referred to above, even if the estate otherwise has sufficient liquid assets to take care of its expenses and taxes. It is often desirable to redeem stock under this special provision because it can otherwise be difficult for the decedent's heirs to withdraw funds from the corporation without paying tax at ordinary income rates.

Installment Payment of Estate Tax. The estate taxes attributable to a decedent's closely-held business can be paid over a 14-year period if certain conditions are met. This 14-year payout offers a favorable interest rate plus a five-year deferral on the first installment of estate taxes. The deferral provision only applies to an "interest in a closely held business." To qualify, the value of the closely held business must exceed 35% of the adjusted gross estate. The amount of estate tax that qualifies for a deferred payout is limited to the portion of the total tax that is attributable to the decedent's business interest. Thus, if the decedent's qualifying stock constitutes 62% of the adjusted gross estate, then 62% of the total estate tax liability may be deferred.

Even though none of the tax attributable to the closely held business interest is paid for five years, the interest on the tax for the first four years must be paid annually. Starting in the fifth year, the estate tax due plus interest may be paid in up to 10 yearly installments.

The interest rate charged on the deferred estate tax attributable to the first $1 million in value of the closely held business interest is 4%. The regular federal interest rate applies to the deferred estate tax in excess of that amount.

E&Y FOCUS: Estate Planning—Steps to Take Now

Here's a handy checklist of estate planning measures you need to consider:

- Review with your spouse your current financial situation and your entire personal financial plan (including plans for your retirement as well as plans for the years after one of you has died).
- If any adult member of your family does not have a will, or if any wills have not been reviewed within the last three years, contact your attorney. This is especially important because of the frequency of tax law changes.
- Compile a list documenting where all your important financial and legal papers are located. Inform all appropriate persons of your list. If you have not already done so, be sure your spouse or whomever you designate as your personal representative knows your attorney, accountant, trust officer, broker, insurance advisor, and other appropriate individuals.
- Compile information on the cost and approximate purchase date of all your assets, including your residence.
- To reduce federal estate taxes, consider assigning ownership rights of your group term life insurance to your spouse, a trust, or other appropriate recipient.
- Review who you have designated as a beneficiary for your employee retirement or Keogh plan and other employee benefits.
- Review how your assets will be passed on to your beneficiaries.
- Make sure that you have provided for the legal guardianship and personal custody of your minor children.

- Review your will or any trust you have set up with your attorney. In particular, you and your spouse should check the provisions in your wills that pertain to what would happen to your estates if both of you died at the same time. Have you, for example, properly divided your assets to take maximum advantage of the marital deduction and the unified estate and gift tax credit (discussed on page 191)?
- If you and your spouse do not have durable powers of attorney, consider having them drawn up soon.

If the answer to any of the following questions is yes, you may need professional assistance to help you determine whether there are tax problems on the horizon. Remember: A 'yes' answer is a warning flag, but not necessarily a signal that there is a problem.

Are you:
- Making significant cash gifts to members of your family that are likely to continue indefinitely?
- Planning to make gifts to grandchildren within the next few years? In your will?
- Anticipating a significant inheritance? Is your spouse?

Do You:
- Hold assets jointly with your spouse, other than your residence and a working banking account?
- Have a simple will that leaves all property you own at the date of your death outright to your spouse?
- Own any real property in a state other than the state of your residence?
- Have a child or other relative with a serious medical problem that may require special consideration in your will or trust instrument?
- Have substantially more or less property than your spouse?

Have you:
- Moved your residence to a different state since you last executed your will?
- Named your estate as the beneficiary of your life insurance or your retirement plan benefits?

III

Tax Strategies for Businesses

One of the most important decisions you make in starting a new business is choosing how to organize your new concern—as a sole proprietorship, a partnership, an S corporation, or a regular corporation (otherwise known as a C corporation). There are, of course, advantages and disadvantages to each and the nature of your business to a considerable extent will determine the choice you make. Yet, you would be well advised to be familiar with each of the different options because the consequences of your choice will be far-reaching.

A sole proprietorship is not a separate legal entity from its owner, and its income is simply included on the owner's individual income tax return. Partnerships and S corporations also are generally not subject to federal taxes at the corporate level. However, income from a regular or C corporation is taxed at the entity level, and generally taxed again when it is distributed to shareholders.

This section of the book is far more than a primer on how different kinds of businesses are taxed. We've included tax-saving strategies that could benefit your company or partnership. There is also a special chapter on S corporations. Like income of a partnership or sole proprietorship, S corporation income, in general, escapes double taxation. But S corporation shareholders, like the shareholders of a regular corporation, are generally sheltered from the liabilities of the corporation.

12

Some Basic Planning Strategies for Businesses

Introduction

A business may generally be conducted as a sole proprietorship, a partnership, or a corporation. This chapter offers some suggestions on how to choose the right structure for your business and, having chosen it, what the tax consequences of that decision are likely to be. In addition, this chapter explains how to compute the income from your business that is subject to tax—either directly to you (for a proprietorship, partnership, or S corporation) or to the business itself (for a regular corporation). Finally, this chapter suggests some planning strategies that will help you minimize the amount of tax you owe.

Choosing the Proper Business Entity

In deciding the form in which you will do business, taxes are an important consideration *but* by no means the only one. In subsequent paragraphs we will discuss the various types of entities you can use in operating a business. Following are some items you need to consider in making that decision:

1. Are there any state laws governing your choice of a particular business entity? (For example, a state may require a business, such as a bank or an insurance company, to be incorporated or preclude certain professionals from limiting their personal liability.)
2. Do you need to protect your personal assets from the potential liabilities of the business?
3. Do you intend to pass on interests in the business to your children or grandchildren or other relatives?

The answer to any of these questions can affect your choice of business enterprise.

You generally may incorporate, on a tax-free basis, an existing proprietorship or partnership, or even a new business. In addition, most property may be transferred to an existing corporation in exchange for the corporation's stock without recognizing any gain in the transferred property if, after the exchange, the existing corporation is controlled by those transferring the property.

How to Choose. The corporate form is generally the form of choice for doing business because it offers flexibility in terms of the free transfer of shares, along with limited liability for its shareholders. However, under the current tax system, corporate income is subject to two levels of tax—at the corporate level when income is earned and at the shareholder level when dividends are paid. Income from an S corporation, on the other hand, is only taxed at the individual level. Nevertheless, because S corporation eligibility requirements limit a corporation's corporate structure, capital structure, and types and number of shareholders, many corporations are C corporations for tax purposes.

In any case, a taxpayer should carefully review the various business entity alternatives in order to make an informed decision regarding the structure of his or her business.

Types of Businesses

Sole Proprietorship

A sole proprietorship is not a separate legal entity from its owner. Accordingly, a sole proprietor has unlimited personal liability for the debts of the business. In other words, a sole proprietor's liability is not limited to business assets; the proprietor's individual assets are also at risk.

A sole proprietorship is not treated as a separate taxable entity for federal income tax purposes. The income generated by the sole proprietorship is simply included on its owner's individual income tax return along with other items of income and deduction. Thus, the income of a sole proprietorship is taxed once, at its owner's individual income tax rate.

You report gross profit or loss for the year from the sole proprietorship on Form 1040, Schedule C, and it becomes part of your adjusted gross income. In addition to owing income tax on such income, you, as the sole proprietor, will usually be liable for self-employment tax (page 158) and will also be required to make payments of estimated taxes (page 145). A net loss from the business can generally be deducted in computing your adjusted gross income.

Your profit (or loss) is computed as income less your allowable deductions. Income includes cash, property, and services received by the business from all sources unless specifically excluded under the tax code. Allowable deductions include all necessary and ordinary expenses incurred in connection with the business. For sole proprietorships in the business of selling goods or inventory, the primary expense will be the cost of goods sold. The cost of goods sold represents the cost of materials, labor, and overhead included in the inventory sold during the year. Other expenses that you deduct on Schedule C include salaries and wages, interest on loans used in the business, rent, depreciation, bad debts, travel and entertainment, insurance, and real estate taxes. (See the discussion on page 238.)

Because a sole proprietorship is not a separate entity, a sale of the business will be treated as if each asset in the business had been sold separately. The gain or loss on such a sale is the total of the gains or losses as separately computed for each individual asset. See the section on sales of business property (page 157) for more information on computing the gain or loss from the sale of assets.

Partnership

In contrast to a sole proprietorship, a partnership is an entity that is separate and apart from the individual taxpayer. A partnership is not a taxable entity; however, it must compute its income each year and file a partnership return (Form 1065) on or before the 15th day of the 4th month after the end of the partnership's tax year. Most decisions affecting the determination of partnership income are made by the partnership and are binding upon the partners.

If you are a member of a partnership, you are individually liable for tax on your share of partnership income as determined under the partnership agreement, even if such income is not distributed to you. You report your share of income or loss for the partnership year that ends with or within your own taxable year. This includes guaranteed payments of interest and salary paid to the partners that are deducted in determining the partnership's income. These payments would normally be considered ordinary income to you on your personal return.

The items listed below are not taken into account by a partnership in computing its income or loss but are reported separately by the partnership so that they can be included in each partner's individual return:

■ Net income or losses from rental real estate activities
■ Net income or losses from other rental activities
■ Portfolio income or losses, including (a) interest, (b) dividends, and (c) royalties
■ Gains and losses from the disposition of property used in a trade or business and certain involuntary conversions

- Charitable contributions
- Foreign income taxes
- Other items as required, such as contributions made on behalf of the partners to a qualified pension or profit-sharing plan and items subject to a special allocation under the partnership agreement that differ from the partnership allocation of profit and loss generally
- Any item that would result in a different tax liability to a partner if not taken into account separately (e.g., investment interest expense or percentage depletion)
- Allowable tax credits
- Deductions relating to the election to expense certain depreciable business assets

In addition, you are required to account separately for your share of items of income and deductions that are considered tax preference items. (See page 138.)

For tax years beginning after 1986, all partnerships must generally conform their tax years to that of their owners unless the partnership can establish, to the satisfaction of the IRS, a business purpose for having a different tax year.

Deductions you claim for losses from the partnership are often limited by the at-risk rules and passive loss provisions. (See the discussion in Chapter 1.)

Partnership interests may be held by *general* partners or *limited* partners. The general partners in a partnership are jointly liable for the debts of the business. In addition, general partners are jointly and individually liable for wrongful acts committed by a general partner in the course of the partnership's trade or business. Like a sole proprietor, the personal assets of a general partner are subject to the claims of the partnership's creditors (although any partner required to pay a partnership liability may assert a right to be indemnified by the other partners). A limited partner is usually subject to the claims of the business's creditors only to the extent of his or her capital contribution to the partnership or to the extent he or she is obligated to contribute in the future under the partnership agreement. To be considered a limited partner rather than a general partner, the partner must not actively participate in the management of the partnership. A limited partnership (i.e., a partnership with limited partners) must have at least one general partner whose assets are subject to the claims of the business's creditors.

Many states have authorized the registration of a limited liability partnership (an LLP) as a new form of partnership. In an LLP the personal assets of a partner are not subject to partnership liabilities for the tortious conduct of other partners. LLPs are generally treated like regular partnerships for tax purposes.

Regular or C Corporation

A C corporation is recognized as a legal and tax entity separate from its owners. Stockholders are generally sheltered from any liabilities of the corporation. (Note: In closely held corporations, lenders often require shareholders to guarantee the payment of the corporation's debt, thus reducing the potential benefit of limited liability—one of the benefits of forming a corporation.) Ownership in a C corporation may be divided into any number of shares of various classes of stock with different rights as to voting and the receipt of dividends. A corporation can also issue debt or equity securities. Convertible bonds, stock rights, stock warrants, and stock options provide investors with alternative forms of investment.

A C corporation is taxed on its taxable income whether or not it is distributed to the stockholders. Earnings distributed to stockholders are taxable as ordinary dividends to the extent of the corporation's earnings and profits. As a result, corporate earnings are generally subject to "double tax"—first at the corporate level and again when distributed to shareholders.

TAXSAVER

Paying higher salaries to shareholders of C corporations, if such remuneration is reasonable, can avoid the double taxation of the business income.

E&Y FOCUS: Executive Compensation

A publicly-held corporation is not allowed a deduction for compensation in excess of $1 million paid or accrued for the tax year to certain employees. The employees covered by the new rule, which was passed as part of the 1993 Tax Act, are the chief executive officer of the corporation (or an individual acting in that capacity) and the four highest compensated officers (other than the C.E.O.) whose compensation is required to be disclosed to shareholders under Securities and Exchange Commission (SEC) rules.

Certain kinds of compensation are excluded from the $1 million cap. These include:

- Compensation payable on a commission basis;
- Certain other performance-based compensation;
- Payments to a tax-qualified retirement plan (including salary reduction contributions);

- Amounts that are excludable from the executive's gross income, such as employer-provided health benefits and certain other fringe benefits, and;
- Any compensation payable under a written binding contract which was in effect on February 17, 1993, and all times thereafter before such compensation was paid. In addition, the contract cannot have been modified in any material way since that date.

Faced with the $1 million cap on deductible compensation, publicly held corporations should consider restructuring their compensation packages for covered employees to ensure that as much compensation as possible is performance-based. In addition, incentive stock options, which do not generate a deduction for employers (where certain holding-period requirements are met) may become increasingly attractive for employers that are running up against the $1 million cap for covered employees.

To the extent that a corporation pays interest to a shareholder, double taxation of the business income is avoided because, although the interest is taxable to the shareholder, interest paid is generally deductible by the corporation. The IRS carefully scrutinizes the characterization of debt from shareholders to be certain it is not equity.

A "hybrid" entity known as the limited liability company (LLC) may be treated as a corporation for legal purposes but as a partnership for tax purposes. Several states have adopted statutes which allow LLCs. You should consult your tax advisor regarding the tax treatment of LLCs.

S Corporation

Shareholders of an S corporation generally have the same advantage of limited liability as shareholders in a regular or C corporation. However, like a partnership, an S corporation is generally not subject to federal taxes at the corporate level. Its items of income, gain, loss, deduction, and credit pass through to its shareholders and are reported by them on their individual income tax returns.

If you expect your business to operate at a loss during its formative years, an S election may make sense. By electing S corporation status, the losses of the company will "flow through" and may be available, subject to limitations, to offset your personal income from other sources. If an S election is not made, the losses remain at the corporate level and can't be used until the corporation has income.

A corporation must formally elect to be taxed as an S corporation by filing Form 2553, "Election by a Small Business Corporation," with the IRS, as well as meeting certain other requirements. The election to be taxed as an S corporation and eligibility requirements are discussed in detail in Chapter 14.

Organizational and Start-Up Expenditures

Organizational and start-up expenditures incurred by a corporation are generally not deductible. An exception to this rule applies to companies that attach the appropriate election with their tax return for the year in which they begin business. These companies can amortize (write off ratably over a period of time) their organizational expenses over a period of not less than 60 months.

Start-up expenses may also be amortized over a period of not less than 60 months. Start-up expenditures are defined as amounts paid (or incurred): (a) that would have been deductible if they had been incurred in connection with the operation of an existing business; and (b) in connection with 1) investigating the creation or acquisition of an active trade or business, 2) creating an active trade or business, or 3) engaging in a profit-making or income-producing activity that is converted into an active trade or business. In this last case (3), the expenses incurred prior to the day on which the active trade or business begins would be deductible. The term "start-up expenditure" does not include any expense for interest, taxes, or research and experimental expenditures.

TaxSaver

You can amortize certain expenses incurred in creating a business or, in the case of partnerships, in anticipation of an activity becoming a business. A partnership can only deduct its organizational expenses if, like a corporation, it makes an election (described above) to do so over a period of not less than 60 months. Start-up expenses that don't qualify as organizational expenditures can be amortized by an electing partnership in computing its income. Expenses involved in investigating the acquisition of a partnership interest may be deducted by the partner on his or her personal return.

Accounting Periods and Methods

Accounting Periods

Taxable income must be reported on the basis of the corporation's taxable year which, with few exceptions, will be an annual 12-month period. Generally, a C corporation may adopt a taxable year ending at the end of any month, assuming an annual accounting period is established. If an annual accounting period is not established, taxable income must be computed on a calendar-year basis.

As a general rule, S corporations and personal service corporations (i.e., corporations whose principal activity is the performance of personal services, primarily by the employee-owners) must use a calendar year. Partnerships must have the same taxable year as that of the partners who own a majority interest in profits and capital. This is usually a calendar year. However, these entities may use a different year if they can establish a business purpose for a fiscal year (e.g., the requested year is a natural business year). In addition, these entities generally may elect to have a fiscal year that does not defer more than three months of income for their owners. A partnership or S corporation that makes such an election must make a deposit with the IRS that is roughly equal to the taxes that are being deferred for the partners or shareholders.

Once an accounting period is chosen, you will generally need to obtain permission from the IRS to change to another year-end.

Accounting Methods

A corporation must compute taxable income in accordance with the method of accounting regularly employed in keeping its books. An "accounting method" includes not only the overall method of computing income, but also the accounting treatment of individual items. Federal tax law permits a variety of methods, including the cash method, the accrual method, the installment method (in limited situations), the special rules for long-term contracts (described below), or any combination of methods that clearly reflect income.

For tax purposes, the choice of the cash method of accounting is restricted to individuals, sole proprietorships, certain farming businesses, certain personal service corporations, S corporations, certain partnerships, and small businesses (i.e., corporations with average gross receipts for the preceding three years of $5 million or less). Corporations, large partnerships with corporate partners, and businesses that are considered "tax shelters" must use the accrual method of accounting. (For a further discussion of the cash and accrual methods, see pages 262–263.)

Unless otherwise required or permitted under the tax law, an accounting method may be changed only after securing permission from the IRS. The IRS may require a change in accounting method if the method used does not clearly reflect income.

Long-Term Contracts. Generally, a long-term contract is defined for tax purposes as a building, installation, construction, or manufacturing contract that is not completed within the tax year in which it was entered into. A company that derives income from long-term contracts normally must report income under the percentage-of-completion method.

Under the percentage-of-completion method, you must include as income during the tax year a portion of the contract price based on the percentage of the contract completed during the year. Expenditures made during the tax year that are allocable to the contract are deducted as they are incurred.

TaxSaver

A company may elect to defer reporting under the percentage-of-completion method until 10% of the estimated contract costs are incurred. A company making this election may be able to defer the reporting of taxable income to a subsequent tax year. In addition, an exception to the required use of the percentage-of-completion method is available for home construction contracts and certain other contracts entered into by small contractors. These entities may use the completed contract method. Under the completed contract method, revenue and expenses from the contract are deferred until the contract is completed.

Special rules apply to taxpayers who overestimate or underestimate the contract price or costs. Such taxpayers must recompute their tax liability using the actual contract price and costs to determine whether they have a liability or are entitled to a refund (the so-called "look-back" rules).

Installment Sales. The installment method of reporting certain sales income generally allows businesses to defer the payment of taxes until the year in which a payment is received rather than the year in which the transaction occurs. An installment sale occurs when property is sold and the buyer is permitted to pay for it over a period of time which extends beyond the tax year in which the sale occurs. (See discussion on page 122.)

Generally, the installment method is mandatory for eligible sales. A taxpayer may elect not to use the installment method, however, by reporting the entire gain for the tax year in which the sale is made on a timely filed return.

TaxSaver

In certain cases, you may wish to "elect out" of the installment method and, instead, recognize the entire gain in the year of sale. This may be beneficial if you have capital losses or expiring net operating losses which can offset the recognized gain or if your tax rate is expected to increase in the year the cash is received.

What to Include and What to Deduct from Income

A corporation must generally report any income it receives unless such income is specifically excluded by a provision in the tax code. Reportable income may be cash, property, or services received and includes interest, dividends, rents, royalties, payments for services, gains from dealings in property, and income from the discharge of indebtedness. However, cash or property received by a corporation is, in certain circumstances, not taxable. For example, cash that is received in exchange for the issuance of stock or through debt financing is not subject to tax.

TAX*SAVER*

The following may result in a deferral of income:
- *Delaying deliveries on sales*
- *Making sales on consignment or approval*

Corporations are entitled to deduct ordinary and necessary business expenses paid or incurred during the taxable year, subject to various limitations. Deductible expenses may include:
- salaries and wages,
- rent,
- repairs,
- bad debts,
- interest—both actual payments and imputed interest,
- taxes,
- charitable contributions,
- casualty losses,
- depreciation and amortization,
- travel and entertainment,
- amortizable bond premium,
- depletion,
- advertising, and
- contributions to pension and profit-sharing plans

Special rules regarding some of these deductions are discussed in the following paragraphs.

TAX*ALERT*

The 1993 Tax Act limited certain business deductions. The business meals and entertainment deduction is re-

duced from 80% to 50% of the total amount for tax years beginning after December 31, 1993. No deduction is permitted for club dues, including airline and hotel clubs. Expenses incurred for lobbying are no longer deductible, except for expenses paid for "technical advice." The new limitations for club dues and lobbying expenses are effective for amounts paid after December 31, 1993.

Bad Debts

Taxpayers are allowed a deduction for specific debts owed to them that become wholly or partially worthless during the tax year.

Ordinary deductions are generally allowed for debts created or acquired in connection with a taxpayer's trade or business (e.g., trade receivables). Capital losses are allowed with respect to nonbusiness debts.

Charitable Contributions

A corporation may deduct charitable contributions if such contributions do not exceed 10% of its taxable income computed before deducting such contributions, the dividend-received deduction (explained later), net operating loss carrybacks (also explained later), and capital loss carrybacks. Charitable deductions in excess of this 10% limitation can be carried over to the next five taxable years, subject to the same 10% limitation.

Deductions for property contributions are subject to the 10% limitation discussed above. However, no deduction is permitted for that portion of a contribution that would constitute ordinary income if the property contributed were sold at its fair market value (e.g., inventory).

Corporations (other than S corporations, personal holding companies, and service organizations) are entitled to claim a deduction for contributions of inventory and certain types of property to a charitable organization. When such property is transferred specifically for the care of the needy, the ill, or infants, the amount of the deduction for such contributions may exceed the corporation's tax basis in the contributed property, but is limited to the basis of the property plus one-half of the unrealized appreciation. Furthermore, the amount of the deduction may not exceed 200% of the basis of the contributed property.

Note: No charitable deduction is allowed in computing a partnership's taxable income, although each partner may claim a deduction for his or her share of the partnership's charitable contribution.

Example: During 1994 Widget Corporation makes a contribution of women's coats to a shelter for the needy. The fair market value of the coats is $1,000 and the basis is $200. The corporation would be permitted to take a $400 deduction for the coats determined as follows: the deduction is limited to the corporation's basis in the property, $200, plus one half of the unrealized appreciation, $400 [($1,000 − $200) ÷ 2]. Therefore, the deduction is limited to $600 ($200 + $400). However, because the amount exceeds 200% of basis, or $400, the second limitation is imposed, and the charitable contribution is limited to $400.

Corporations (other than S corporations, personal holding companies, and service organizations) are also entitled to claim a charitable deduction for contributions of research property. To be eligible for the deduction, the equipment must be constructed by the taxpayer and contributed to a qualifying educational institution such as a college, university, or a qualifying tax-exempt scientific research organization. The recipient must be the first to use the property. In addition, the contribution must be made within two years of substantial completion of construction and must be substantially used by the receiving institution for research purposes. The deduction for scientific contributions is limited to the donated property's basis plus one-half of the unrealized appreciation. However, the deduction may not exceed 200% of the basis.

An accrual-basis corporation for which the board of directors authorizes a charitable contribution during the taxable year and then makes the contribution within two and a half months after year-end may elect to treat the deduction as if it were made in the year authorized.

Depreciation

Depreciation is the annual deduction allowed for recovering the cost of fixed assets. Generally, depreciation deductions can be claimed on property purchased for business use. These deductions are calculated using the "cost recovery" systems that are explained in this section. The amount of the tax deduction will depend on which "cost recovery" system is used.

Tangible Property. The depreciation allowance in the case of tangible property applies only to that part of the property which is subject to wear and tear, to decay or decline from natural causes, to exhaustion, or to obsolescence. The allowance does not apply to inventories or stock in trade, or to land apart from most improvements added to it. The allowance does not apply to natural resources which are subject to an allowance for depletion. No deduction for depreciation is allowed on automobiles or other vehicles used solely for pleasure, on a building used by the taxpayer solely as his or her residence, or on furniture or furnishings therein.

Intangibles. Because of the Tax Act of 1993, most acquired intangible assets—including goodwill and going-concern value—may be amortized on a straight-line basis over a uniform 15-year period. The new tax act also repealed rules that allowed amortization of the cost of franchises, trademarks or trade names over a 10- or 25-year period. The effect of the new law is that certain intangible assets that were not able to be amortized, can now be amortized over a 15-year period. Other intangible assets that were able to be amortized over longer or shorter periods, must now be amortized over a 15-year period. Generally, a business is not entitled to an amortization deduction for self-created assets—i.e., assets created by the taxpayer as opposed to assets that have been obtained through a business acquisition.

The following is a list of some of the intangible assets that can be amortized over a 15-year period using the straight-line method if the assets were acquired after August 10, 1993, the day the 1993 Tax Act was enacted:

- Goodwill;
- Going-concern value;
- Workforce in place;
- Information base, including business books and records;
- Know-how and similar items, including secret formulas, processes, designs, and patterns;
- Franchises, trademarks, and trade names; and
- Covenants not to compete and similar agreements entered into in connection with the direct or indirect acquisition of an interest in a trade or business.

Accelerated Cost Recovery System (ACRS).

The cost of assets placed in service after December 31, 1980, and before January 1, 1987, must generally be recovered according to the accelerated cost recovery system (ACRS). To qualify for deductions under ACRS, capital expenditures must be for "recovery property," which is any depreciable, tangible property that is used in a business or held for the production of income.

Under ACRS, capital expenditures are generally recovered over periods of 3, 5, 10, 15, 18, or 19 years. The applicable recovery period depends on the type of property and the date it was placed in service.

Modified Accelerated Cost Recovery System (MACRS).

The modified accelerated cost recovery system (MACRS) generally applies to tangible property placed in service after December 31, 1986.

Each item of property depreciated under MACRS is assigned to a property class. The property class establishes the period of time over which the cost basis of an item in the class is recovered. The class to which property is assigned is determined by its asset depreciation range (ADR) class life (a classification system established by the IRS). The ADR class life determines the property's recovery period and the method of depreciation that is used.

Under MACRS, tangible property falls into one of the following classes:

1. *3-year property.* This class includes property such as tractor units for over-the-road use, and certain horses.

2. *5-year property.* This class includes property such as automobiles, trucks, property used in connection with research and experimentation, computers and peripheral equipment, and office machinery (typewriters, calculators, copiers, etc.). It does not include office furniture and fixtures.

3. *7-year property.* This class includes property such as office furniture and fixtures (desks, files, etc.), and as designated, any single-purpose agricultural or horticultural structure. Note: This class also includes any property that does not have a class life and that has not been designated by law as being in any other class.

4. *10-year property.* This class includes single-purpose agricultural or horticultural structures, any tree or vine bearing fruit or nuts, vessels, barges, tugs, and similar water transportation equipment.

5. *15-year property.* This class includes roads, shrubbery, municipal wastewater treatment plants, and certain telephone distribution plants.

6. *20-year property.* This class includes property such as farm buildings, and, as designated, any municipal sewers.

7. *Residential rental property.* This class includes any real property that is a rental building or structure (including mobile homes) for which 80% or more of the gross rental income for the tax year is rental income from dwelling units. If you live in any part of the building or structure, the gross rental income includes the fair rental value of the part you live in. A dwelling unit is a house or apartment used to provide living accommodations in a building or structure, but does not include hotels, motels, and inns in which more than half of the units are used on a transient basis. Residential rental property is depreciated over 27.5 years.

8. *Nonresidential real property.* This class includes any real property that is not residential rental property (defined above), and any real property that is Section 1250 property with a class life of 27.5 years or more. Section 1250 property includes all real property that is subject to an allowance for depreciation and that is not or has never been Section 1245 property (i.e., property subject to an

allowance for depreciation that includes personal property and other tangible property used as an integral part of manufacturing, production, extraction, or the furnishing of transportation, communications, electrical energy, gas, water, or sewage disposal services). It also includes leased property (such as a building) to which the lessee has made improvements that are subject to an allowance for depreciation and the cost of acquiring a lease. This property is depreciated over 39 years.

TAXALERT

For property placed in service before May 13, 1993, the depreciation deduction for nonresidential real estate is determined by using a recovery period of 31.5 years.

The rate of recovery under MACRS is dependent upon three factors:
1. depreciation method,
2. recovery period, and
3. the applicable convention.

There are three simplifying conventions: half-year, mid-month, and mid-quarter. These designations refer to when the property is deemed to have been placed in service during the year. All property within an individual class placed in service in a given taxable year must be depreciated using the same recovery method, period, and convention. Real estate is an exception to this rule. The recovery method and period are determined on a property-by-property basis.

Alternative Depreciation System. The alternative depreciation system (ADS), which utilizes the straight-line depreciation method and longer recovery periods, must be used for property used predominantly outside the United States, tax-exempt use property, tax-exempt bond-financed property, imported property restricted by presidential executive order, and listed property (defined below) used 50% or less for business purposes. In addition, you may elect to apply ADS in lieu of post-1986 MACRS deductions to any other class of property. ADS is also used for the purpose of computing the depreciation adjustment for post-1986 assets in connection with the alternative minimum tax rules. See Chapter 13.

If you lease property, your depreciation deductions for any leasehold improvements you may make are determined under MACRS without regard to the term of your lease. Thus, the costs of the improvements are depreciated over the applicable recovery period.

Short Tax Year. If property was placed in service during a short taxable year (i.e., a tax year of less than 12 months) or used in a new trade or business, the first-year deduction must be allocated by calculating the depreciation deduction using the applicable method for the number of months the property was used.

Recapture. For a discussion of recapture of depreciation on the sale of an asset, see page 234.

"Listed" Property. Any "listed" property placed in service after June 18, 1984, that is not used more than half the time in a qualified business use during any tax year cannot qualify for MACRS depreciation, or for the asset expensing election (explained below). Instead, the property must be depreciated using the alternative depreciation system described above.

Listed property includes: (1) any passenger automobile; (2) any other property used as a means of transportation; (3) any property of a type generally used for entertainment, recreation, or amusement; (4) any computer and related peripheral equipment used exclusively at a regular business establishment that is owned or leased by the person operating the establishment; (5) any cellular telephone or other similar telecommunications equipment; and (6) any other property specified by IRS regulations.

Miscellaneous. If you claim accelerated depreciation in excess of straight-line depreciation on certain pre-1987 leased real or personal property, the deduction will be considered a tax preference item for purposes of computing the alternative minimum tax. (See pages 251–252.)

Sales or transfers of used property among related taxpayers for the purpose of receiving increased depreciation deductions are subject to certain restrictions, known as antichurning rules. The rules generally disqualify the property from being depreciated under a more rapid recovery method.

Expensing Assets Acquired (Section 179)

Instead of claiming a depreciation deduction, you may elect to expense (i.e., deduct currently) up to $17,500 per year of the cost of tangible personal property and other tangible property placed in service and used primarily in a trade or business. Before 1993, the amount was $10,000. A depreciation deduction provides a recovery over a period of years, while expensing provides for a more immediate recovery. A deduction is not available for real property or property held for investment.

TAXSAVER

If you have incurred a loss in the current year, the expense will not be allowed in the current year, but can *be carried over. If you expect to have taxable income in the following year, it may be more advantageous to take the $17,500 expense in the current year and obtain the full benefit of that expense in the following year, as opposed to depreciating the asset over five or seven years.*

Certain Restrictions. The amount of the expense cannot be greater than the income derived from the active conduct of any trade or business (computed without regard to the property to be expensed). Costs disallowed under this income limitation are carried forward to the succeeding taxable year and added to the allowable amount of such year.

In addition, the $17,500 maximum amount is reduced (but not below zero) by $1 for each $1 of property placed in service in a tax year exceeding $200,000. Therefore, the $17,500 expense is not available for taxpayers who place qualifying property that costs more than $217,500 in service during a given year.

TAXSAVER

You should carefully consider the timing of your purchases of Section 179 property to maximize the tax deductions available.

In the case of a partnership or S corporation, the limitation applies to the partnership or corporation as well as to each partner or shareholder.

The dollar limitation on expensing must be apportioned among the component members of a controlled group. (See Chapter 13, page 248.)

TAXSAVER

An individual who is both a partner in a partnership and a sole proprietor should be careful to avoid a permanent disallowance that may result if the total election amount exceeds the limitations discussed above.

Inventories

If you are in a business in which the production, purchase, or sale of merchandise produces income, you must identify the particular goods in inventory so that the proper costs can be calculated. The cost of merchandise sold during the year is determined by taking into account your inventory at the beginning of the year, adding to that the cost of goods purchased or produced during the year, and by subtracting the inventory remaining on hand at the end of the year.

When goods are so intermingled that they cannot be identified with particular purchases, the goods sold or used in manufacture are deemed to be the goods purchased first and the goods that remain in the inventory are deemed to be the goods purchased last—the first-in, first-out (FIFO) method. A taxpayer may elect to compute his or her goods remaining on hand at the end of the year as being those purchased first—the last-in, first-out (LIFO) method. Under this method, the cost of goods sold during the year is deemed to be those purchased or used in manufacture last.

TaxSaver

In periods of rising costs, a LIFO inventory method will generally reduce taxable income. In certain cases a company using LIFO can affect taxable income by timing the purchase of goods.

In times of decreasing prices, the FIFO method of accounting will generally provide a larger tax benefit than the LIFO method.

Taxpayers with inventories must use the accrual basis of accounting for purchases and sales. The inventory method used must conform to the best accounting practices in that particular trade or business and must clearly reflect income. Manufacturers are required to include both direct costs (such as material and labor) and indirect costs (such as those listed below) in inventory.

Uniform Inventory Capitalization Rules.

According to the uniform inventory capitalization rules enacted by Congress in 1986, certain indirect costs previously allowed as "period costs" must be capitalized into inventory. These indirect costs are generally associated with the cost of running a business over a specific time period, rather than costs associated with the production and sale of a product. To the extent the inventory remains unsold these indirect costs may not be deducted. Among these costs are:

- Costs related to purchasing and storing inventory
- Interest on debt either incurred or continued to finance the production of real property or certain tangible personal property
- Taxes (other than income taxes)
- Successful bidding expenses
- Depreciation
- Utilities related to equipment or facilities
- Engineering and design costs (other than research and experimentation)
- Compensation paid to officers attributable to production
- Insurance costs related to equipment or facilities

- Deductible contributions to pension, profit-sharing, stock bonus, or annuity plans for current service costs
- Past service pension costs incurred after December 31, 1987

These rules generally relate to either real or tangible personal property you produce, or property acquired for resale. There are some exceptions, including: (1) property you produce for use other than in a trade or business; (2) self-constructed assets if substantial construction began before March 1, 1986; (3) property produced under a long-term contract; (4) certain development and other costs of oil and gas wells or other mineral property; (5) certain farming activities; and (6) property acquired by a small business (less than $5 million in gross receipts) and held for resale to customers. The uniform inventory capitalization rules generally apply to all types of taxpayers (i.e., individuals, corporations, and partnerships), although special capitalization rules apply to farmers.

Imputed Interest

If you hold a debt instrument issued for nonpublicly traded property and the interest rate is not stated or is insufficient, a portion of each payment is treated as unstated interest rather than principal. The result is recognized as interest income to the seller, and interest expense to the borrower. The imputed interest rules apply to payments due more than six months after a sale or exchange of property where some or all of the payments are due more than one year after the date of sale. In addition, the imputed interest rules generally apply only to sales where payments are more than $3,000, but no greater than $250,000. (Where payments are greater than $250,000, the original issue discount rules, discussed below, may apply.)

Computing Unstated Interest. As a general rule, unstated interest is computed by taking the sum of the installment payments and discounting them using the applicable federal rate (AFR). The AFR, which is published monthly by the U.S. Treasury Department, is based on the average yield on marketable U.S. obligations during the preceding month. The AFR is limited to 9%, compounded semiannually, for debt instruments that have a principal amount under $2,800,000 and that have been annually adjusted for inflation since 1990 based upon the consumer price index. Special rules apply for sales of land between family members, sales of farms by individuals and small businesses, and sales of principal residences.

Accrual-method taxpayers must report interest income (expense) as it accrues, while cash-basis taxpayers must recognize interest income (expense) as payments are made.

(The accrual and cash methods of accounting are explained on page 218.)

Original Issue Discount (OID). The original issue discount (OID) provisions follow the imputed interest rules discussed above. OID rules apply to long-term debt instruments, such as bonds or notes, that either pay no interest, pay interest at a lower rate than the market rate, or are not required to pay interest at least annually. For example, OID rules apply to zero-coupon bonds. The OID rules also apply to instruments issued at a discount from their face amount. OID is computed by considering the yield to maturity of the debt instrument in order to determine the portion of the redemption price that represents interest. This interest is recognized as an interest expense by the issuing party, and as interest income by the debt holder, as it accrues, without regard to their method of accounting (cash or accrual).

Special rules, enacted in response to the explosive growth of so-called "junk bonds," apply to debt instruments issued after July 10, 1989, that have a term of more than five years, significant OID, and a yield that is more than five points over the AFR. A regular corporation that issues such an instrument may not deduct any portion of the OID on the instrument until interest is actually paid in property other than stock or obligations of the issuing corporation. Further, to the extent that the debt instrument's yield is more than six points over the AFR, no deduction is allowed for that portion of the OID, even when paid in cash.

Dividends-Received Deduction

In order to reduce the multiple taxation of corporate dividends, the law allows, with certain exceptions, a corporation receiving a dividend from a domestic corporation to deduct 70% of the dividend. In the case of any dividend from a domestic corporation owned 20% or more by another corporation, 80% may be deducted. This deduction is limited to 70% (80% if a 20%-or-more owned corporation is involved) of taxable income computed without regard to certain adjustments, including the dividends-received deduction itself.

Dividends-received deductions that are limited as a result of the net income limitation are lost forever. However, this rule does not apply where the recipient corporation would have a net operating loss (NOL) (see discussion later in this chapter) after taking into account the dividends-received deduction. In such a case, the dividends-received deduction is allowable and increases the NOL carryover. A corporation with qualifying dividend income should plan carefully to ensure that the dividends-received deduction is not lost because of these rules.

The dividends-received deduction must be reduced by an amount that reflects the percentage of the cost of the investment directly financed with borrowed money.

An affiliated group may elect a 100% dividends-received deduction on intragroup dividends that are paid out of earnings of taxable years ending after 1963. This applies as long as the distributing corporation and the recipient corporation were members of the group on each day of the taxable year.

Qualified Pension, Profit-Sharing, and Stock Bonus Plans

Payments made by an employer to qualified employee retirement plans are deductible as long as the plans satisfy the qualification requirements established by the tax laws and IRS regulations. Investment earnings and gains attributable to contributions made under a qualified plan are not taxable to the employer or to the trust that holds the investment. In addition, accumulated amounts are not taxable to the employee until such amounts are distributed.

Research and Experimental Expenses

If you incur research and experimental expenditures that cannot be charged to a capital account in connection with a trade or business, you may elect to treat these expenditures as either (1) deductions in the year the expenses are paid or incurred or (2) deferred expenses that will be amortized over a period of not less than 60 months, beginning with the month you first realize benefits from the expenditures. The election will apply to all research and experimental expenditures you pay or incur, or, if so limited by the election, to all expenditures for a particular project.

TaxSaver

Once made, the election applies to all such expenditures you incur unless a different method is authorized by the IRS. If you fail to make an election, your research and experimental expenditures must be capitalized. Expenditures for acquiring or improving land or depreciable or depletable property for use in connection with research and experimentation are not considered qualifying research and experimental expenditures. Depreciation (cost recovery) and depletion expenses attributable to such property, however, do qualify as research expenditures.

Qualified research expenditures may also be eligible for a tax credit. (See pages 247–248 for additional information.)

Leasing Expenditures

Leasing expenses are deductible as incurred. Consequently, the IRS reviews leasing transactions carefully to ensure that they are not sales-financing arrangements set up to produce a lease expense deduction. Typically, a leasing transaction does not transfer the benefits and burdens of ownership to the lessee. This is different than in a financing arrangement where the parties contemplate a transfer as an indication of ownership. Court decisions on leasing expenditures have generally focused on the intentions of the parties, the substance, rather than the form of the transaction, and whether and under what terms there is an option to purchase at the end of the lease term. The courts have looked unfavorably at arrangements that permit the lessee to purchase the leased asset at the end of the lease term for a nominal or "bargain" amount.

Lobbying Expense Deduction

For amounts paid or incurred during 1994, no deduction is allowed for amounts paid or incurred for participation or intervention in a political campaign on behalf of a candidate for public office (campaign expenses) or for attempts to influence the general public, or segments thereof, with respect to legislative matters, elections, or referenda (grass roots lobbying expenses). In addition, no deduction is allowed for lobbying of foreign governments.

Furthermore, no deduction is allowed for the costs of any attempt to influence state or federal legislation and any communications with a *covered executive branch official* in an attempt to influence official actions or positions of that official. Covered executive branch officials include the President, Vice President, certain White House officials, cabinet-level officials, the two most senior officials in each Executive agency, and certain other officials.

The ordinary and necessary business expenses of those in the business of lobbying on behalf of others are exempted from the new disallowance rules. If a taxpayer has *de minimis* amounts ($2,000 or less) of in-house lobbying expenses (not counting payments to a professional lobbying organization or organization dues allocable to lobbying activities), those in-house expenses are exempt from the general disallowance, and may be deductible business expenses.

TaxSaver

A number of contacts with the government should not be considered lobbying contacts, including (but not limited to) those compelled by subpoena, statute, regulation, etc.; those made in response to public notices soliciting communications to the public; those made to a federal official with regard to judicial proceedings, criminal or civil law enforcement inquiries, investiga-

tions, or proceedings. Congress has expressed an intent that such contacts should not be considered lobbying. Thus, expenses incurred in dealing with the IRS and Treasury Department on matters involving private letter rulings, technical advice memoranda, and regulation commentary would remain deductible.

Business Capital Gains and Losses

Two requirements must be met for the capital gain or loss provisions to apply: (1) there must be a sale or exchange, and (2) the property sold or exchanged must be treated by the Internal Revenue Code as a capital asset.

A sale or exchange is defined for this purpose in generally the same manner as it is for ordinary business transactions. A sale is a transfer of property for money or for a mortgage, note, or other promise to pay money. An exchange is a transfer of property for other property or for services.

The rules for figuring a taxable gain or a deductible loss apply to both sales and exchanges. Capital assets generally include all assets owned and used by a corporation for business purposes. Capital assets do not include the following: 1) inventory, 2) depreciable property, 3) real estate used in a business, 4) notes and accounts receivable acquired in the ordinary course of a business for services rendered or from the sale of inventory, or 5) in certain cases, copyrights or literary, musical, or other artistic compositions. Letters and memorandums prepared by or for you are also not classified as capital assets.

Net capital gains on sales or exchanges of business assets recognized after 1986 are taxed at a corporation's ordinary income tax rate. Net capital losses, on the other hand, may not be deducted from ordinary income. They may, however, generally be carried back three years and any excess losses may be carried forward and applied against net capital gains recognized during the following five years. The loss carryovers are treated as short-term capital losses and are offset against any net capital gains in the carryback and carryforward years. Special limitations on the carryover of net capital losses apply following certain corporate acquisitions and changes in ownership. (See page 249.)

TaxSaver

Corporations should review their tax positions before year end and consider additional sales of capital assets to coordinate the timing of gains and losses and prevent the expiration of unused losses.

Depreciation Recapture

Any gain realized on sales and certain other dispositions of depreciable personal or other tangible business property (except buildings and their structural components that are "real property") is treated as ordinary income to the extent of depreciation deductions taken prior to the sale. Expensing certain assets in the year the property was placed in service is treated as depreciation for purposes of these rules. (See page 226.)

Gains realized on the disposal of depreciable real property, such as a building, must be recaptured under rules that are both more complicated and more beneficial than the rules for depreciable personal property. The rules also differ depending on when the property was acquired and how much depreciation has been claimed. In general, any gain equal to the excess depreciation over straight line depreciation is ordinary income and any remaining gain on the disposition is a capital gain. One important exception to this rule is nonresidential real property acquired from 1981 through 1986 under the Accelerated Cost Recovery System (ACRS). Depreciation on this ACRS property is recaptured up to the lesser of either the gain or the total depreciation taken on the property.

Net Operating Loss Deduction

If the corporation's deductions for the year exceed its income for the year, the resulting amount is a net operating loss. Net operating losses generally may be carried back 3 years and forward 15 years and may be used to reduce taxable income incurred in those years. You may elect to forgo the 3-year carryback period and carry forward the entire loss.

TaxSaver

The election to forgo a net operating loss (NOL) carryback is irrevocable. Therefore, when deciding whether to forgo a net operating loss carryback consider:

1) The marginal tax brackets in the carryback years versus the tax brackets in the carryforward years.
2) The time value of money (what will you be able to earn with the refund money).
3) The effect on tax credits.

In general, a 10-year carryback period is available for the portion of the loss that is attributable to the costs of investigating, defending, or settling product liability claims and certain other statutory or tort liabilities. In lieu of the 10-year carryback, the corporation may either elect a 3-year carryback or forgo the carryback period altogether, as mentioned above. Special limitations apply to the carryover of a net operating loss of a corporation that is a party to an acquisition or that experiences a change in ownership. (See page 250.)

A corporation generally may not carry back the portion of a net operating loss created by interest deductions arising from a major stock acquisition or significant distribution or redemption (referred to as a corporate equity reduction transaction, or CERT).

13

Determining Income, Deductions, and Taxes for Your Business

Introduction

Once the taxable income of your business has been determined, you must next calculate the tax on such income. This chapter tells you how to determine the tax for all business entities: sole proprietorships, partnerships, and corporations. While regular or C corporations are tax-paying entities, your share of the income from a proprietorship, a partnership, or an S corporation is included and taxed on your individual return.

The chapter explains which federal tax forms each corporate entity is required to file, and it suggests strategies that you might bear in mind while completing the forms that could help you reduce your taxes.

Sole Proprietorship Income

You must report your business income for the year from a sole proprietorship on Form 1040, Schedule C. In addition to owing income tax, you as the sole proprietor may also be liable for self-employment tax (see page 158). You may also be required to estimate your tax liability in advance and make payments during the year, instead of waiting until April 15th of the following year (see pages 145–148). A net loss from the business can generally be deducted in computing your adjusted gross income. (Also see the discussion of sole proprietorships in Chapter 12.)

Who Has to File Schedule C? You have to file Schedule C if you are the owner of a business or are a self-employed professional. This includes a wide variety of activities, such as owning a store; being a self-employed lawyer, doctor, accountant, or other professional; working as a freelance writer or independent consultant; or owning a manufacturing company. Schedule C must be filed whether you pursue this activity full- or part-time and whether or not you also have another job. Farmers use a special schedule, Schedule F. Schedule C cannot be filed if your business, trade, or professional practice is in the form of a corporation, partnership, or joint venture.

If you operate your own business while you are also employed by another one, you have to separate your deductions relating to each business.

Example: A freelance writer who is also employed as a newspaper reporter needs to segregate deductible expenses relating to the freelance writing activity from the reimbursable expenses relating to being a reporter.

If you operate more than one sole proprietorship, you must file a separate Schedule C for each trade or business.

Example: During the day, Dave operates a store that sells party favors. At night, he operates a security service. The businesses are separate and distinct and a separate Schedule C should be filed for each one.

Who Doesn't Have to File Schedule C? Not every income-producing activity is considered a trade or business. For example, investing in stocks and other securities for you own account (rather than for clients) is not considered a trade or business. It doesn't matter if you pursue this activity full-time or whether you generate substantial profits. Your income from these activities will be considered dividends, interest, or capital gains, as appropriate. Your deductions, if any, will be treated as miscellaneous itemized deductions and will only be deductible to the extent that they exceed 2% of your adjusted gross income.

An activity that you pursue as a hobby—even if you make money at it—will not be classified as a business by the IRS, and you do not need to file Schedule C. Expenses of a hobby, however, may be deductible to the extent that the activity produces any income. To determine whether an activity is a trade or business or a hobby, the IRS is likely to consider several factors. If, for example, you do not keep careful records of your income and expenses, do not maintain a separate bank account, and spend little time on the activity, the IRS may not consider the activity to be a trade or business. All the facts in regard to the activity are taken into account. No one factor alone is decisive. Here are a few:

Whether your losses from the activity are due to circumstances beyond your control (or are normal in the start-up phase of your type of business).

Whether you change your methods of operation in an attempt to improve the profitability of the activity.

Whether the activity makes a profit in some years, and how much profit it makes.

Whether you can expect to make a future profit from the appreciation of the assets used in the activity.

Example: John is a successful doctor. He is also an avid fox hunter. He raises horses which he uses in fox hunting but he also sells them to his hunting friends. Over the years the expenses of raising and selling the horses have exceeded his income from this source. The IRS will probably view the horse-raising operation as a hobby.

How to Complete Schedule C. Schedule C contains four basic sections. A line-by-line discussion of how to fill out the form is beyond the scope of this book but is provided in *The Ernst & Young Tax Guide,* published annually. What follows are some suggestions to bear in mind when completing the form:

Business Address. You should use your home address if you use part of your home as your principal place of business. If you don't, you may have a difficult time claiming a home office deduction (see page 64). If you plan to claim a deduction for expenses of a home office, you must also complete Form 8829, *Expenses for Business Use of Your Home.* Although filing a Form 8829 will not automatically result in an audit, the return may be more closely scrutinized.

Accounting Method. Most small businesses use the cash method of accounting, i.e., reporting income when it is actually received and expenses when they are actually paid. Remember that you are also required under the cash method to report income when it is "constructively" received. For example, if interest is credited to your business money market account on December 31, 1994, it must be reported as income in 1994, even though you don't get your bank statement until 1995. Or, if you receive checks from customers in 1994, you must generally report income, even though you don't deposit the checks in your business account until 1995. If your business involves inventory, then you must ordinarily use the accrual method of accounting for purchases and sales (see page 218). In some cases, you may use a combination of the cash and accrual methods. You should consult with your tax advisor.

Income. If your business provides only services, you will have no cost of goods sold. Your gross receipts will equal your gross profit.

What Can be Deducted. For an expense to be deducted, it (1) must be paid by you within the taxable year in carrying on your trade or business, (2) must not be a capital investment, and (3) must be ordinary and necessary. Extravagant expenses run the risk of being disallowed. While the 1986 Tax Act stipulated that certain costs in manufacturing or producing property must be capitalized, this provision does not apply to writers, artists, and photographers. The IRS is on the alert for taxpayers who try to claim deductions on Schedule C that would otherwise be subject to the 2% floor on miscellaneous itemized deductions.

Advertising. You do not have to prove that the advertising immediately led to increased sales in order to claim a deduction.

Bad Debts. You cannot deduct losses from bad debts for receivables that you have not yet reported as income if you are a cash-method taxpayer. Accrual-method taxpayers include items in income where they have done everything required of them. If a customer subsequently refuses to pay them, a bad debt deduction can eventually be claimed, in effect reversing the original inclusion in income.

Car and Truck Expenses. You cannot deduct expenses for the personal use of a car or truck but can deduct those expenses incurred during the course of business.

Depreciation. A discussion of depreciation is provided in Chapter 12. Remember that, under certain circumstances, in the first year you acquire tangible personal property, you can deduct up to $17,500 of its cost.

Employee Benefit Programs. In most instances as a sole proprietor, you may not deduct the amount you pay for your own benefits. If your spouse or children work for you, the cost of their benefits is deductible, as are payments for benefits of your other employees. Until December 31, 1993, you were allowed a deduction for 25% of your health insurance premiums for you and your family, but they could not exceed your net earnings from the business.

Insurance. Generally, business-related insurance premiums—for fire, theft, malpractice and liability insurance, etc.—are deductible. Insurance premiums prepaid for a year are deductible when paid, even though the coverage carries over to the succeeding year. Premiums paid for more than a 12-month period must be deducted *pro rata.*

Interest. Interest on business loans is deductible; however, you may deduct only the part of your prepaid interest that relates to the current tax year. Special rules apply if you borrow to construct or manufacture assets. You should consult with your tax advisor.

Legal and Professional Services. You can deduct immediately most fees for professional services (legal, accounting, etc.) incurred in your trade or business. However, fees paid in connection with the acquisition of a capital asset (title insurance, for example) should be added to the cost of that asset. Fees for advice on personal matters are generally not deductible.

Pension and Profit-Sharing Plans. Contributions for your employees (but not for yourself) to qualified plans are deductible. Remember, in order to obtain a 1994 deduction for your contributions, your plan must be in existence by December 31, 1994. For more information about pension and profit-sharing, Keogh, and SEP plans, see Chapter 2.

Rent or Lease. You may deduct amounts paid as rent for business premises. The IRS says that prepaid rent is only immediately deductible to the extent that it relates to the year in which it is paid. The balance is deductible over the period to which the payment relates.

Taxes and Licenses. Federal income taxes can never be deducted, but certain other taxes—including real property, payroll, and your contribution as an employer to FICA (Social Security)—are deductible.

Depositing Payroll Taxes. Payroll taxes, withheld income taxes, and Social Security taxes are paid to the government either directly to the IRS or to a depository bank. The payee and frequency of deposits depend on the total amount of payroll taxes withheld each pay period. You should check with your tax advisor for how these rules apply to your situation.

Travel, Meals, and Entertainment. Business-related expenses of this nature can generally be deducted, subject to a 50% ceiling. Note that dues paid for memberships in clubs after December 31, 1993, are no longer deductible as business expenses. See Chapter 2 for more about travel and entertainment.

Utilities. Utility and telephone bills are generally deductible. You cannot claim a deduction for the basic monthly charge you pay for local telephone service for the first telephone line in your home, even if it is partly (or solely) used for business. Charges for extra services—such as call-forwarding, three-way calling, call-waiting—are deductible to the extent they relate to business use. A cellular phone installed for business purposes may be depreciated under the MACRS method of depreciation (see Chapter 12 for an explanation) to the extent that business use of the telephone exceeds 50%. If your business use is less, you must use the straight-line method of depreciation over 5 years. If your business usage of the phone falls below 50% for any one year, you must add back part of the depreciation you've claimed in prior years to your income.

Wages. You can deduct wages, salaries, and other compensation—including amounts paid to your relatives—as long as the amounts are reasonable for the services provided. You cannot deduct any amount paid by your sole proprietorship to yourself.

Other Expenses. There are a variety of business expenses not specifically listed on Schedule C that can be claimed. Some of the more common ones: (1) union dues and dues for professional associations; (2) subscriptions to business-related publications; (3) bank service charges on business accounts; (4) security and refuse removal fees; and (5) laundry and dry-cleaning fees for uniforms you are required to wear on the job, as long as the clothes are not suitable for off-the-job use.

Partnership Income

Even though a partnership is not a tax-paying entity (see discussion in Chapter 12), it must compute its income each year and file a partnership return (Form 1065). Form 1065 is due on the 15th day of the 4th month following the close of the partnership's taxable year (April 15th for calendar-year partnerships). Extensions of time are available. The partnership also may have to file state and local returns in each jurisdiction in which it does business and where its partners reside. Failure to do so may subject the partnership (and each partner) to significant penalties.

Schedule K-1. A Schedule K-1 shows each partner's distributive share of the partnership's income or loss, deductions, and credits. A Schedule K-1 for each partner should accompany the partnership return sent to the IRS, and each partner should receive a copy of his or her own Schedule K-1. Each partner's distributive share is generally determined by the partnership agreement. Each partner needs to enter the information provided on Schedule K-1 in the appropriate place on his or her personal tax return.

A partner is considered to be self-employed, rather than an employee of the partnership. Therefore, if you are a general partner, your share of partnership income will be subject to self-employment tax (see discussion earlier in this chapter). In addition, you cannot exclude from your income the value of certain fringe benefits—health insurance, for example—that the partnership provides for you and your family.

Limitation on Deduction of Partnership Loss.
A partner may not deduct losses in excess of his or her adjusted basis for his or her partnership interest. Generally, one's basis in a partnership is the original capital contribution. This basis is adjusted to take into consideration any additional capital contribution, allocable shares of partnership debts and previously reported partnership gains, and cumulative shares of previously reported losses and any distributions. The computation should be made by your accountant.

Special Allocation of Losses and Other Items.
Under certain circumstances, the partnership agreement can provide for tax benefits to flow disproportionately to one or more of the partners. This special allocation of partnership items must be equalized at some point in the future.

S Corporation Income

Corporations electing S corporation status are generally not subject to corporate income taxes. (S corporations are discussed in Chapter 12 and in greater detail in Chapter 14.) However, an S corporation must file an annual tax return on Form 1120S for its taxable year. Form 1120S is generally due on the 15th day of the third month following the close of the taxable year (March 15th for calendar-year S Corporations). Extensions of time are available. Attached to the return is a Schedule K-1 for each shareholder, showing his or her share of the S corporation's income, loss, deductions, and credits. The S corporation must also send each shareholder a copy of his or her Schedule K-1.

Regular or C Corporations

Filing Requirements
A corporation's federal income tax return (Form 1120) is due on the 15th day of the third month following the end of its taxable year (e.g., March 15, 1995, for the calendar year 1994). An automatic extension of time to file of up to six months may be granted if an extension request (Form 7004) is properly filed. An extension of time to file, however, does not extend the time to pay the tax due. Corporations must pay the balance of tax due as shown on their tax return on or before the original due date of the return.

Penalties are imposed for failure to pay corporate income taxes when due under the same circumstances and at the same rates as for individuals. (See page 148.)

Tax Rates

The current corporate tax rates are included in the appendices at the back of this book.

Estimated Tax Requirements

Any C corporation is required to make estimated tax payments if it expects to have a year-end tax bill of $500 or more. Form 1120-W is available from the IRS to assist you in estimating your company's tax and in determining the deposits to be made. Payments are due on the 15th day of the 4th, 6th, 9th, and 12th months of the corporation's taxable year. (See Tax Payments below.)

Computing Quarterly Installments. Corporations may be penalized for not paying enough tax for an installment period. In general, the required quarterly installment is the lesser of:

1. One-fourth of the tax shown on the return for the current year, or
2. 25% of the tax shown on the return for the preceding year.

In order to calculate the required quarterly installment based on the prior year's tax, the following conditions must be met:

1. The prior year's return must have covered a 12-month period;
2. A tax liability of $1 or more must have been shown on the prior year's return; and
3. The corporation cannot be a "large" corporation, although a large corporation may use this method for the first installment for the year. A "large" corporation is a corporation with taxable income of at least $1 million in at least one of the three preceding tax years. (See page 245.)

The required quarterly installment may also be based on either annualized or seasonal income. If it is based on the company's annualized income, the required quarterly installment is equal to 100% of the tax, allocated evenly and cumulatively to each of the quarterly periods. To calculate its annualized income, the company must place its taxable income for the corresponding portion of the tax year on an annualized basis (i.e., multiply taxable income for the corresponding portion of the tax year by 12 and divide by the number of months in the period), compute the tax, and, after deducting prior installments for the year, pay the tax according to cumulative percentages.

Only certain corporations with a seasonal pattern in income can base their required quarterly installments on seasonal income. If it is based on seasonal income, the required quarterly installment is computed by annualizing income, assuming that income earned in the current year is earned in the same seasonal pattern as in the three preceding tax years. One hundred percent of the tax, allocated evenly and cumulatively to each quarterly period, and computed by using annualized seasonal income, must be paid under this method.

If estimated payment installments are determined by using either the annualized method or the seasonal income method, and some other method is used for a subsequent installment (i.e., 100% of the current year liability or 100% of the prior year liability), you may need to make an adjustment to the amounts paid. IRS rules require that 100% of the reduction in estimated taxes resulting from using the annualized or seasonal income methods for previous installments must be paid with the subsequent installment to avoid an underpayment penalty. The tax computed under each exception includes all taxes such as the alternative minimum tax (AMT), minus any allowable credits.

Underpayment Penalties. Corporations will be penalized for paying less than the required quarterly installment. The penalty is equal to the amount of the underpayment multiplied by the applicable federal rate (AFR). (See page 229 for more about the AFR.) The penalty is assessed from the installment due date to the earlier of the date on which a subsequent installment is paid or the original due date of the return.

A payment of estimated tax is applied against underpayments of required installments in the order in which the installments are required to be paid, regardless of the installment to which the payment relates. Thus, if an underpayment exists for a corporation's first quarter, any second quarter payment will first be applied to the underpayment for the first quarter. An overpayment of a required installment may be applied to subsequent underpayments, unless the overpayment is already allocated to an earlier underpayment. No penalty is imposed for an underpayment of estimated tax if the tax shown on the return is less than $500.

In addition for tax years beginning after December 31, 1993, the income annualization methods used to determine estimated tax payments have been modified. First, there is a new set of periods over which a corporation may elect to annualize income. Thus, there are now three alternative sets of periods a corporation may use to annualize income. Second, corporations are required to annually elect which of the three alternative periods they will use.

Special Rules for "Large" Corporations. Large corporations may not use the prior year's tax exception, except to determine the amount of the first installment for the tax year.

Quick Refund of Overpaid Estimated Tax

If a corporation overpays its total tax liability by making estimated tax payments that are higher than necessary, it may apply for a quick refund on Form 4466. The refund request must be made within two-and-a-half months after the close of the corporation's taxable year and before the date on which the corporation files its tax return. In addition, the overpayment must be equal to at least 10% of the corporation's expected tax liability and, in any case, must not be less than $500.

Tax Credits

Certain nonrefundable credits are available to businesses. They are presented below in the order in which they are applied against the tax. Any corporation claiming a credit should consult with its tax advisor.

Foreign Tax Credit. At the option of the corporation, foreign income taxes imposed on foreign source income may either be deducted in computing taxable income or taken as a credit against U.S. taxes. In addition, foreign income taxes paid by certain foreign corporations from which dividends are received or deemed to be received will be considered "paid" by the corporate shareholder and may be included in computing its foreign tax credit.

TaxSaver

In general, it will be preferable for a corporation to elect the credit against U.S. taxes rather than to claim a deduction for foreign taxes paid. A credit offsets tax liability on a dollar-for-dollar basis. A deduction will bring a benefit of only 35 cents on the dollar at the top marginal tax rate.

A foreign tax may be allowed as a credit against a corporation's U.S. tax only if it is treated as an income tax under U.S. tax law. The same is true if it is an income tax substitute for an income tax imposed on the general population of a foreign country. Under U.S. tax law, a "creditable" tax is any foreign tax that attempts to tax net realized gains. Examples of creditable taxes include: income-withholding taxes; flat or progressive taxes on gross income less reasonable deductions; and gross-receipt taxes that are "in lieu" of an income tax. Noncreditable foreign taxes are capital, stamps, sales, VAT, or other consumption taxes.

Foreign taxes that are not creditable taxes are still allowed as a deduction from income.

Limits on the Credit. The foreign tax credit that may offset U.S. tax liability is generally limited to the ratio of foreign-source taxable income to worldwide taxable income times the U.S. tax. The limitation restricts the foreign tax credit to the effective U.S. rate of tax. An excess foreign tax credit arising in any year may ordinarily be carried back two years and forward five years. Limitations on the carryover of unused credits in certain corporate acquisitions and reorganizations are explained on page 250.

A separate foreign tax credit limitation must be calculated if the corporation has the following types of income:
- passive income,
- high withholding tax interest,
- financial services income,
- shipping income dividends from each non-controlled foreign corporation,
- dividends from a DISC (Domestic International Sales Corporation) or former DISC, and
- taxable income attributable to foreign trade income of a Foreign Sales Corporation (FSC).

Puerto Rico and Possessions Tax Credit. If a U.S. corporation meets certain conditions, it is entitled to a tax credit equal to the amount of U.S. tax on its taxable income derived from sources outside the U.S. from the active conduct of a business in a U.S. possession, such as Puerto Rico. For tax years beginning after 1993, the possessions credit has been modified. Consult your tax advisor.

Credit for Clinical Testing. A credit equal to 50% of certain qualified clinical testing expenses paid or incurred on or before December 31, 1994, related to drugs for rare diseases or conditions is allowed. The deduction for such expenses must be reduced by the credit taken.

Nonconventional Fuel Credit. Subject to certain limitations, taxpayers producing fuel from nonconventional sources (shale oil, tar sands, etc.) are generally allowed a credit of $3 per barrel for the fuel produced that is equivalent to a barrel of oil.

General Business Credit. Each of the five credits discussed below (investment, targeted jobs, alcohol fuel, credit for increased research, and low-income housing) is calculated separately and then combined for purposes of applying an overall limitation. Unused general business credits may be carried back 3 years and forward 15 years. Transition rules are provided for pre-1984 credit carryforwards under prior law. General business credits are deemed to be used in the order listed below:

Investment Credit. The investment credit is made up of the following three components: (1) the rehabilitation credit; (2) the energy credit; and (3) the reforestation credit. See page 68.

Targeted Jobs Credit. A credit is allowed for 40% on the first $6,000 of first-year qualified wages paid to employees hired from certain disadvantaged groups who begin work on or before December 31, 1994. The wage expense deduction must be reduced by the amount of the credit. The disadvantaged groups include:
  (1) handicapped individuals undergoing vocational rehabilitation;
  (2) economically disadvantaged youths;
  (3) youths participating in a qualified cooperative education program;
  (4) general assistance recipients.

TaxSaver

In many cases, employers hire qualifying individuals yet fail to take advantage of the credit. Be sure you take advantage of the credit if you meet all of the requirements.

Alcohol Fuel Credit. A credit is allowed for certain sales and use of alcohol as a fuel.

Credit for Increased Research. A nonrefundable credit equal to 20% of the excess of the qualified research expenses (paid or incurred before July 1, 1995) for the taxable year over a base amount is allowed. The base amount is generally calculated using historical research and development expenses, and gross receipts. The costs eligible for the credit are limited to those expenses that represent an increase over the prior years' expenditures. The base amount cannot be less than 50% of the costs for the current year.

The term "qualified research" refers to experimental and laboratory research and development. The deduction allowed for research and development expenditures must be reduced by the research credit claimed. However, you may elect not to claim the full amount of the credit to avoid the reduction of the deduction.

In addition, certain corporations are allowed an additional 20% credit for basic research payments. In general, basic research payments are payments in cash to certain qualified organizations for basic research.

There is also a new rule regarding the determination of the base percentage for start-up companies. A start-up company is assigned a base percentage of .03 for each of its first five tax years after 1993 in which it incurs qualified research expenses. For subsequent tax years, the base percentage will be computed based on its actual levels of research spending.

Disabled Access Credit. Certain small businesses are allowed a 50% credit against their income tax for "eligible access expenditures" that are at least $250 but no more than $10,250. Eligible expenditures are those paid to enable small businesses to comply with the Americans with Disabilities Act of 1990. Allowable expenditures would include amounts paid to remove architectural barriers which affect a disabled person's access to a business or costs for special services and equipment for the disabled. Businesses with gross receipts under $1 million or 30 or fewer full-time employees during the preceding tax year are eligible for the credit.

Companies that spend more than $15,000 to eliminate architectural barriers or are too large to qualify for the credit may deduct expenditures up to $15,000 each year.

Special Rules and Taxes for Corporations

This section is intended to familiarize a business executive with some of the special rules and taxes that can apply to corporations. In all cases, the rules and taxes only apply in a limited number of situations. In addition, you should consult with a professional tax advisor if any of the items discussed are applicable to your company or personal situation. Whenever possible, we have tried to point out tax strategies that you and your tax advisor may want to discuss. Taxpayers who are involved with closely-held corporations should pay particular attention to the special rules discussed below.

Special Rules

Controlled Groups of Corporations

Controlled groups are corporations that are related by common ownership. To prevent abuses that could result from the establishment of multiple corporations, restrictions are placed on certain tax benefits available to controlled groups of corporations.

A controlled group can only benefit from lower tax rate brackets to the extent that it would if it were taxed as a single corporation. In addition, the benefit of the graduated tax rate structure must be divided equally among the group of controlled corporations, unless the corporations consent to a different allocation. The income of a controlled group must be aggregated for purposes of computing the 5% surtax on income between $100,000 and $335,000.

Members of a controlled group are also limited to one $40,000 exemption for purposes of calculating the alternative minimum tax. (See page 251.) Controlled corporations are also subject to the following additional limitations:

(1) one $250,000 accumulated earnings credit;

(2) one $2 million exemption for purposes of computing the environment tax (page 253);

(3) one $17,500 limitation for the expensing of fixed asset additions (page 227); and

(4) one $1 million base amount for the large corporation test related to the calculation of estimated taxes (page 243).

S corporations are generally excluded from a controlled group for purposes of the above restrictions.

Consolidated Returns

Corporations that make up an "affiliated group" (which uses a different qualification test than a controlled group) may elect to report their income and deductions on a consolidated income tax return. The primary benefits of filing a consolidated return are: the ability to offset income of profitable group members with losses of unprofitable group members; the ability to postpone reporting gains on intercompany sales; and the ability to offset capital gains with capital losses between members. In general terms, an affiliated group is one or more chains of corporations connected through stock ownership with a common parent corporation. To be considered connected through stock ownership, the parent corporation must directly own 80% of at least one other corporation. Direct stock ownership of at least 80% in the aggregate is also required for all other members of the group. The ownership is computed in terms of voting power and value of stock. For this purpose, certain preferred stock is not counted in calculating the 80% threshold. An election to file a consolidated return is generally binding on the affiliated group for all future years.

The Treasury Department has established extensive regulations governing the filing of consolidated tax returns. These regulations set forth rules for using net operating loss carryovers, computing intercompany profits and losses where the group has sales among its members, establishing accounting periods and methods, determining earnings and profits of group members, and numerous other matters.

Tax-Free Changes in Corporate Ownership

Corporations can in certain cases reorganize, liquidate, or acquire other corporations without the corporation itself or its shareholders recognizing either gain or loss. The recognition of the gain or loss is deferred because the corporation's or the shareholder's original basis is carried over to the new entity. Income taxes are not payable until some future date when a taxable sale, exchange, or termination occurs.

The IRS has issued complex regulations dealing with the change in ownership rules and prescribing the manner of applying the limitations to capital losses and excess credits. It is important that corporations with losses carefully evaluate any recent or prospective transactions (including transactions involving the parent corporation) that could cause a change in ownership in light of the regulations. These regulations also impose reporting and record-keeping requirements on these corporations.

Certain Carryovers. A successor corporation in a tax-free reorganization, liquidation, or acquisition can generally carry over unused net operating losses, general business credits, job credits, foreign tax credits, and capital losses from the predecessor corporation. This transfer of tax attributes is limited if there has been a substantial change in stock ownership or, in some cases, if there has been a change in the corporation's business. In addition, if the principal purpose of an acquisition is to obtain tax benefits that would not otherwise be available, those benefits may be disallowed by the IRS.

TAXSAVER

If you are seeking to acquire a corporation with net operating losses or other carryforward items, you should plan carefully to avoid the limitations that apply when a substantial percentage of the corporation's stock changes hands.

Likewise, corporations seeking outside equity investors need to exercise care in planning transactions. If the change in corporate ownership exceeds certain limits, the ability to use the loss and credit carryovers may be limited or denied.

Special Taxes

Accumulated Earnings and Personal Holding Company Taxes

Certain corporations that do not distribute their earnings for a taxable year may be subject to either a tax on an excess accumulation of earnings or to a tax on undistributed personal holding company income. In computing these taxes, the amount of earnings is determined in accordance with specific provisions of the Internal Revenue Code. Consideration is given to dividends paid and certain other adjustments.

TAXSAVER

Throughout the year, corporations should monitor their accumulation of earnings and the types of income they receive in order to detect potential exposure to these taxes. If a corporation determines that one of these taxes may apply, there are methods available to reduce or eliminate any resulting tax liability.

For example, if a corporation is vulnerable to the accumulated earnings tax, the use of "consent" dividends may be appropriate. "Consent" dividends are hypothetical (in that they are not actually paid) distributions to a shareholder who consents to treat some or all of the corporation's income as a dividend even though no cash is received. Since special rules apply to consent dividends, you should consult a professional tax advisor.

Corporate Alternative Minimum Tax

The Tax Reform Act of 1986 revised the minimum tax on corporations. Under prior law, corporations were subject only to an "add-on" minimum tax (i.e., a tax that was in addition to the corporation's regular income tax). However, for tax years beginning after December 31, 1986, the add-on minimum tax no longer applies, and an alternative minimum tax (AMT) is imposed.

In general, the AMT is based on the corporation's regular taxable income increased by tax preference items and increased or decreased by adjustments to arrive at an amount upon which the corporate AMT rate of 20% is applied.

It is beyond the scope of this book to explain how the AMT is calculated. In any case, you will need to get professional tax advice. What follows is a listing of AMT preference and adjustment items that may determine whether or not a company is subject to the AMT.

Preferences:

1. The excess of accelerated depreciation deductions over straight-line depreciation on real property (and leased personal property for personal holding companies) placed in service before 1987.
2. Tax-exempt interest on certain private activity bonds (other than qualified bonds issued on behalf of certain charitable organizations) issued after August 7, 1986.
3. Depletion to the extent that it exceeds the adjusted basis of the property involved.
4. The amount by which excess intangible drilling costs exceed 65% of the taxpayer's net income from oil, gas, and geothermal properties for the taxable year.

Adjustments. Adjustments are items of income or deductions that are recomputed for AMT purposes. The adjustments that must be made include the following:

1. An alternative depreciation deduction (using less accelerated methods and longer depreciation lives) for real and personal property and certified pollution-control facilities placed in service after 1986.
2. The percentage-of-completion method of accounting must be used for most long-term contracts entered into on or after March 1, 1986.
3. Gain or loss on the disposition of property must be recalculated using an adjusted basis that takes into account AMT depreciation allowances and other AMT methods of accounting.
4. Net losses and income from passive activities must be recomputed using the AMT measurements of income and deductions. (See pages 18–19 for an explanation of the passive loss rules.)
5. Net losses from tax shelter farming activities for personal service corporations must be added back.
6. A special adjustment for earnings calculated under a separate system called adjusted current earnings (ACE) is necessary.
7. The alternative tax net operating loss must be recalculated.

A special minimum tax credit (MTC) is available to offset a future year's regular tax liability for years in which it exceeds its AMT liability.

TaxSaver

A company should be aware that planning techniques used to reduce its regular tax might not provide a current tax benefit if the company is subject to the alternative minimum tax. Moreover, in certain cases, regular tax planning techniques can even subject the company to the AMT. For example, the use of Modified Accelerated Cost Recovery System depreciation could result in AMT liability.

While traditional regular tax planning techniques (e.g., accelerating deductions and deferring income) can result in an AMT liability, the company may, nevertheless, want to make sure that such techniques are employed because the minimum tax credit can be used to offset a future year's regular tax liability.

TaxSaver

The AMT is, in effect, an independent income tax system apart from the regular income tax. This requires that the company keep separate records for items such as depreciation on assets acquired after 1986, AMT net operating loss carryovers, and AMT foreign tax credit carryovers. Specifically, since different amounts of depreciation are allowed under the two systems, separate basis amounts must be tracked for purposes of computing gain or loss upon a sale of such assets.

While many companies have recognized the need to maintain a separate set of records for AMT purposes (since the AMT system has been with us since 1986), it may not be as widely known that a third set of records is required for adjusted current earnings (ACE) purposes.

TaxAlert

The new tax law eliminates the depreciation component of the adjusted current earnings (ACE) adjustment. As under prior law, unless the straight-line method of depreciation was used for regular tax purposes, corporations will compute depreciation for MACRS tangible personal property for AMT purposes by using the 150% declining-balance method over the class life of the property.

This rule is effective for property placed in service after December 31, 1993. While this change should simplify the calculation of depreciation for alternative minimum tax purposes, taxpayers must continue to make the ACE adjustment for depreciation for property placed in service before January 1, 1994.

TaxSaver

In certain cases, a corporation can reduce its AMT exposure by leasing equipment rather than purchasing it. Regular tax depreciation deductions could be partially disallowed for AMT purposes, but lease payments should be fully deductible for both regular tax and AMT purposes.

Environmental Tax

For tax years beginning after December 31, 1986, and before January 1, 1996, a 0.12% environmental tax is imposed on the excess of a corporation's modified alternative minimum taxable income, with certain adjustments, over $2 million.

A corporation may be liable for the environmental tax even if it is not subject to AMT. Further, no tax credits are allowed against the tax. The tax may be deducted from the corporation's gross income.

14

S Corporations

Introduction

Income earned by regular C corporations is taxed at the corporate level when earned and taxed again at the shareholder level when distributed as dividends. An S corporation election permits a corporation to avoid this "double taxation." S corporation income generally is only taxed at the shareholder level. This in itself can be a tremendous tax-saving opportunity.

Yet, for legal purposes, an S corporation is indistinguishable from any other corporation. S corporation shareholders have limited liability and other rights and protections similar to shareholders of regular corporations. If your corporation meets the requirements to qualify for S corporation status, you should seriously consider making an S election.

This chapter discusses how to elect S corporation status, the advantages of being an S corporation, and other considerations associated with operating as an S corporation.

Electing S Corporation Status

A corporation must meet certain requirements in order to be an S corporation. Specifically, a corporation can elect S corporation status only if the following conditions are met:

- The corporation is a domestic corporation.
- The corporation has only one class of stock.
- The corporation has no more than 35 shareholders. (A husband and wife are treated as one shareholder for this purpose.)
- The corporation is not a member of an affiliated group of corporations. (An affiliated group is basically one in which two or more corporations are connected by 80% or greater ownership.)
- The corporation's shareholders are individuals, estates, and certain qualifying trusts.
- The corporation's shareholders are citizens or residents of the United States.
- The corporation is not a Domestic International Sales Corporation (DISC) or former DISC, a financial institu-

tion, an insurance company, or a corporation that claims the Puerto Rico or possessions tax credit.

In order to elect S corporation status, the corporation must meet all of the above requirements on the day the S election is filed and on every day of each year for which the election is to be effective.

To be effective for the current year, an S election must be made during the preceding year, or within the first two-and-a-half months of the current tax year. All persons who are shareholders on the day the election is made must consent to the election. In addition, if the election is filed within the first two-and-a-half months of the year in which it is to be effective, all persons who held stock prior to the filing of the election must consent, even if they don't own stock on the day the S election is filed. An S election is made on a Form 2553, *Election by a Small Business Corporation.*

Advantages of Being an S Corporation

Income earned by a regular corporation is taxed at the corporate level when earned, and is generally taxed again at the shareholder level when distributed as dividends. Thus, the income of a regular corporation is subject to "double taxation." An S corporation's income or loss is reported directly on the shareholders' returns, generally escaping tax at the corporate level. The income is taxable to the shareholders even if it is not distributed, but generally it is not taxed again when distributed. The income increases the shareholder's stock basis, potentially reducing gain or increasing loss when the stock is sold. Additionally, the shareholders may be able to shelter the income with losses from other sources. If a corporation is profitable, electing S status can be especially advantageous because the double taxation of its income may be eliminated.

Example: Assume Corporation A earns $500,000 during its 1994 tax year and distributes its after-tax earnings to its shareholders. If Corporation A operates as a regular corporation, the total amount of tax the corporation and its shareholders will pay is $300,680 ($170,000 + $130,680), and only $199,320 of the earnings are available to the shareholders, computed as follows:

Corporation A taxable income	$500,000
Corporate level tax at 34%	170,000
Income distributed and taxed to shareholders	$330,000
Shareholder level tax at 39.6%	130,680
Remaining income available	$199,320

On the other hand, if Corporation A operates as an S corporation, the total amount of tax incurred by the corporation and its shareholders is only $198,000, leaving

$302,000 available for the shareholders—a savings of $102,680. This is computed as follows:

Corporation A taxable income	$500,000
Corporate level tax at 34%	N/A
Income distributed and taxed to shareholders	$500,000
Shareholder level tax at 39.6%	198,000
Remaining income available	$302,000

Note, however, that the highest individual tax rate (39.6%) currently exceeds the highest corporate tax rate (35%).

If the corporation is incurring losses, an S election may also be advantageous. Like S corporation income, S corporation losses are reported directly on the shareholders' individual returns. The losses may be usable to offset income from other sources. However, a shareholder's currently deductible share of the corporation's losses is limited to his or her basis in the corporation's stock and debt of the corporation owed to the shareholder and may be subject to other limitations as well. See the discussion of the at-risk and passive activity loss rules in Chapter 1.

TAXSAVER

Shareholders of S corporations that incur losses often find themselves unable to claim deductions if the losses exceed the shareholder's basis in the corporation's stock. An S corporation shareholder generally can obtain basis in S corporation debt only by actually loaning money to the corporation. If an S corporation borrows money from a bank, the loan does not provide the shareholders with basis against which a loss could be claimed, even if the shareholders guarantee such loans. Consult your tax advisor about restructuring these loans so that the shareholders can utilize the losses being passed through by the company.

TAXSAVER

If your corporation can qualify as an S corporation, you should consider making the election if:
1. *The shareholders expect their individual tax rates to be lower than the applicable regular corporate tax rate in the future or they want to avoid the double taxation on income;*
2. *The corporation anticipates having losses from operations that can be used by the shareholders to greater advantage than being carried back or forward by a regular corporation;*

3. *Most of the income to be earned by the corporation will be distributed to the shareholders; or*
4. *Your regular corporation might be vulnerable to the accumulated earnings tax. (See page 250 for details.)*

You should consider not *making the S corporation election if:*

1. *You anticipate that losses will result in greater benefits if the corporation is a regular corporation. This might be the case when the losses can be carried back or forward to offset income of the regular corporation in other years and the use of the losses by the individual shareholders to offset other income is limited.*
2. *You expect to retain the net income in the business and the corporate tax rate will be lower than the individual rate of the S corporation's shareholders. Currently, the highest individual tax rate (39.6%) exceeds the highest corporate tax rate (35%).*

State Tax Considerations

While S corporation income generally is exempt from corporate tax at the federal level, not all states exempt S corporations from state taxes at the corporate level. This can result in double state taxation on corporate earnings or dividend distributions.

Most states recognize S corporation status. However, several states tax S corporations in the same way they tax C corporations.

Some states require a separate S election at the state level while others base their acceptance on the federal election. Because corporations engaged in multi-state commerce are subject to the tax rules of many states, state corporate tax can be *very* complicated. Please consult your tax advisor.

Operating as an S Corporation

Pass-Through of Income and Losses. S corporation income is taxable directly to the corporation's shareholders based on their respective ownership percentages. A loss for the corporation's taxable year is deductible on a *pro rata* basis, but may be limited to the shareholder's basis, amount at risk, or passive activity income. In cases where a shareholder either joins or leaves the S corporation during the year, income or loss for that shareholder is usually allocated in proportion to the number of days that the shareholder held the stock during the taxable year. In certain cases, however, the corporation may elect or be required to "close the books," and treat its tax year as two separate years for purposes of allocating income or loss.

An S corporation is required to separately identify items that would be subject to special treatment on the shareholders' individual returns. These items include interest, dividend, and royalty income; capital gains and losses; gains and losses on business property; investment interest expense; and charitable contributions. Items not subject to any special limitations are passed through in aggregate. Tax credits also generally pass through directly to the shareholders.

Health insurance premiums paid by an S corporation for the benefit of shareholder-employees owning more than 2% of its stock are deductible by the S corporation and includable in the shareholder's income as additional compensation.

Taxable and nontaxable income that flows from the S corporation to the individual shareholder increases the shareholder's basis in his stock. According to the IRS, however, an S corporation's nontaxable cancellation of indebtedness ("COD") income does not increase any shareholder's stock basis. Likewise, deductible and nondeductible expenses decrease a shareholder's basis in his stock. Distributions from an S corporation are generally tax-free to the extent of a shareholder's basis (however, such distributions reduce basis). If the S corporation was a regular corporation prior to electing S status, a distribution in excess of the earnings accumulated since electing S corporation status may be taxed as a dividend to the shareholder.

Corporate Level Taxes. S corporations generally are not subject to corporate tax, but if an S election is made for a corporation that operated as a regular corporation for a period of time, certain taxes may apply. A brief discussion of these taxes follows:

LIFO Recapture Tax. If a regular corporation using the LIFO (last-in first-out) method of accounting for inventory elects S corporation status, the corporation must include its LIFO reserve in income for its last taxable year as a regular corporation. The LIFO reserve amount that must be included in income is the excess of the inventory value computed under the FIFO (first-in first-out) inventory method over the value computed under the LIFO method. The increase in tax attributable to including the reserve in income is payable over four tax years, with the first payment due on the due date (without extensions) of the last regular corporate return.

Built-In Gains Tax. S corporations that were formerly regular corporations, and that elected S corporation status after December 31, 1986, may be subject to a special "built-in gains" tax. The tax is paid at the corporate level. It generally applies to income or gain accrued in the corporation's assets *before* it elected S status, to the extent that the income or gain is recognized during the corporation's first 10 years as an S corporation.

The tax does not apply to the appreciation of assets occurring after the date the corporation makes its S election.

The tax, if applicable, will be imposed using the highest regular corporate rate, currently 35%.

The corporate level tax reduces the amount of the gain from the disposition of an asset that passes through to the S corporation's shareholders.

In addition, there is a "net income limitation" to the amount of the built-in gains subject to this tax. The taxable built-in gains are limited to the current year's taxable income. If the S corporation election was made on or after March 31, 1988, any recognized built-in gain not subject to tax because of this taxable income limitation must be carried over to the subsequent tax year and is subject to that year's taxable income limitation. If the taxable income limitation prevents the recognition of built-in gain income beyond the 10-year period, these gains will escape tax at the corporate level.

Unexpired net operating losses, capital losses, business credit carryforwards and alternative minimum tax credit carryforwards may be used to offset the built-in gains tax.

Passive Investment Income Tax. An S corporation with regular corporation earnings and profits and passive investment income (for example, interest and dividends) exceeding 25% of its gross receipts may have to pay a special tax. If those conditions exist for three consecutive tax years, the corporation's S election terminates.

Investment Tax Credit Recapture. Any investment tax credit recapture on assets placed in service during any period as a regular corporation must generally be paid by the S corporation.

TAXSAVER

Any new corporation that can qualify for S corporation status can reap a huge tax benefit on the subsequent sale of corporate assets. A regular corporation would have to pay tax at the corporate level on any gain from the sale of assets; an S corporation would not. That can amount to an enormous tax benefit for an S corporation. But, as explained above, an existing corporation that has been a regular corporation and did not elect to become an S corporation by December 31, 1986, cannot simply elect S status and hope to avoid the corporate tax on gains from the sale of asset it held at that time unless the corporation waits at least 10 years before selling the assets.

Taxable Year. Generally, an S corporation is required to report on a calendar year basis unless it can demonstrate to the satisfaction of the IRS a valid business purpose for a fiscal year-end. However, a newly formed S corporation can elect a year-end (ending not earlier than September 30) by making a "required payment" to the IRS, which is intended to eliminate the tax benefit from the deferral.

TAXSAVER

In most cases, an S corporation or partnership would have to demonstrate to the IRS that the different fiscal year is its "natural business year."

The use of a year other than a calendar year can result in a deferral of taxes, and, with a natural business year the corporation does not have to make a "required payment" to offset the benefit of the deferral.

Terminating S Corporation Status. Once an S election is made, it is generally effective for all subsequent tax years. However, a corporation's S election will terminate if the corporation violates any of the eligibility requirements explained earlier in this chapter. In addition, an S election will terminate if the corporation has regular corporation earnings and profits and more than 25% of its gross receipts is from passive investment income for three consecutive years. Shareholders of an S corporation, who hold more than one-half of the number of issued and outstanding shares, may also revoke the corporation's S election.

TAXSAVER

A company should take steps to safeguard against unwanted transfers of stock that would terminate its S election. For example, a minority shareholder not otherwise able to individually revoke the company's S election could nevertheless do so by transferring stock to a shareholder not qualified to hold S corporation stock. One way of protecting against unwanted transfers is to ratify agreements limiting the shareholder's ability to transfer stock.

TAXSAVER

When To Consider Terminating S Corporation Status. *The following factors should be taken into account when evaluating whether you should terminate an S election:*

■ *Since the passage of the 1993 Tax Act, the top corporate tax rate (35%) is now lower than the top individual tax rate (39.6%). In addition, the alternative minimum tax rate for C corporations can be lower than the applicable individual rate for S corporation shareholders. Before the 1993 Act, the top individual rate was lower than the top corporate rate.*

- *Because a C corporation is not subject to the rules limiting the number and kind of shareholders discussed earlier, it has much more flexibility and more financing alternatives and opportunities.*

- *Preferred stock is prohibited in an S corporation and not in a C corporation. S corporations cannot have more than one class of stock. Unlike C corporations, all outstanding shares generally must have the same rights to distributions and liquidation proceeds.*

- *Certain dividend income eligible for a 70% dividend received deduction is available to C corporations but not S corporations.*

- *A C corporation has more favorable exclusions for certain employee benefits (e.g., exclusion of health insurance benefits).*

Once a corporation's S election has terminated, the corporation generally cannot elect S status again for five years. However, under certain limited conditions, the IRS may permit the corporation to re-elect S status before five years have passed. In addition, if the event that caused the S election to terminate was inadvertent, the IRS may grant a waiver of the inadvertent termination and allow the corporation to continue to be treated as an S corporation.

15

Year-End Tax Planning for Businesses

Introduction

The political climate will undoubtedly dictate whether business taxes are changed. If they are, in addition to raising tax rates, Congress will probably continue its efforts to raise revenue from businesses by technical changes in the tax code. These changes might include further restrictions on accounting methods that permit businesses to defer payment of taxes. In addition, businesses with foreign operations are likely to face continued scrutiny.

Timing of Income and Deductions

A business's overall accounting method can substantially affect tax planning. Most individuals and many owners of service businesses use the cash method of accounting for tax purposes. However, most other businesses must use the accrual method of accounting.

Under the cash method, items of income are reported when actually or "constructively" received (that is, when unrestricted use of the funds is available). Items of expense are reported when actually paid. Under the accrual method, the right to receive an income item and the liability to pay an expense item generally determine when those items are reported. For tax purposes, however, an accrual method taxpayer usually may not deduct a liability until goods or services are provided.

The typical business will want to defer income and accelerate expenses (although this strategy would need to be reevaluated if it appeared likely that tax rates were going to rise substantially). Consider the following potential suggestions for accomplishing this goal:

■ Delay deliveries on sales (but consider the potential property tax effect).

- Make sales on consignment or approval (thus delaying billing and payment).
- Make the maximum deductible charitable contributions.
- Contribute the maximum deductible amount to tax-qualified retirement plans.
- In certain cases, corporations on the LIFO (last-in, first-out) inventory method can affect taxable income by timing the purchase of inventory.

TaxAlert

Remember to consider the impact of the alternative minimum tax (AMT). With the relatively small differences between the AMT rate and the regular corporate tax rate, more corporations are subject to AMT than ever before. However, because the corporate AMT tax can be fully credited against future corporate income tax, its effect may not be very severe.

Depreciation

The date new property is placed in service can significantly affect the amount of your 1994 depreciation deduction. In general, personal property is treated as if it was placed in service at the midpoint of a tax year (July 1 for calendar-year taxpayers) no matter when it was actually purchased and placed in service. However, it's not always that simple. If more than 40% of the property purchased during the tax year is placed in service during the last three months of the year, different procedures apply. Under these circumstances, all property purchased and placed in service throughout the year will be treated as being placed in service in the middle of the quarter in which it was placed in service. This will usually result in a lower first-year depreciation deduction than if the property were treated as having been placed in service at the midpoint of the tax year.

In certain situations, however, having depreciable property subject to the more-than-40% rule is advantageous. Thus, you should review your fourth quarter acquisition plans to determine whether you want the more-than-40% rule to be activated. In general, real property is treated as placed in service in the middle of the month in which it is actually placed in service.

For tax purposes, depreciation is calculated using the modified accelerated cost recovery system (MACRS). An alternative depreciation system must be used when determining if the AMT applies. The difference between depreciation calculated under MACRS and the alternative depreciation system is an adjustment item used in computing the AMT. If you wish to avoid the AMT you should consider leasing instead of purchasing depreciable assets.

Taxpayers may expense up to $17,500 of capital purchases for tangible personal property in the year acquired, provided such expenses do not exceed the taxable income derived from the business. To limit this write-off for larger businesses, the $17,500 is reduced dollar-for-dollar by the cost of eligible property in excess of $200,000.

Other Business Expenses. If you employ your children in your unincorporated business, their earned income will be taxed at their tax rates, and you will get a deduction for their salaries. Also, for children under age 18, neither you (as employer) nor they will be subject to FICA tax on wages you pay to them.

Capital Asset Transactions

Corporations generally compute capital gains and losses in the same manner as individuals. For capital losses, however, corporations may only offset such losses against capital gains and not any portion of ordinary income as is true with individuals. Excess capital losses can be carried back three years and forward five years to offset capital gains. Unused capital losses expire and are lost forever.

Corporations should review their tax positions before year end. Additional sales or exchanges of capital assets should be considered to coordinate the timing of gains and losses and prevent expiration of unused losses.

Charitable Giving

Your corporation may be able to reap special benefits from its charitable contributions. As a means of accelerating the maximum deduction (generally 10% of taxable income) into the current tax year, a corporation that uses the accrual method of accounting may deduct contributions made within 2½ months after the close of the tax year, provided the contributions have been authorized by the board of directors by year end. The IRS requires that a statement regarding the board's action be attached to the return. For a corporation whose tax year coincides with the calendar year, contributions must be made by March 15, 1995. In addition, gifts of *current* inventory may not be subject to the 10% limitation. For more information, see Chapter 12.

Executive Compensation

In general a taxpayer may claim a business deduction for a reasonable allowance for salaries or other compensation for personal services rendered. However, a publicly-held corporation is precluded, subject to some exceptions, from taking a deduction for compensation in excess of $1 million paid to its chief executive officer and the four other most highly compensated officers. Excepted from this rule are 1) payments to a tax-qualified plan, 2) fringe benefits that are excludable from gross income, and 3) qualified performance-based compensation, including stock options or other stock appreciation rights, provided it meets certain independent director and shareholder approval requirements.

In general, compensation must meet the following four requirements in order to be considered performance-based: (1) it must be paid solely on account of the attainment of one or more preestablished objective performance goals, (2) the performance goal(s) must be established by a compensation committee comprised solely of two or more outside directors, (3) the material terms of the performance goal(s) must be disclosed to and subsequently approved by the shareholders, and (4) the compensation committee must certify in writing prior to payment that the performance goals have, in fact, been satisfied.

TaxSaver

There are a number of strategies companies and top executives can consider to minimize the effect of the $1 million annual cap on compensation deductions.

One strategy is to use nonqualified deferred compensation arrangements to minimize or completely avoid the new $1 million limitation with respect to base salary. These arrangements could be elective, nonelective, or a combination of both. The goal would be to defer base salary to a point in time when it is deductible.

There are two basic structures that can be used. First, base salary could be deferred under an agreement which provides that it will be paid when the employee is no longer a covered employee. Alternatively, the deferral agreement could provide that the deferred base salary will be paid at the first point in time that it is deductible. This approach could create problems in administration, however, since deductibility will depend on the other components of the employee's compensation package, e.g., bonuses and stock option exercises.

Highly paid employees and employers should also consider converting their bonus plans to arrangements that meet the requirements for performance-based compensation.

Companies should also consider granting stock options and stock appreciation rights (SARs) at fair market value. If the options or rights are granted at fair market value and the other requirements for performance-based compensation are met, the income from the exercise of the stock options or SARs will not be counted as part of the $1 million limitation.

TaxAlert

Compensation that is tied to pre-established performance goals is exempted from the $1 million deductibility limitation. However, in order for 1995 incentive plans to receive an exemption, performance goals must be established and approved by the compensation committee no later than December 31, 1994.

Dividends-Received Deduction

The law permits a corporation to deduct 70% (or, in some cases, 80% or 100%) of qualifying dividend income that it receives from taxable domestic corporations. A special provision limits this to 70% of the recipient corporation's taxable income, computed without regard to certain adjustments, including the dividends-received deduction itself.

Dividends-received deductions that are limited as a result of the net income limitation are lost forever. However, this rule does not apply if the recipient corporation would have a net operating loss (NOL) after taking into account the dividends-received deduction. In such a case, the dividends-received deduction is allowable and increases the NOL carryover.

A corporation with qualifying dividend income should plan carefully to ensure that the dividends-received deduction is not lost because of these rules. For more information, see Chapter 12.

Estimated Tax Filing Requirements

Businesses should conserve cash by making payments only when taxes are owed and only in the required amounts. Overpayments are essentially interest-free loans to the government, while underpayments may result in a nondeductible penalty.

A lower estimated installment amount may be paid if it is shown that use of an annualized income method or, for corporations with seasonal incomes, an adjusted seasonal method would result in a lower required installment. See Chapter 13.

State Tax Considerations

In your year-end business tax planning, you should consider the substantial role state taxes play in a business's overall tax liability.

Taking Advantage of Net Operating Losses. A

company may be able to utilize losses generated by an affiliated company in states in which the companies are required to file separate returns. To do so, income-generating assets may have to be transferred to the company with the loss, certain other intercompany transactions may have to occur, or the companies may have to merge. You will need to consult your tax advisor to plan how to maximize your tax benefits.

Distributions and Transactions Between Different Companies. Intercompany transactions that are not subject to federal taxes under the federal consolidated return rules may be subject to direct or indirect state taxes. Some states tax a portion of dividends paid by one company to another. On the other hand, some sales of tangible property between companies and some management fees that one company pays another may be exempt from state taxes. You should consult your tax advisor to determine whether state taxes could be reduced or eliminated by restructuring certain distributions and other transactions between companies.

Appendices

1994 Income Tax Rates

Single Individuals*

If 1994 taxable income is:		The tax is:	
Over—	But not over—		Of excess over—
$ 0	$ 22,750	$ 0 + 15%	$ 0
22,750	55,100	3,412.50 + 28%	22,750
55,100	115,000	12,470.50 + 31%	55,100
115,000	250,000	31,039.50 + 36%	115,000
250,000	—	79,639.50 + 39.6%	250,000

Unmarried (or Legally Separated) Individuals Who Qualify as Heads of Households*

If 1994 taxable income is:		The tax is:	
Over—	But not over—		Of excess over—
$ 0	$ 30,500	$ 0 + 15%	$ 0
30,500	78,700	4,575.00 + 28%	30,500
78,700	127,500	18,071.00 + 31%	78,700
127,500	250,000	33,199.00 + 36%	127,500
250,000	—	77,299.00 + 39.6%	250,000

Married Individuals Filing Joint Returns and Certain Widows and Widowers*

If 1994 taxable income is:		The tax is:	
Over—	But not over—		Of excess over—
$ 0	$ 38,000	$ 0 + 15%	$ 0
38,000	91,850	5,700.00 + 28%	38,000
91,850	140,000	20,778.00 + 31%	91,850
140,000	250,000	35,704.50 + 36%	140,000
250,000	—	75,304.50 + 39.6%	250,000

Married Individuals Filing Separate Returns*

If 1994 taxable income is:		The tax is:	
Over—	But not over—		Of excess over—
$ 0	$ 19,000	$ 0 + 15%	$ 0
19,000	45,925	2,850.00 + 28%	19,000
45,925	70,000	10,389.00 + 31%	45,925
70,000	125,000	17,852.25 + 36%	70,000
125,000	—	37,652.25 + 39.6%	125,000

*Does not take into account the alternative minimum tax; net capital gain taxed at maximum of 28%.

1994 Income Tax Rates

Estates and Nongrantor Trusts*

If 1994 taxable income is:		The tax is:	
Over—	But not over—		Of excess over—
$ 0	$ 1,500	$ 0 + 15%	$ 0
1,500	3,600	225.00 + 28%	1,500
3,600	5,500	813.00 + 31%	3,600
5,500	7,500	1,402.00 + 36%	5,500
7,500	—	2,122.00 + 39.6%	7,500

*Does not take into account the alternative minimum tax; net capital gain taxed at maximum of 28%.

Corporations**

If taxable income is:		The tax is:	
Over—	But not over—		Of excess over—
$ 0	$ 50,000	$ 0 + 15%	$ 0
50,000	75,000	7,500 + 25%	50,000
75,000	100,000	13,750 + 34%	75,000
100,000	335,000	22,250 + 39%	100,000
335,000	10,000,000	113,900 + 34%	335,000
10,000,000	15,000,000	3,400,000 + 35%	10,000,000
15,000,000	18,333,333	5,150,000 + 38%	15,000,000
18,333,333	—	6,416,667 + 35%	18,333,333

**Does not take into account the alternative minimum tax.

Social Security Taxes

Old-Age Benefit Tax on Employers and Employees

Social Security rate on the first $60,600[a] of wages	6.20%
Medicare rate on all wages	1.45%

Self-Employment Tax[b]

Social Security rate on the first $60,600[a] of self-employment income	12.4%
Medicare rate on all self-employment income	2.9%

[a]The wage base can increase based on a statutory formula. Any change is published in the *Federal Register* no later than November 1 each year.
[b]A self-employed individual may deduct one-half of his or her self-employment tax for the year as a business expense in arriving at adjusted gross income.

Unified Estate and Gift Tax Rates

Taxable transfers over (1)	But not over (2)	Tentative tax on amount in col. (1) (3)	Rate of tax on excess over amount in col. (1) (4)
$0	$10,000	$0	18%
10,000	20,000	1,800	20%
20,000	40,000	3,800	22%
40,000	60,000	8,200	24%
60,000	80,000	13,000	26%
80,000	100,000	18,200	28%
100,000	150,000	23,800	30%
150,000	250,000	38,800	32%
250,000	500,000	70,800	34%
500,000	750,000	155,800	37%
750,000	1,000,000	248,300	39%
1,000,000	1,250,000	345,800	41%
1,250,000	1,500,000	448,300	43%
1,500,000	2,000,000	555,800	45%
2,000,000	2,500,000	780,800	49%
2,500,000	3,000,000	1,025,800	53%
3,000,000	—	1,290,800*	55%

*Plus 5% of the cumulative transfers in excess of $10,000,000 but not exceeding $21,040,000.

Unified Estate and Gift Tax Credit

The unified estate and gift tax credit is $192,800. This has the effect of exempting estates of $600,000 or less from estate taxes.

Computation of Maximum Federal Estate Tax Credit for State Death Taxes

Adjusted taxable estate* more than— (1)	But not more than (2)	Maximum credit amount in col. (1) (3)	Rate of credit on excess over amount in col. (1) (4)
$0	$40,000	$0	None
40,000	90,000	0	.8%
90,000	140,000	400	1.6%
140,000	240,000	1,200	2.4%
240,000	440,000	3,600	3.2%
440,000	640,000	10,000	4.0%
640,000	840,000	18,000	4.8%
840,000	1,040,000	27,600	5.6%
1,040,000	1,540,000	38,800	6.4%
1,540,000	2,040,000	70,800	7.2%
2,040,000	2,540,000	106,800	8.0%
2,540,000	3,040,000	146,800	8.8%
3,040,000	3,540,000	190,800	9.6%
3,540,000	4,040,000	238,800	10.4%
4,040,000	5,040,000	290,800	11.2%
5,040,000	6,040,000	402,800	12.0%
6,040,000	7,040,000	522,800	12.8%
7,040,000	8,040,000	650,800	13.6%
8,040,000	9,040,000	786,800	14.4%
9,040,000	10,040,000	930,800	15.2%
10,040,000	—	1,082,800	16.0%

*The taxable estate less $60,000.

Note: The 1995 tax rate schedules for individual taxpayers and estates and trusts have not been compiled. The rate brackets are indexed each year to account for inflation in the consumer price index. Under the Internal Revenue Code, the indexed 1995 tax rate tables must be available by December 15.

Tax Calendar

Your 1994 individual income tax return is due on April 17, 1995, if you are a calendar-year taxpayer. You shouldn't wait until then to get your tax affairs in order, however. The calendar that follows is designed to highlight what you need to file and when. It includes important tax dates not only for individuals but for corporations as well. Key dates for employers are also highlighted. Taxpayers whose years end on dates other than December 31 must adjust these dates to their situation. Due dates that fall on a Saturday, Sunday, or legal holiday are automatically extended to the next business day.

Individuals

January 16
- Form 1040-ES (declaration of estimated tax) for fourth quarter of prior year

April 17
- Form 1040 (individual income tax return) for prior year or Form 4868 (request for automatic four-month extension)
- Form 709 or 709A (gift tax return) for prior year or extension request (Form 4868 or letter)
- Form 1040-ES for first quarter of current year

June 15
- Form 1040-ES for second quarter

August 15
- Form 1040 for prior year, if previously extended by Form 4868 (if additional time is needed, a further two-month extension may be obtained by filing Form 2688)
- Form 709 or 709A, if previously extended by Form 4868 or letter (alternatively, request additional time to file by filing Form 2688 or by letter)

September 15
- Form 1040-ES for third quarter

October 16
- Form 1040 for prior year, if request for automatic four-month extension and additional two-month extension were previously filed

Corporations

March 15
- Form 1120 (corporate income tax return) (Form 1120S for an S corporation) for prior year or Form 7004 (request for automatic six-month extension)

April 17
- Deposit estimated tax for first quarter of current year

May 15
- Form 8752 (Required Payment or Refund Under Section 7519) for an S corporation using a year other than a calendar year

June 15
- Deposit estimated tax for second quarter of current year

September 15
- Form 1120 (Form 1120S for an S corporation) if previously extended by Form 7004
- Deposit estimated tax for third quarter of current year

December 15
- Deposit estimated tax for fourth quarter of current year

Employers

(Includes businesses and individuals, as well as employers of household employees)

January 31
- Form 941 (employer's quarterly federal tax return) or Form 942 (employer's quarterly tax return for household employees) for fourth quarter of prior year
- Form 940 (employer's federal unemployment tax return) for prior year
- Distribute Forms W-2 (Wage and Tax Statement), W-2P (Statement for Recipients of Annuities, Pensions, Retired Pay, or IRA Payments), and 1099-R (Total Distributions from Profit-Sharing Retirement Plans, Individual Retirement Arrangements, Insurance Contracts, etc.) to employees

February 28
- File Form W-3 (Transmittal of Income and Tax Statements) with Forms W-2 and/or W-2P and for prior year with IRS and Social Security Administration

■ File Form 1096 (Annual Summary and Transmittal of U.S. Information Returns) with Form 1099-R for prior year with IRS

May 1
■ Form 941 or Form 942 for first quarter of current year

July 31
■ Form 941 or Form 942 for second quarter

October 31
■ Form 941 or Form 942 for third quarter

Index